The Barbra Streisand Record & C
1962-2014
A Six-Decade Celebration
By Paul Busa

ISBN 10 : 150317848X

ISBN 13 : 9781503178489

Copyright © 2014, 2012 by Paul Busa
All rights reserved. No part of this book may be reproduced without permission.
Second edition
Cover Design: Steven Baxter
Photos Credits: Firooz Zahedi Front Cover & pg. 4; William Claxton Back Cover; Steve Schpiro pg. 1, 125, & 143; Russell James pg. 3; Greg Gorman pg. 85 & 87; Hank Parker pg. 175; Francesco Scavullo pg. 117, 175 & 201; Mario Casilli pg. 65, 159 & 202.
All photographs appear courtesy of Columbia Records/SONY
All covers, picture sleeves, and record labels appear courtesy of Columbia/SONY, Capital, 20th Century Fox, and Arista Records.

Table of Contents

Introduction	*Page 5*
The Albums	*Page 6*
7" Singles US	*Page 25*
7" EP's US	*Page 41*
7" Singles International	*Page 42*
7" EP's International	*Page 72*
12" Singles US & International	*Page 80*
Cassette Singles	*Page 86*
CD Singles US & International	*Page 88*
Movie Radio Spots	*Page 96*
Acetate Records	*Page 98*
12" LP's US	*Page 100*
12" LP's International	*Page 128*
CD's US Release	*Page 157*
CD's International Release	*Page 168*
Sheet Music	*Page 192*
An American Institution (Closing)	*Page 200*

Introduction

Welcome to what has been years in the making and a total labor of love. I have been collecting Barbra Streisand memorabilia for over 30 years, and have focused on the worldwide singles and album releases. I first had an idea to do a book in the early 1990's. Then a fan from Holland was putting together a Record Collector's Guide to which I contributed. This motivated me to do my own book; one that would include all the US singles.

I tried to make this as complete as possible. A few items I was unable to acquire and made references. Some of the International records do not list year or country, so what's listed is based on research through Record Dealers and Collectors over the years. While this book focuses on the vinyl and compact disc releases, other formats her albums were issued in include reel-to-reel tapes, 8 tracks, cassette tapes, and the short-lived mini-disc. The book starts with all Streisand's albums listed with song titles, release dates, Billboard Chart position and Gold/Platinum status. Then the singles/EP's 7" & 12" US & International are listed in order of release, followed by the CD Singles. It's interesting to note that most of the recent promo CD singles are being pressed on a cheap disc (CDR) with a blue backing. Apparently the record companies are doing this due to the low demand for pressed CD's versus digital downloads. This is referred to by dealers as an 'acetate pressing'.

And recent full CD's are issued as promos in plain red card sleeves, which are not very collectable. Next are the 12" LP's International & US with catalog numbers & record labels. One LP I was unable to confirm exists is Yentl pressed on red vinyl from South America. Listed next are the albums on CD US & International with catalog numbers and record labels. The following are credited as references: Barbra-archives.com; RIAA.Com; Barbra Now & Then #2 1984 (Magazine); Barbra Streisand Record Collector's Guide Book 1962-1999 by Helena den Ouden-Ton (Holland, no ISBN #).

People who need people. Special thanks to Rodger Landers for all his technical help and support. I'd also like to thank the following people who have contributed to this book: Sue Cragg, Steven Baxter, Dennis Berno, Robert DeLucca, Alan Carmack, Matt Howe, Don Gunderson, Jose Mora & Allison J. Waldman.

This book is dedicated to Helen & Sam Busa

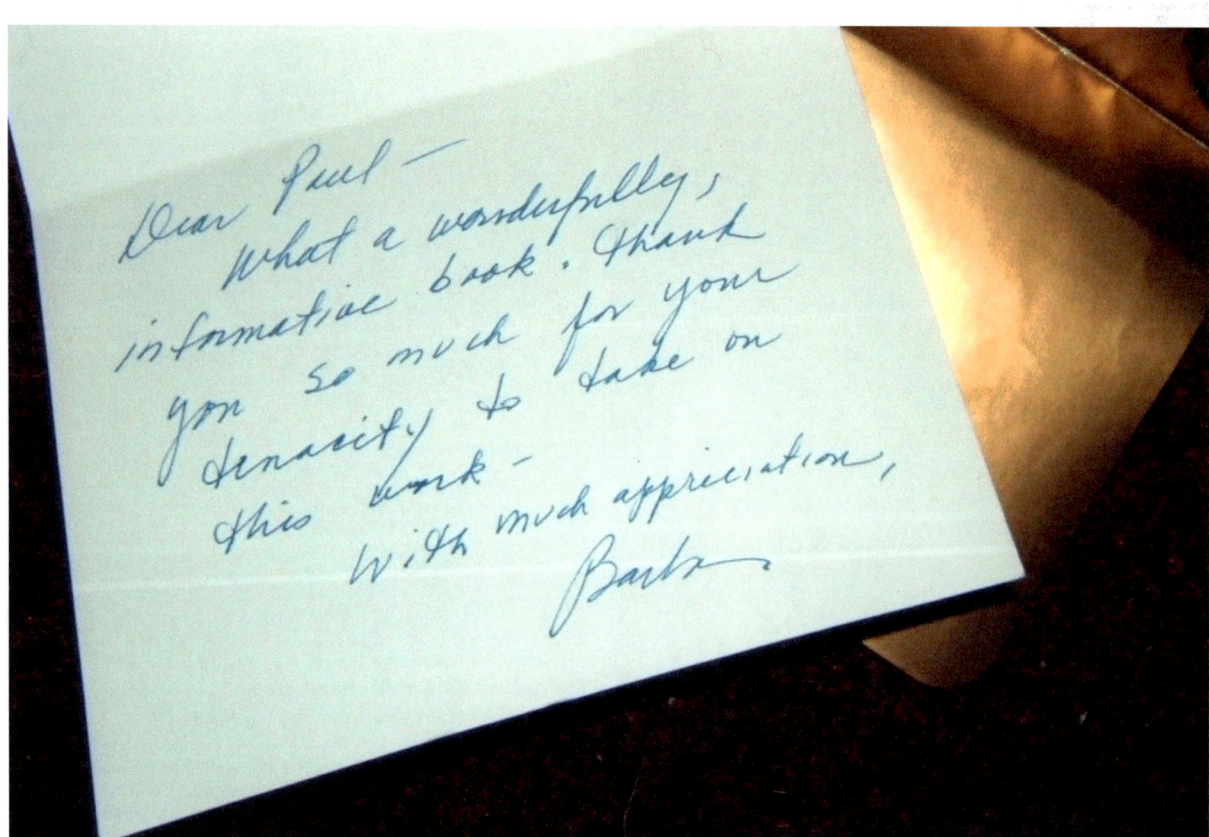

The Albums

This is the complete album catalog. Note: One Night Only is considered a DVD release. All records labels/catalog numbers in CD/LP sections.

I Can Get It For You Wholesale-Original Broadway Cast Recording
Released April 1962   Billboard #125

(Overture/I'm Not A Well Man (Barbra & cast)/Way Things Are/ When Gemini Meets Capricorn/Momma, Momma, Momma/ The Sound Of Money/Too Soon/The Family Way/Who Knows?/ Ballad Of The Garment Trade (Barbra/Cast)/Have I Told You Lately?/ A Gift Today/Miss Marmelstein (Barbra)/A Funny Things Happened/ What's In It For Me?/Eat A Little Something/What Are They Doing To Us (Barbra & cast))

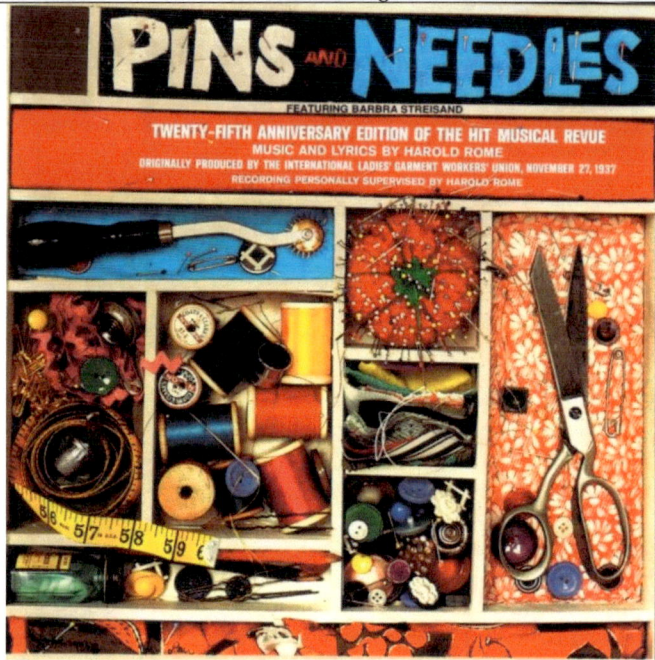

Pins And Needles-25th Anniversary Edition Of The Hit Musical Revue   Released May 1962

(Sing Me A Song/Doing The Reactionary (Barbra)/One Big Union For Two/It's Better With A Union Man/Nobody Makes A Pass At Me (Barbra)/I've Got The Nerve To Be In Love/Not Cricket To Picket (Barbra)/Back To Work/Status Quo (Barbra)/When I Grow Up/Chain Store Daisy/Four Little Angles Of Peace (Barbra)/Sunday In The Park/What Good Is Love (Barbra)/Mene, Mene, Tekel)

The Barbra Streisand Album   Released Feb.25, 1963
Billboard #8 (Certified Gold & Platinum)

(Cry Me A River/My Honey's Loving Arms/I'll Tell The Man In The Street/A Taste Of Honey/Who's Afraid Of The Big Bad Wolf?/ Soon It's Gonna Rain/Happy Days Are Here Again/Keepin' Out Of Mischief Now/Much More/Come To The Supermarket (In Old Peking)/A Sleepin' Bee)

The Second Barbra Streisand Album   Released Aug. 1963
Billboard #2 (Certified Gold & Platinum)

(Any Place I Hang My Hat Is Home/Right As The Rain/Down With Love/Who Will Buy?/When The Sun Comes Out/Gotta Move/My Coloring Book/I Don't Care Much/Lover, Come Back To Me/I Stayed Too Long At The Fair/Like A Straw In The Wind)

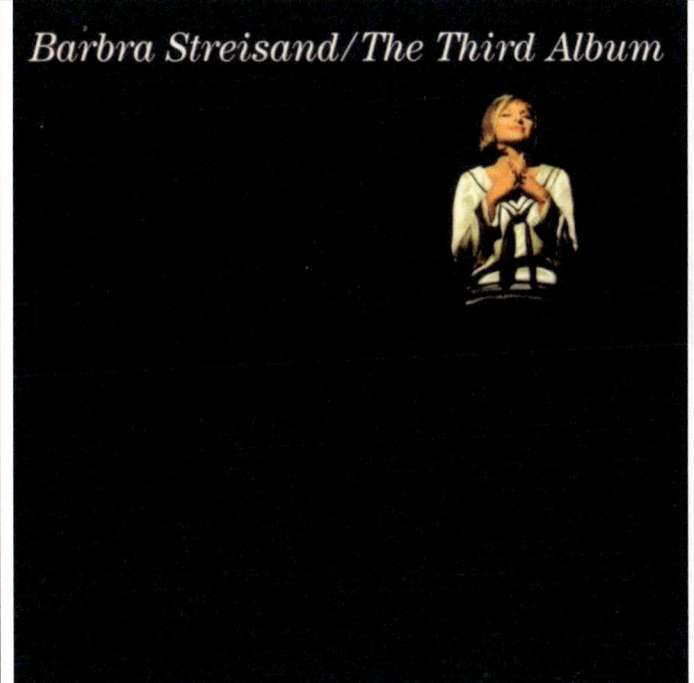

The Third Album   *Released Feb. 1964*
Billboard #5 (Certified Gold)

(My Melancholy Baby/Just In Time/Taking A Chance On Love/ Bewitched (Bothered And Bewildered)/Never Will I Marry/As Time Goes By/Draw Me A Circle/It Had To Be You/Make Believe/I Had Myself A True Love)

Funny Girl Original Broadway Cast Recording
Released April 1964   *Billboard #2 (Certified Gold)*

(Overture/If A Girl Isn't Pretty/I'm The Greatest Star/Cornet Man/Who Taught Her Everything? /His Love Makes Me Beautiful/ I Want To Be Seen With You Tonight/Henry Street/People/You Are Woman/Don't Rain On My Parade/Sadie, Sadie/Find Yourself A Man/Rat-Tat-Tat-Tat/Who Are You Now? /The Music That Makes Me Dance/Don't Rain On My Parade (Reprise))

People   *Released Sept. 1964*
Billboard #1 (Certified Gold & Platinum)

(Absent Minded Me/When In Rome/Fine And Dandy/Supper Time/Will He Like Me/How Does The Wine Taste?/I'm All Smiles/Autumn/My Lord And Master/Love Is A Bore/Don't Like Goodbyes/People)

My Name Is Barbra   *Released May 1965*
Billboard #2 (Certified Gold)

(My Name Is Barbra/A Kid Again-I'm Five/Jenny Rebecca/My Pa/Sweet Zoo/Where Is The Wonder/I Can See It/Someone To Watch Over Me/I've Got No Strings/If You Were The Only Boy In The World/Why Did I Choose You/My Man)

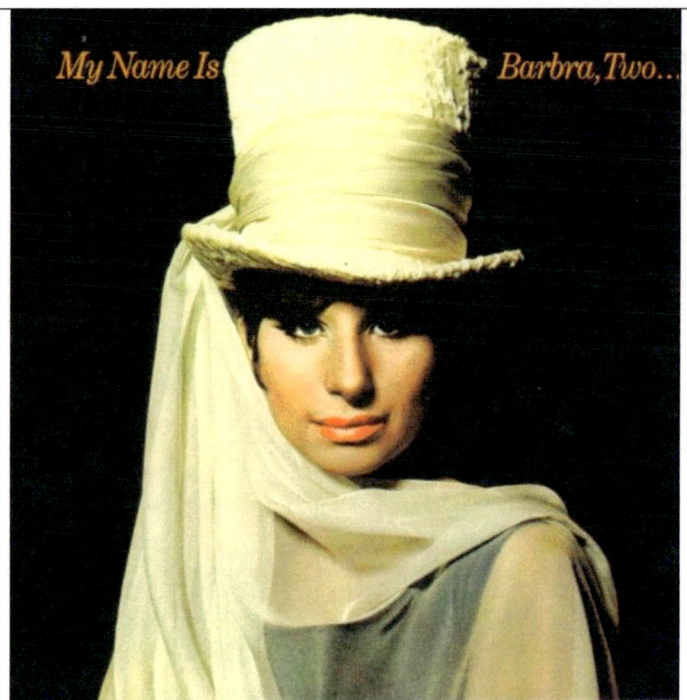

My Name Is Barbra, Two   Released Oct. 1965
Billboard #2 (Certified Gold & Platinum)

(He Touched Me/Shadow Of Your Smile/Quiet Night/I Got Plenty Of Nothin'/How Much Of The Dream Comes True?/Second Hand Rose/The Kind Of Woman Needs/All That I Want/Where's That Rainbow?/No More Songs For Me/Medley-Second Hand Rose/Give Me The Simply Life/ I Got Plenty Of Nothin'/Brother Can You Spare A Dime?/Nobody Knows You When You Down & Out/Second Hand Rose/Best Things In Life Are Free)

Color Me Barbra   Released March 1966
Billboard #3 (Certified Gold)

(Yesterdays/One Kiss/The Minute Waltz/Gotta Move/Non C'est Rien/Where Or When/Medley Animal Crackers In My Soup-Funny Face/That Face-They Didn't Believe Me-Were Thine That Special Face I've Grown Accustomed To Her Face-Let's Face The Music-Sam, You Made The Pants Too Long-What's New Pussycat-Small World/I Love You I Stayed Too Long At The Fair-Look At That Face/C'est Si Bon/Where Am I Going?/Starting Here, Starting Now)

Harold Sings Arlen (With Friend)   Released March 1966

Contains two Streisand tracks House Of Flowers and Ding-Dong! The Witch Is Dead (duet with Arlen). Both appear on Just For The Record.

Je m'appelle Barbra   Released Oct. 1966
Billboard #5 (Certified Gold)

(Free Again/Autumn Leaves/What Now My Love/Ma Premiere Chanson/Clopin Clopant/Le Mur/I Wish You Love/Speak To Me Of Love/Love And Learn/Once Upon A Summertime/Martina/ I've Been Here)

Simply Streisand   *Released Oct. 1967*
Billboard #12 (Certified Gold)

(My Funny Valentine/The Nearness Of You/When Sunny Gets Blue/Make The Man Love Me/Lover Man (Oh, Where Can You Be?)/More Than You Know/I'll Know/All The Things You Are/The Boy Next Door/Stout-Hearted Man)

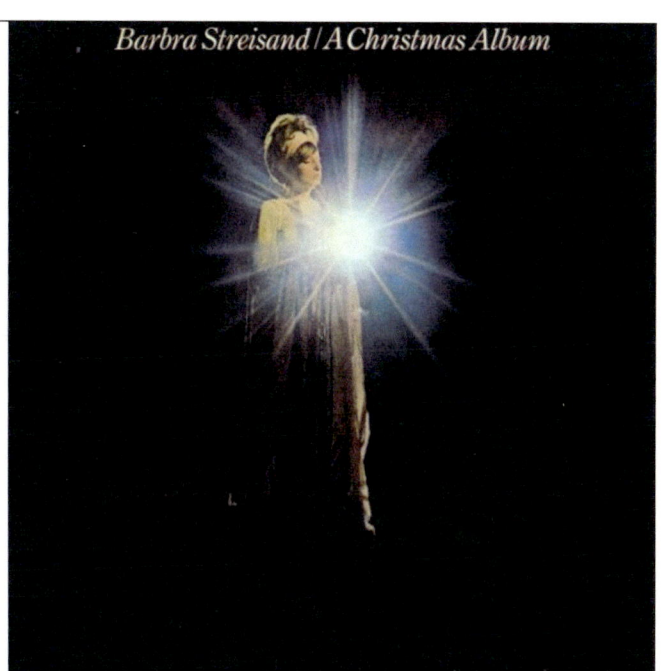

A Christmas Album   *Released Oct. 1967*
Billboard Holiday Album Chart #1
(Certified Gold & Multi-Platinum x5)

(Jingle Bells?/Have Yourself A Merry Little Christmas/The Christmas Song/White Christmas/My Favorite Things/The Best Gift/Sleep In Heavenly Peace (Silent Night)/Gounod's Ave Maria/O Little Town Of Bethlehem/I Wonder As I Wander/The Lord's Prayer)

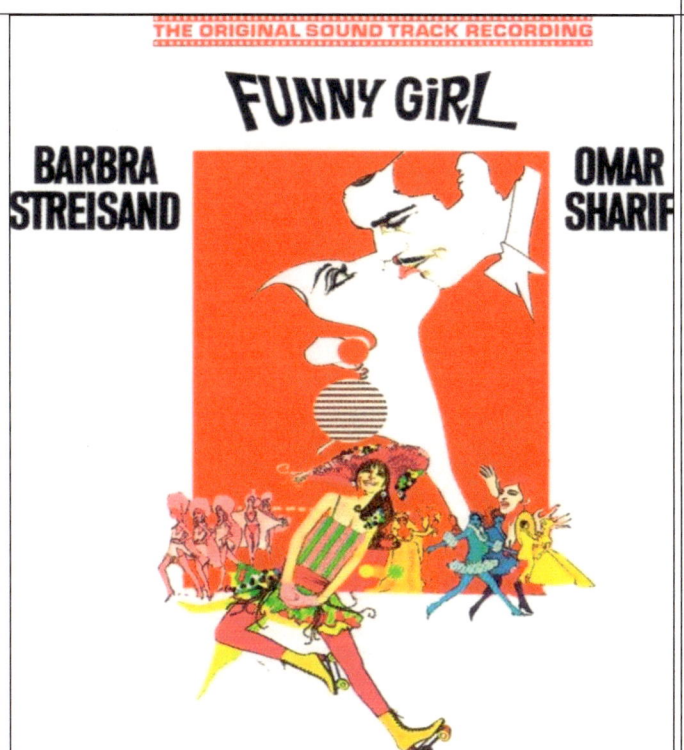

Funny Girl Original Soundtrack Recording   *Released Aug. 1968*
Billboard #12 (Certified Gold & Platinum)

(Overture/I'm The Greatest Star/If A Girl Isn't Pretty/Roller Skate Rag/I'd Rather Be Blue Over You/His Love Makes Me Beautiful/People/You Are Woman, I Am Man/Don't Rain On My Parade/Sadie, Sadie/The Swan/Funny Girl/My Man/Finale)

A Happening In Central Park   *Released Sept. 1968*
Billboard #30 (Certified Gold)

(I Can See It/Love Is Like A New Born Child/Folk Monologue/Value/Cry Me A River/People/He Touched Me/Marty The Martian/The Sound Of Music/Mississippi Mud/Santa Claus Is Comin' To Town/Natural Sounds/Second Hand Rose/Sleep In Heavenly Peace (Silent Night)/Happy Days Are Here Again)

What About Today?   *Released July 30, 1969*
Billboard #31

(What About Today?/Ask Yourself Why/Honey Pie/Punky's Dilemma/Until Its Time For You To Go/That's A Fine Kind O' Freedom/Little Tin Soldier/With A Little Help From My Friends/Alfie/The Morning After/Goodnight)

Hello Dolly Original Motion Picture Soundtrack
Billboard #49   Released Oct. 1969

(Just Leave Everything To Me/It Takes A Woman/It Takes A Woman Reprise/Put On Your Sunday Clothes/Ribbons Down My Back/Dancing/Before The Parade Passes By/Elegance/Love Is Only Love/Hello Dolly/It Only Takes A Moment/So Long Dearie/Finale)

Greatest Hits   *Released Jan 1970*
Billboard #32 (Certified Gold & Multi-Platinum x2)

(People/Second Hand Rose/Why Did I Choose You/He Touched Me/Free Again/Don't Rain On My Parade/My Coloring Book/Sam, You Made The Pants Too Long/My Man/Gotta Move/Happy Days Are Here Again)

On A Clear Day You Can See Forever Original Soundtrack Recording
Released July 1970
Billboard #108

(Hurry! It's Lovely Up Here/On A Clear Day Main Title/Love With All The Trimmings/Melinda/Go To Sleep/He Isn't You/What Did I Have That I Don't Have/Come Back To Me/On A Clear Day/On A Clear Day Reprise)

The Owl And The Pussycat Original Soundtrack Recording
Released Jan 1971

(Contains comedy highlights from film-no Streisand vocals)
Music by Blood, Sweat & Tears
(The Confrontation/The Warmup/The Seduction/The Morning After/The Reunion)

Stoney End *Released Feb. 1971*
Billboard #10 (Certified Gold & Platinum)

(I Don't Know Where I Stand/Hands Off The Man/If You Could Read My Mind/Just A Little Lovin' (Early In The Mornin')/Let Me Go/Stoney End/No Easy Way Down/Time And Love/Maybe/Free The People/I'll Be Home)

Barbra Joan Streisand *Released Aug. 1971*
Billboard #11 (Certified Gold)

(Beautiful/Love/Where You Lead/I Never Meant To Hurt You/One Less Bell To Answer-A House Is Not A Home/Space Caption/Since I Fell For You/Mother/The Summer Knows/I Mean To Shine/You've Got A Friend)

Live At The Forum *Released Oct. 1972*
Billboard #19 (Certified Gold & Platinum)

(Sing-Make Your Own Kind Of Music/Starting Here, Starting Now/Don't Rain On My Parade/Monologue/On A Clear Day/Sweet Inspiration-Where You Lead/Didn't We/My Man/Stoney End/Sing-Happy Days Are Here Again/People)

Barbra Streisand…And Other Musical Instruments
Billboard #64   Released Nov. 1973

(Piano Practicing/I Got Rhythm/Johnny One Note-One Note Samba/Glad To Be Unhappy/People/Second Hand Rose/ Don't Rain On My Parade/Don't Ever Leave Me/Monologue/ By Myself/Come Back To Me/I Never Has Seen Snow/ Lied: Auf Dem Wasser Zu Singen/The World Is A Concerto -Make Your Own Kind Of Music/The Sweetest Sounds)

The Way We Were   Released Jan. 1974
Billboard #1 (Certified Gold & Multi-Platinum x2)

(Being At War With Each Other/Something So Right/The Best Thing You've Ever Done/The Way We Were/All In Love Is Fair/What Are You Doing The Rest Of Your Life?/ Summer Me, Winter Me/Pieces Of Dreams/I've Never Been A Woman Before/My Buddy-How About Me)

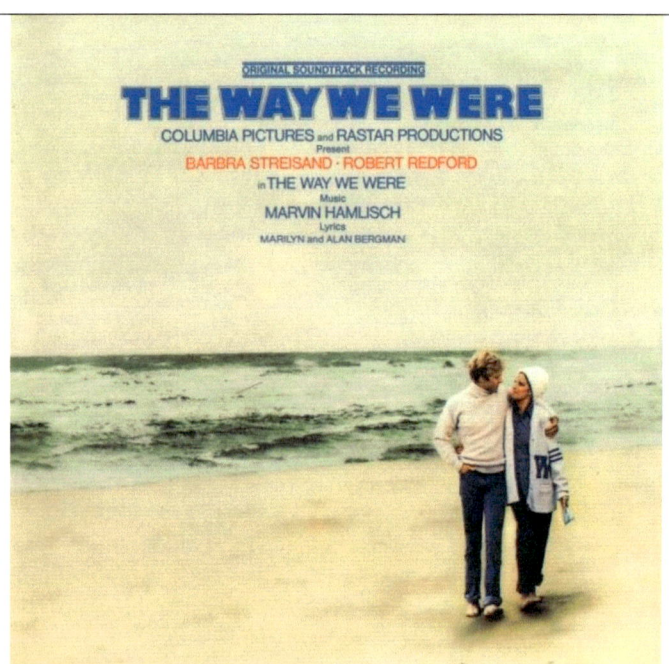

The Way We Were Original Soundtrack Recording
Released Jan. 1974
Billboard #20 (Certified Gold)

(Contains two vocal versions of The Way We Were, the rest of the album is instrumental)

Butterfly   Released Oct.28, 1974
Billboard #13 (Certified Gold)

(Love In The Afternoon/Guava Jelly/Grandma's Hands/I Won't Last A Day Without You/Jubilation/Simple Man/Life On Mars/Since I Don't Have You/Crying Time/Let The Good Times Roll)

Funny Lady Original Soundtrack Recording   Released Mar. 1975
Billboard #6 (Certified Gold)

(Blind Date/More Than You Know/It's Only A Paper Moon-I Like Him/
It's Only A Paper Moon-I Like Her/I Found A Million Dollar Baby
(In A 5 & 10 Cent Store)/So Long Honey Lamb/I Got A Code In My
Doze/Clap Hands, Here Comes Charley/Great Day/How Lucky Can
You Get/Am I Blue/Isn't It Better/If I Love Again/
Let's Hear It For Me/Me And My Shadow)

Lazy Afternoon   Released Oct. 1975
Billboard #12 (Certified Gold)

(Lazy Afternoon/My Father's Song/By The Way/Shake Me,
 Wake Me/I Never Had It So Good/Letters That Cross In
The Mail/You And I/Moanin' Low/A Child Is Born/
Widescreen)

Classical Barbra   Released Feb. 1976
Billboard #46 (Certified Gold)

(Beau Soir/Brezairola/Verschwiegene Liebe/Pavane/Apres un
Reve/In Trutina/Lascia ch'io Pianga/Mondnacht/Dank sei
Dir, Herr/I Loved You)

A Star Is Born Original Soundtrack Recording
Released Nov. 1976
Billboard #1 (Certified Gold & Multi-Platinum x4)

(Watch Closely Now/Queen Bee/Everything/Lost Inside
Of You/Hellacious Acres/Evergreen/The Woman In The
 Moon/I Believe In Love/Crippled Crow/With One More Look
At You-Watch Closely Now/Evergreen-Reprise)

Superman   Released June 1977
Billboard #3 (Certified Gold & Multi-Platinum x2)

(Superman/Don't Believe What You Read/Baby My Baby/I Found You Love/Answer Me/My Heart Belongs To Me/Cabin Fever/Love Comes From The Unexpected Places/New York State Of Mind/Lullaby For Myself)

Songbird   Released May 1978
Billboard #12 (Certified Gold & Platinum)

(Tomorrow/A Man I Loved/I Don't Break Easily/Love Breakdown/You Don't Bring Me Flowers/Honey Can I Put On Your Clothes/One More Night/Stay Away/Deep In The Night/Songbird)

Greatest Hits Volume 2   Released Nov. 1978
Billboard #1 (Certified Gold & Multi-Platinum x5)

(Evergreen/Prisoner/My Heart Belongs To Me/Songbird/ You Don't Bring Me Flowers (with Neil Diamond)/The Way We Were/Sweet Inspiration-Where You Lead/All In Love Is Fair/ Superman/Stoney End)

The Main Event Original Soundtrack Recording
Released June 1979
Billboard #20 (Certified Gold)

(The Main Event-Fight/The Body Shop/Main Event-Short version/Instrumental Copeland Meets Coasters-Get A Job/Big Girls Don't Cry/It's Your Foot Again/Angry Eyes/ I'd Clean A Fish For You/The Main Event-Ballad version)

Wet *Released Oct. 1979*
Billboard #7 (Certified Gold & Platinum)

(Wet/Come Rain Or Come Shin/Splish Splash/On Rainy Afternoons/After The Rain/No More Tears (Enough Is Enough) (Duet with Donna Summer)/Niagara/I Ain't Gonna Cry Tonight/Kiss Me In The Rain)

Guilty *Released Sept. 1980*
Billboard #1 (Certified Gold & Multi-Platinum x5)

(Guilty (with Barry Gibb)/Woman In Love/Run Wild/ Promises/The Love Inside/What Kind Of Fool (with Barry Gibb) /Life Story/Never Give Up/Make It Like A Memory)

Memories *Released Nov. 1981*
Billboard #10 (Certified Gold & Multi-Platinum x5)

(Memory/You Don't Bring Me Flowers/My Heart Belongs To Me/New York State Of Mind/No More Tears (Enough Is Enough)/ Comin' In And Out Of Your Life/Evergreen/Lost Inside Of You/The Love Inside/The Way We Were)

Yentl Original Soundtrack Recording *Released Nov. 1983*
Billboard #9 (Certified Gold & Platinum)

(Where Is It Written?/Papa, Can You Hear Me?/This Is One Of Those Moments/No Wonder/The Way He Makes Me Feel/No Wonder (Part two)/Tomorrow Night/Will Someone Ever Look At Me That Way?/No Matter What Happens/No Wonder (Reprise)/A Piece Sky/The Way He Makes Me Feel (studio version)/No Matter What Happens (studio version)

Emotion Released Oct. 1984
Billboard #19 (Certified Gold & Platinum)

(Emotion/Make No Mistake, He's Mine (Duet with Kim Carnes)/ Time Machine/Best I Could/Left In The Dark/Heart Don't Change My Mind/When I Dream/You're A Step In The Right Direction/ Clear Sailing/Here We Are At Last)

The Broadway Album Released Nov. 4, 1985
Billboard #1 (Certified Gold & Multi-Platinum x4)

(Putting It Together/If I Loved You/Something's Coming/ Not While I'm Around/Being Alive/I Have Dream-We Kiss In A Shadow-Something Wonderful/Adelaide's Lament/Send In The Clowns/Pretty Woman-The Ladies Who Lunch/Can't Help Lovin' That Man/I Loves You Porgy-Porgy, I's Your Woman Now (Bess, You Is My Woman)/Somewhere)

One Voice Released April 20, 1987
Billboard #9 (Certified Gold & Platinum)

(Somewhere/Evergreen/Something's Coming/People/Send In The Clowns/Over The Rainbow/Guilty & What Kind Of Fool with Barry Gibb/Papa, Can You Hear Me?/The Way We Were/It's A New World/Happy Days Are Here Again/ America The Beautiful)

Nuts Original Soundtrack Recording Released Dec. 21, 1987

(Instrumentals by Streisand-no vocals)
(The Apartment/The Bar/The Hospital/The Finale/The End Credits)

Till I Loved You   Released Oct. 25, 1988
Billboard #10 (Certified Gold & Platinum)

(The Places You Find Love/On My Way To You/Till I Loved You (Duet with Don Johnson)/Love Light/All I Ask Of You/You And Me For Always/Why Let It Go?/Two People/What Were We Thinking Of/Some Good Things Never Last/One More Time Around)

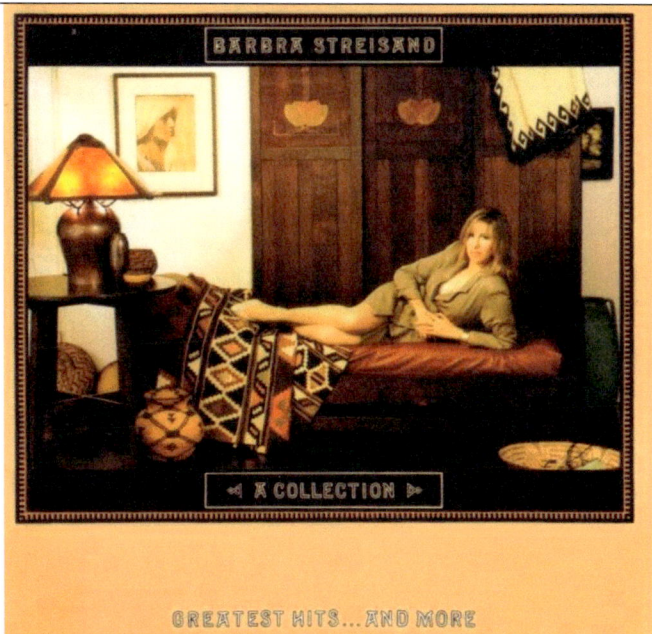

A Collection Greatest Hits…And More   Released Oct. 3, 1989
Billboard #26 (Certified Gold & Multi-Platinum x2)

(We're Not Makin' Love Anymore/Woman In Love/All I Ask Of You/Comin' In And Out Of Your Life/What Kind Of Fool/The Main Event/Someone That I Used To Love/By The Way/Guilty/Memory/The Way He Makes Me Feel/Somewhere)

Just For The Record
Released Sept. 24, 1991
Billboard #38 (Certified Gold & Platinum)

The 60's
You'll Never Know/A Sleepin' Bee/Moon River/Miss Marmelstein/Happy Days Are Here Again/Keepin' Out Of Mischief/I Hate Music/Nobody's Heart Belongs To Me/Value/Cry Me A River/Who's Afraid Of The Big Bad Wolf?/I Had Myself A True Love/Lover, Come Back To Me/Spring Can Really Hang You Up The Most/My Honey's Lovin' Arms/Any Place I Hang My Hat Is Home/When The Sun Comes Out/Judy Garland-Be My Guest/Get Happy-Happy Days Are Here Again (with Judy Garland)

The 60's part two
I'm The Greatest Star/My Man—Auld Lang Syne/People/Family Recording-My Name Is Barbra Medley/1965 Emmy Awards/He Touched Me/You Wanna Bet/House Of Flowers/Ding-Dong! The Witch Is Dead (with Harold Arlen)/Have I Stayed Too Long At The Fair/Starting Here, Starting Now/A Good Man Is Hard To Find-Some Of These Days/I'm Always Chasing Rainbows/Silent Night/Don't Rain On My Parade/Funny Girl/1969 Academy Awards/1969 Friars Club Tribute/Hello Dolly/On A Clear Day/When You Gotta Go-In The Wee Small Hours Of The Morning

The 70's
The Singer/I Can Do It/Stoney End/Close To You (with Burt Bacharach)/We've Only Just Begun/Since I Fell For You/You're The Top (with Ryan O'Neal)/What Are You Doing The Rest Of Your Life?/If I Close My Eyes/Between Yesterday And Tomorrow/Can You Tell The Moment/The Way We Were (soundtrack)/Cryin' Time (with Ray Charles)/God Bless This Child/A Quiet Thing-There Won't Be Trumpets/Lost Inside Of You/Evergreen (demo/soundtrack)/1977 Academy Awards/Hatikvah

The 80's
You Don't Bring Me Flowers (live 1980 Grammy's)/The Way We Weren't (live)-The Way We Were/Guilty/Papa, Can You Hear Me? (demo)/The Moon And I (demo)/A Piece Of Sky (demo/soundtrack)/I Know Him So Well/If I Loved You/Putting It Together/Over The Rainbow/Nuts theme (End Credits)/Here We Are At Last/Warm All Over/You'll Never Know

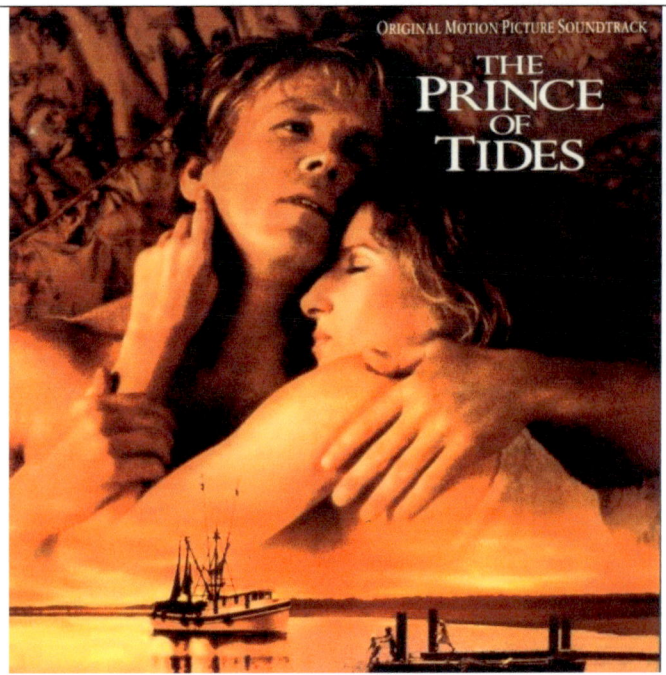

The Prince Of Tides Original Motion Picture Soundtrack
Released Nov. 12, 1991
Billboard #84

(Contains two Streisand tracks Places That Belong To You & For All We Know. Original score by James Newton Howard.)

Highlights From Just For The Record
Released June 30, 1992

(Contains 24 tracks taken from the box set)

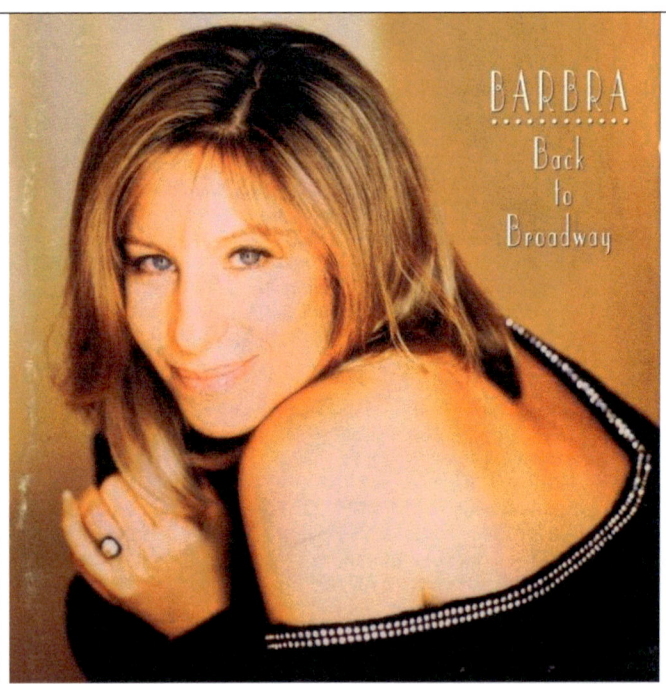

Back To Broadway   ***Released June 29, 1993***
Billboard #1 (Certified Gold & Multi Platinum x2)

(Some Enchanted Evening/Everybody Says Don't/The Music Of The Night (with Michael Crawford)/Speak Low/As If We Never Said Goodbye/Children Will Listen/I Have A Love-One Hand, One Heart (with Johnny Mathis)/I've Never Been In Love Before/Luck Be A Lady/With One Look/The Man I Love/ Move On)

The Concert   ***Released Sept. 27, 1994***
Billboard #10 (Certified Gold & Multi-Platinum x3)

(Act I: Overture/As If We Never Said Goodbye/I'm Still Here-Everybody Says Don't-Don't Rain On My Parade/Can't Help Lovin' That Man Of Mine/I'll Know/People/Lover Man/Therapist Dialogue #1/Will He Like Me? Therapist Dialogue #2/He Touched Me/Evergreen/Therapist Dialog #3/ The Man That Got Away/On A Clear Day/Act II: Entr'acte/ The Way We Were/You Don't Bring Me Flowers/Lazy Afternoon/When You Wish Upon A Star-Someday My Prince Will Come/Not While I'm Around/Ordinary Miracles/Where Is It Written-Papa, Can You Hear Me-Will Someone Ever Look At Me That Way-A Piece Of Sky/Happy Days Are Here Again/ My Man/For All We Know/Somewhere)

The Concert-Highlights Released May 2, 1995
Billboard #81 (Certified Gold)

(Contains 20 tracks taken from The Concert)

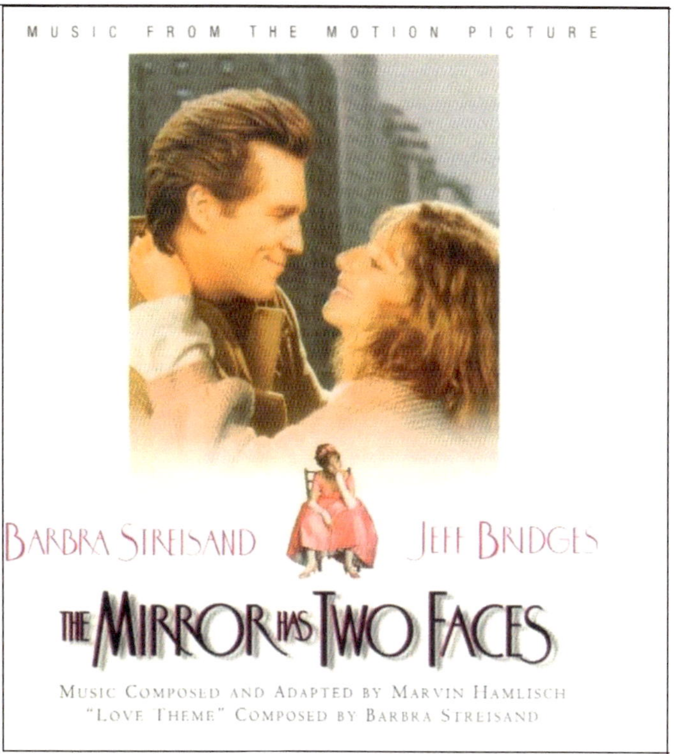

The Mirror Has Two Faces Soundtrack Recording
Released Nov. 12, 1996
Billboard #16 (Certified Gold & Platinum)

(Contains two Streisand songs I Finally Found Someone with Bryan Adams & All Of My Life. Instrumentals by Marvin Hamlisch)

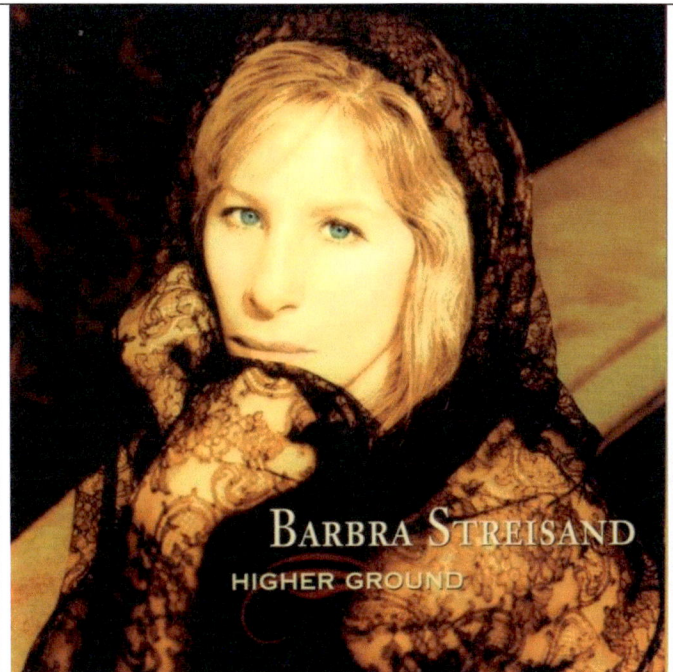

Higher Ground Released Nov. 11, 1997
Billboard #1 (Certified Gold & Multi-Platinum x3)

(I Believe-You'll Never Walk Alone/Higher Ground/At The Same Time/Tell Him (with Celine Dion)/On Holy Ground/ If I Could/Circle/The Water Is Wide-Deep River/Leading With Your Heart/Lessons To Be Learned/Everything Must Change/ Avinu Malkeinu)

A Love Like Ours Released Sept. 21, 1999
Billboard #6 (Certified Gold & Platinum)

(I've Dreamed Of You/Isn't It A Pity?/The Island/Love Like Ours/ If You Ever Leave Me (with Vince Gill)/We Must Be Loving Right/ If I Never Met You/It Must Be You/Just One Lifetime/If I Didn't Love You/Wait/The Music That Makes Me Dance (with Kenny G)

Act One:
(Opening-You'll Never Know (Lauren Frost)/Something's Coming (with Lauren Frost)/The Way We Were/Shirley Maclaine Y1K/Cry Me A River/Lover, Come Back To Me/A Sleepin' Bee/Miss Marmelstein/I'm The Greatest Star-Second Hand Rose-Don't Rain On My Parade/Something Wonderful-Being Alive/As Time Goes By-Speak Low/Alfie/Evergreen/Dialogue (Father part #1/Papa, Can You Hear Me-You'll Never Know (with Frost)/A Piece Of Sky (with Frost)

Act Two:
(Overture-Putting It Together/On A Clear Day (You Can See Forever)/Send In The Clowns/Duets (medley)/Sing (with Jason Gould-I've Got A Crush On You (with Frank Sinatra)/Technology (dialogue)/The Clicker Blues/Simple Pleasures/The Main Event-Fight/Dialogue (Father Part #2/ I've Dreamed of You/At The Same Time/Auld Lang Syne (Ballad)/Dialogue (with Brother Time)/People/Auld Lang Syne (New Years Celebration)/Every Time You Hear Auld Lang Syne/Happy Days Are Here Again/Don't Like Goodbyes/I Believe-Somewhere (with Lauren Frost)

Timeless- Live In Concert   Released Sept. 19, 2000
Billboard #21 (Certified Gold & Platinum)

Christmas Memories   Released Oct. 30, 2001
Billboard #15 (Certified Gold & Platinum)

(I'll Be Home For Christmas/A Christmas Love Song/What Are You Doing New Year's Eve?/I Remember/Snowbound/It Must Have Been The Mistletoe/Christmas Lullaby/Christmas Mem'ries/Grown-Up Christmas List/Ave Maria/Closer/One God)

Duets   Released Nov. 26, 2002
Billboard #38 (Certified Gold)

(I Won't Be The One To Let Go (Barry Manilow)/Guilty (Barry Gibb)/You Don't Bring Me Flowers (Neil Diamond)/I Finally Found Someone (Bryan Adams)/Cryin' Time (Ray Charles)/I've Got A Crush On You (Frank Sinatra)/Tell Him (Celine Dion)/No More Tears (Donna Summer)/What Kind Of Fool (Gibb)/I Have A Love-One Hand, One Heart (Johnny Mathis)/One Less Bell-A House Is Not A Home (Barbra)/Lost Inside Of You (Kris Kristofferson)/Till I Loved You (Don Johnson)/Make No Mistake, He's Mine (Kim Carnes)/If You Ever Leave Me (Vince Gill)/The Music Of The Night (Michael Crawford)/Ding-Dong! The Witch Is Dead (Harold Arlen)/Get Happy-Happy Days Are Here Again (Judy Garland)/All I Know Of Love (Josh Groban)

Disc 1
(A Sleepin' Bee/Cry Me A River/I Stayed Too Long At The Fair/Lover, Come Back To Me/People/My Man/Second Hand Rose/He Touched Me/Don't Rain On My Parade/Happy Days Are Here Again/On A Clear Day/Stoney End/Since I Fell For You/What Are You Doing The Rest Of Your Life?/The Way We Were/All In The Love Is Fair/Lazy Afternoon/Evergreen/My Heart Belongs To Me/You Don't Bring Me Flowers/The Main Event-Fight/No More Tears (Enough Is Enough)

Disc 2
(Woman In Love/Guilty/Comin' In And Out Of Your Life/Memory/Papa, Can You Hear Me?/A Piece Of Sky/Putting It Together/Not While I'm Around/Send In The Clowns/Somewhere/All I Ask Of You/Children Will Listen/As If We Never Said Goodbye/I Finally Found Someone/Tell Him/I've Dreamed Of You/Someday My Price Will Come/You'll Never Walk Alone)

The Essential   Released Jan. 29, 2002
Billboard #15 *(Certified Gold & Platinum)*

The Movie Album   Released Oct. 14, 2003
Billboard #5 *(Certified Gold)*

(Smile/Moon River/I'm In the Mood For Love/Wild Is The Wind/Emily/More In Love With You/How Do You Keep The Music Playing?/But Beautiful/Calling You/The Second Time Around/Goodbye For Now/You're Gonna Hear From Me)

Guilty Pleasures   Released Sept. 20, 2005
Billboard #5 *(Certified Gold)*

(Come Tomorrow (with Barry Gibb)/Stranger In A Strange Land/Hideaway/It's Up To You/Night Of My Life/Above The Law (with Barry Gibb)/Without Your Love/All The Children/Golden Dawn/(Our Love) Don't Throw It All Away/Letting Go)

Act 1
(Overture/Starting Here, Starting Now/Down With Love/The Way We Were/Ma Premiere Chanson/Evergreen (with Il Divo)/Come Rain Or Come Shine/Funny Girl/The Music That Makes Me Dance/My Man/People)

Act 2
(Overture/The Music Of The Night (with Il Divo)/Jason's Theme/Carefully Taught-Children Will Listen/Unusual Way/What Are You Doing The Rest Of Your Life? /Happy Days Are Here Again/Have I Stayed Too Long At The Fair/The Time Of Your Life (Dialogue) /A Cockeyed Optimist/Somewhere (with Il Divo)/My Shinning Hour/Don't Rain On My Parade (Reprise)/Smile)

Live In Concert 2006   *Released May, 8, 2007*
Billboard #7

Love Is The Answer   *Released Sept. 29, 2009*
Billboard #1 (Certified Gold)

(Here's To Life/In The Wee Small Hours Of The Morning/Gentle Rain/If You Go Away/Spring Can Really Hang You Up The Most/Make Someone Happy/Where Do You Start?/A Time For Love/Here's That Rainy Day/Love Dance/Smoke Gets In Your Eyes/Some Other Time/You Must Believe In Spring)

What Matters Most   *Released Aug. 23, 2011*
Billboard #4

(The Wind Mills Of Your Mind/Something New In My Life/Solitary Moon/Nice N' Easy/Alone In The World/So Many Stars/The Same Hello, The Same Goodbye/That Face/I'll Never Say Goodbye/What Matters Most)

Release Me Released Oct. 9, 2012
Billboard #7

(Being Good Isn't Good Enough/Didn't We/Willow Weep For Me/Try To Win A Friend/I Think It's Going To Rain Today/With One More Look At You/Lost In Wonderland/How Are Things In Glocca Morra?-Heather On The Hill/Mother And Child/If It's Meant To Be/Home)

Back To Brooklyn Released Nov. 25, 2013

Although released as a single album, the DVD/CD Deluxe Edition only charted on Billboard, not on the Top Album 200, but on the Top Music Videos at #1.

(I Remember Barbra #1/As If We Never Said Goodbye/Nice 'n' Easy-That Face/The Way He Makes Me Feel/Bewitched, Bothered and Bewildered/Didn't We/Marvin Hamlisch intro/The Way We Were- Through The Eyes Of Love/Jule Styne intro/Being Good Isn't Good Enough/Rose's Turn-Some People-Don't Rain On My Parade/I Remember Barbra #2/You're The Top/What'll I Do-My Funny Valentine (w/Chris Botti)/Lost Inside Of You-Evergreen w/Chris Botti)/Jason Gould intro/How Deep Is The Ocean (w/Jason Gould)/People/Here's To Life (w/intro)/Make Our Garden Grow/Some Other Time (w/intro)

Partners Released Sept. 16, 2014
Billboard #1 (Certified Gold)

(It Had To Be You (Michael Buble)/People (Stevie Wonder)/Come Rain Or Come Shine (John Mayer)/Evergreen (Babyface)/New York State Of Mind (Billy Joel)/I'd Want It To Be You (Blake Shelton)/The Way We Were (Lionel Richie)/I Still Can See Your Face (Andrea Bocelli)/How Deep Is The Ocean (Jason Gould)/What Kind Of Fool (John Legend)/Somewhere (Josh Groban)/Love Me Tender (Elvis Presley)

23

7" Singles US

This is a complete discography of Streisand's US singles (45's) released on vinyl, all on the Columbia label unless noted. The commercial release is shown first, followed by the promotional copy. The promo copies were sent to radio stations and have the same catalog numbers as the regular releases. Some titles were reissued as Columbia Hall Of Fame singles. There has been mention of a Columbia promo single of For Pete's Sake (Don't Let Him Down) (#93028), but unable to confirm.

(Label with extra 'a' in Barbra)

Miss Marmelstein/Who Knows? (Marilyn Cooper)
(JZSP 57067) Promotional-only Released 4-62

 *Happy Days Are Here Again/When The Sun Comes Out (alternate takes)* *#4-42631 Released 11-62*	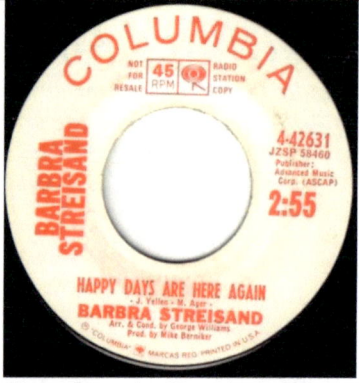 *Happy Days Are Here Again/When The Sun Comes Out* *Promotional copy (Radio Station copy)*	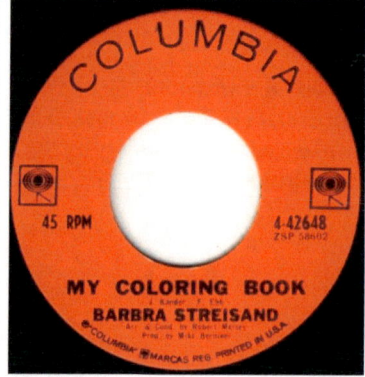 *My Coloring Book/Lover Come Back To Me (alternate takes)* *#4-42648 Released 11-62*
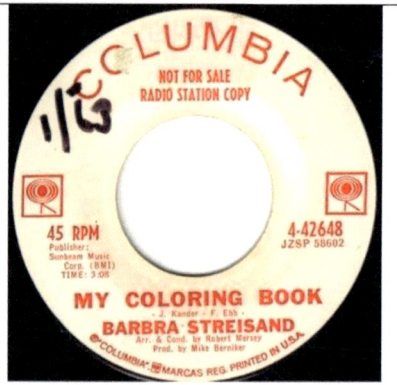 *My Coloring Book/Lover Come Back To Me* *Promotional copy*	 *Lover, Come Back To Me/Any Place I Hang My Hat Is Home Jukebox release* *#3-8854 Released 1963 33 1/3 rpm single*	 *Gotta Move/I Don't Care Much* *Promotional-only* *#JZSP 115999 Released 8-63*
 *My Melancholy Baby/Never Will I Marry* *Special Jukebox 33 1/3 rpm release* *#3-38954 Released 1964*	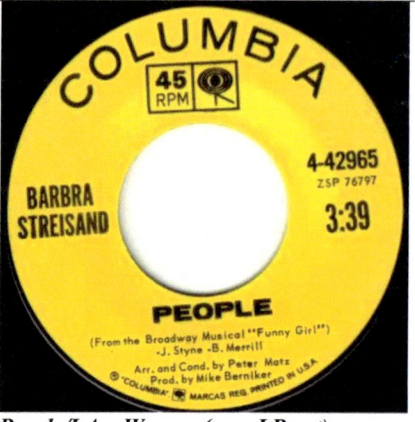 *People/I Am Woman (non-LP cut)* *#4-42965 Released 1-64*	 *People/I Am Woman* *Promotional copy*
 *Special Open End Interview People* *30-minute program on 33 1/3 rpm* *#ZLP 79581 (1964)*	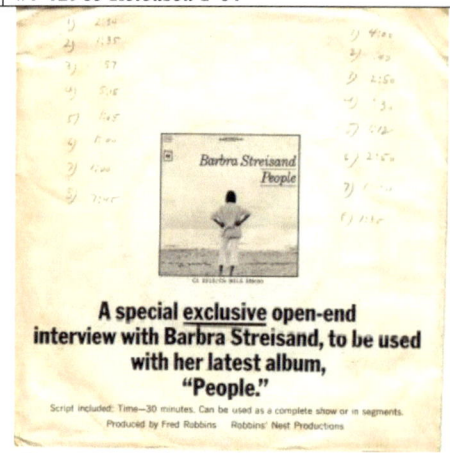 *(Front picture sleeve of People Interview 7")*	 *(Back of picture sleeve)*

 People/I Am Woman (same catalog # 1964) Special purple vinyl promo-only release	 People/I Am Woman #4-42965 Rarely seen on red label	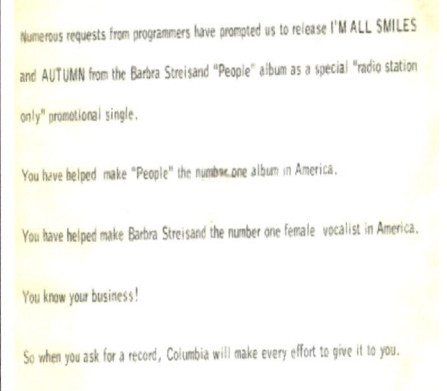 I'm All Smiles/Autumn (JZSP #79184) 1964 White label promo-only release in plain text sleeve
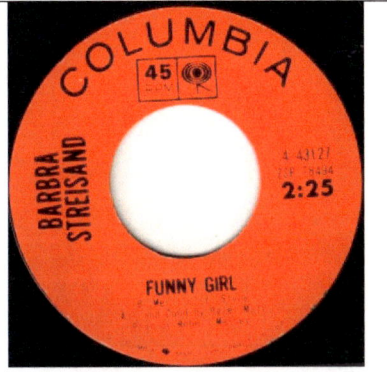 Funny Girl (non-LP cut)/Absent Minded Me #4-43127 Released 8-64	 Funny Girl/Absent Minded Me Promotional copy	 Why Did I Choose You/My Love (non-LP cut) #4-43248 Released 3-65
 Why Did I Choose You/My Love Promotional copy	 Why Did I Choose You special promo-only Blue vinyl release (1965)(same catalog #) Issued as 3:49 and also 2:49	 My Man/Where Is The Wonder #4-43323 Released 6-65
 My Man/Where Is The Wonder Promotional copy	 He Touched Me/I Like Him (non-LP cut) #4-43403 Released 9-65	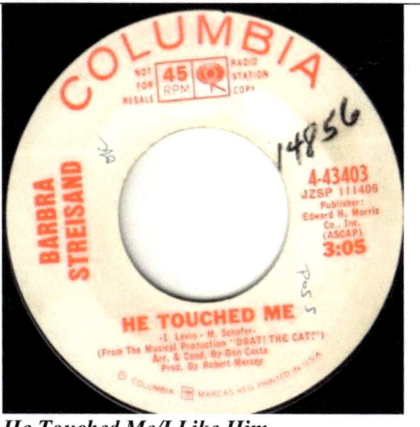 He Touched Me/I Like Him Promotional copy

Second Hand Rose/The Kind Of Man A Woman Needs
#4-43469 Released 11-65

Second Hand Rose/The Kind Of Man A Woman Needs
Promotional copy

Second Hand Rose (both sides)
Rare promotional-only red vinyl issue
(Same catalog #)

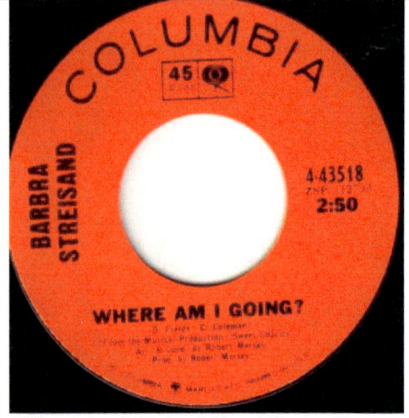
Where Am I Going?/You Wanna Bet
#4-43518 Released 1-66

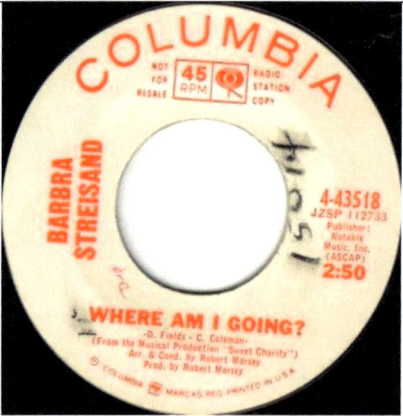
Where Am I Going?/You Wanna Bet
Promotional copy

Sam, You Made The Pants Too Long/The Minute Waltz
#4-43612 Released 4-66

Sam, You Made The Pants Too Long/The Minute Waltz
Promotional copy

Non…C'est Rien/Le Mur
#4-43739 Released 7-66

Non…C'est Rien/Le Mur
Promotional copy

Free Again/I've Been Here
#4-43808 Released 9-66

Free Again/I've Been Here
Promotional copy

Silent Night/Ave Maria
#4-43896 Red label with text sleeve
Released 10-66

Stout-Hearted Men/Look (non-LP cut)
#4-44225 Released 6-67

Stout-Hearted Me/Look
Promotional copy

Lover Man (Oh, Where Can You Be?)/
My Funny Valentine
#4-44331 Released 10-67

Lover Man (Oh, Where Can You Be?)/
My Funny Valentine
Promotional copy

Jingle Bells?/White Christmas
#4-44350 Released 11-67

Jingle Bells?/White Christmas
Promotional copy with promo-only
picture sleeve (white label)

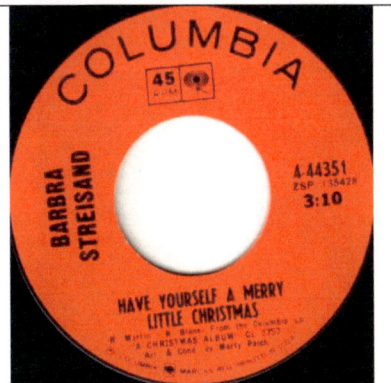
Have Yourself A Merry Little Christmas/
The Best Gift
#4-44351 Released 11-67

Have Yourself A Merry Little Christmas/
The Best Gift
Promotional copy promo sleeve (white label)

My Favorite Things/The Christmas Song
#4-44352 Released 11-67

My Favorite Things/The Christmas Song
Promotional copy promo sleeve (white label)

The Lord's Prayer/I Wonder As I Wander
#4-44354 Released 11-67

The Lord's Prayer/I Wonder As I Wander
Promotional copy promo sleeve (white label)

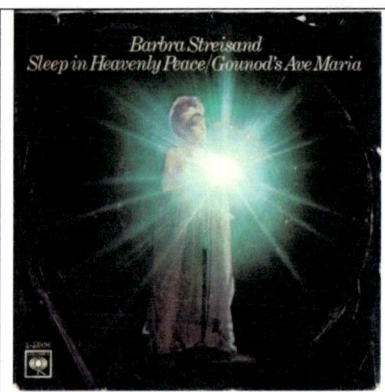
Sleep In Heavenly Peace/Gounod's Ave Maria white label promo copy & sleeve (Catalog # same as '66 release) 11-67

Our Corner Of The Night/He Could Show Me (both non-LP cuts) #4-44474 Released 2-68

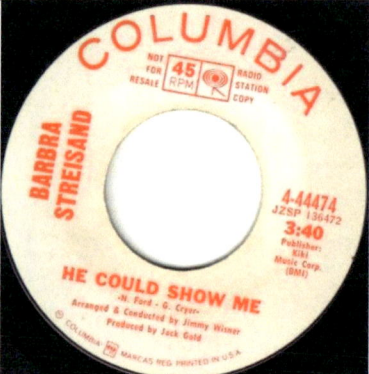
Our Corner Of The Night/He Could Show Me Promotional copy

Our Corner Of The Night/He Could Show Me Rare promotional copy yellow label #ZSP-118643

The Morning After/Where Is The Wonder #4-44532 Released 4-68

The Morning After/Where Is The Wonder Promotional copy

Funny Girl/I'd Rather Be Blue (both alternate takes) #4-44622 Released 7-68

Funny Girl/I'd Rather Be Blue Promotional copy

My Man/Don't Rain On My Parade #4-44704 Red label Released 11-68

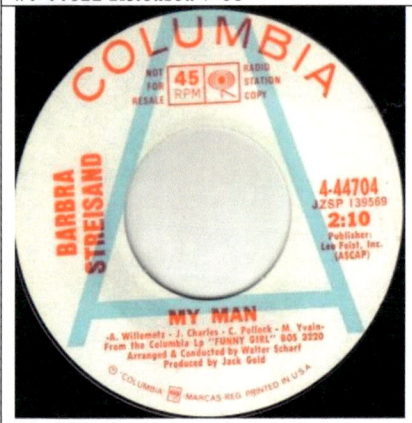
My Man/Don't Rain On My Parade Promotional copy

Frank Mills (non-LP cut)/Punky's Dilemma #4-44775 Released 2-69

Frank Mills/Punky's Dilemma Promotional copy

Little Tin Soldier/Honey Pie
#4-44921 Released 7-69

Little Tin Soldier/Honey Pie
Promotional copy

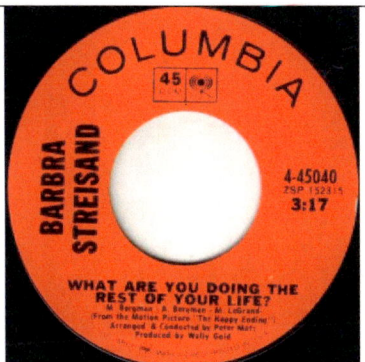
What Are You Doing The Rest Of Your Life?
/What About Today?
#4-45040 Released 10-69

What Are You Doing The Rest Of Your Life?
/What About Today? Promotional copy
Also blue label promo issued

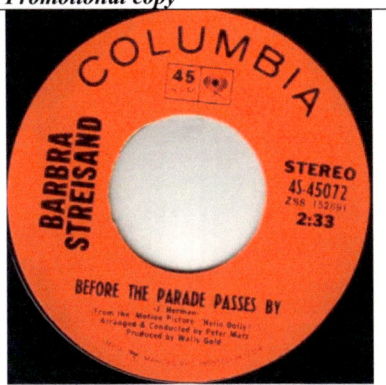
Before The Parade Passes By/Love Is Only Love (alternate takes)
#4S-45072 Released 12-69

Before The Parade Passes By/Love Is Only Love
Promotional copy

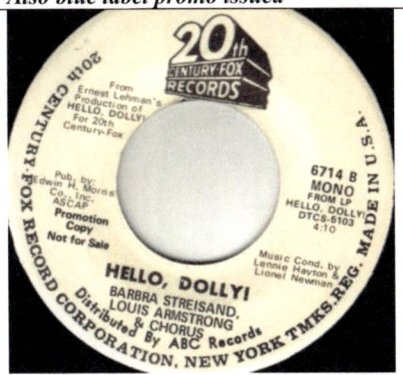
Hello, Dolly! (stereo/mono)
Promotional-only 20th Century Fox Records
#6714 Released 12-69

The Best Thing You've Ever Done/Summer Me, Winter Me
#4-45147 Released 4-70

The Best Thing You've Ever Done/Summer Me, Winter Me
Promotional copy

On A Clear Day (You Can See Forever)
(Stereo/mono) (Alternate take)
Rare promo-only Released 7-70 #AE 24

Love With All The Trimmings (stereo/mono)
Promotional-only (1970)
#AS 1

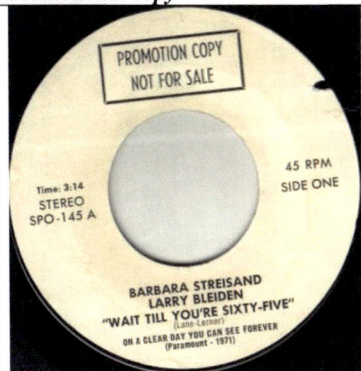
Wait Till You're Sixty-Five (non-LP cut)
/Dean Martin Guiding Star
Promotional-only bootleg (1970's)
#SPO-145 A

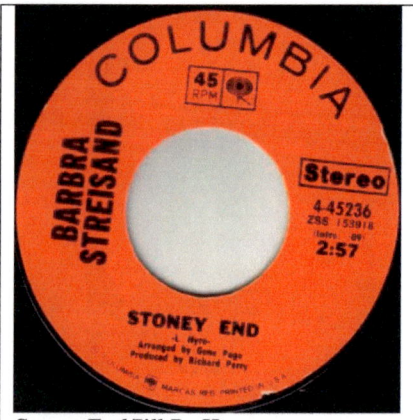
Stoney End/I'll Be Home
#4-45236 Released 9-70

Stoney End (both sides)
Promotional copy

Time And Love/No Easy Way Down
#4-45341 Released 2-71

Time And Love (stereo/mono versions)
Promotional copy

Flim Flam Man/Maybe
#4-45384 Released 4-71

Flim Flam Man (stereo/mono versions)
Promotional copy

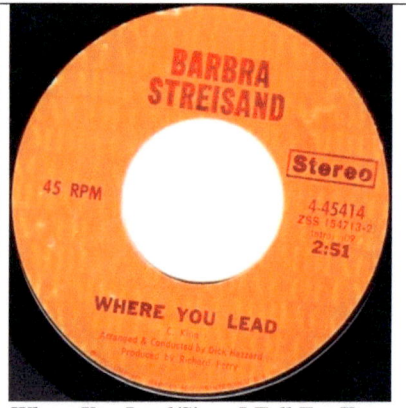
Where You Lead/Since I Fell For You
#4-45414 Released 6-71

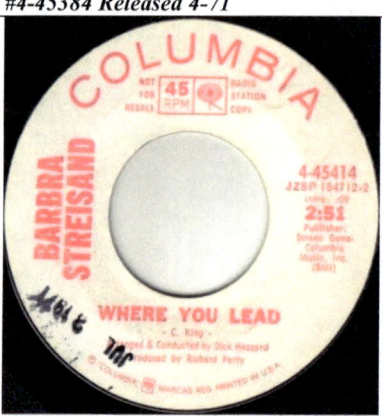
Where You Lead/Since I Fell For You
Promotional copy

Mother/The Summer Knows
#4-45471 Released 9-71

Mother (stereo/mono versions)
Promotional copy

*Space Captain/One Less Bell To Answer-
A House Is Not A* #4-45511 Released 11-71

*Space Captain/One Less Bell To Answer-
A House Is Not A Home*
Promotional copy

Sweet Inspiration-Where You Lead/Didn't We
#4-45626 Released 5-72

Sweet Inspiration-Where You Lead (Stereo/mono versions)
Promotional copy

Sing A Song-Make Your Own Kind Of Music/Starting Here, Starting Now
#4-45686 Released 8-72

Sing A Song-Make Your Own Kind Of Music (Stereo/mono versions)
Promotional copy

Didn't We/On A Clear Day (You Can See Forever)
#4-45739 Released 11-72

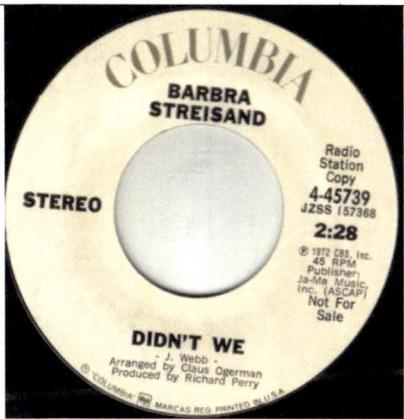
Didn't We (stereo/mono versions)
Promotional copy

If I Close My Eyes/instrumental
#4-45780 gray label
Released 1-73

If I Close My Eyes (stereo/mono versions)
(Issued with picture sleeve same as regular copy except no photo collage on right corner)

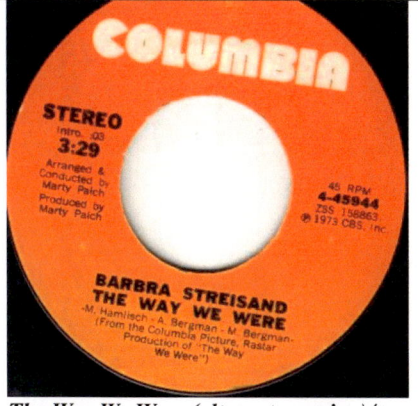
The Way We Were (alternate version)/What Are You Doing The Rest Of Your Life?
#4-45944 Released 9-73

The Way We Were (stereo/mono versions)
Promotional copy

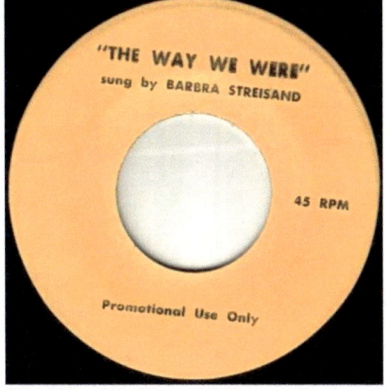
The Way We Were (different alternate take)
Rare 1-sided promo-only single sent to Movie theaters (1973) No catalog #

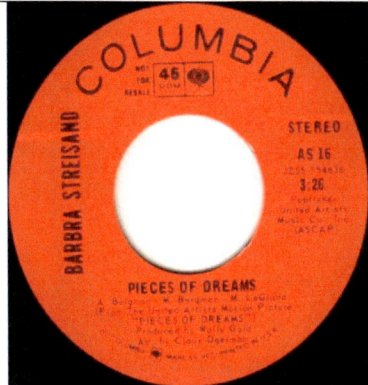
Pieces Of Dreams (both sides)
Rare promotional-only single #AS 16
Sent to Academy Awards members in 1971

33

All In Love Is Fair/My Buddy-How About Me
#4-46024 Released 3-74

All In Love Is Fair (stereo/mono versions)
Promotional copy

Guava Jelly/Love In The Afternoon
#3-10075 Released 12-74

Guava Jelly (stereo/mono versions)
Promotional copy

Jubilation/Let The Goods Times Roll
#3-10130 Released 4-75

Jubilation (stereo/mono versions)
Promotional copy

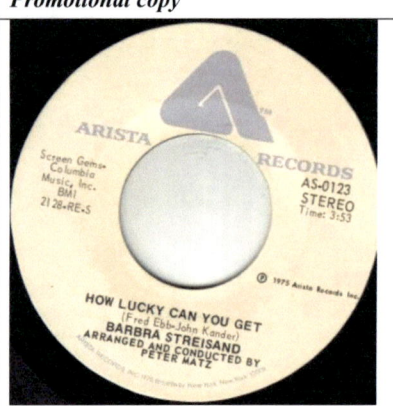
How Lucky Can You Get (alternate)/More Than You Know
Arista #AS-0123 Released 4-75

How Lucky Can You Get/More Than You Know (both in mono)
Promotional copy

If I Love Again/Let's Here It For Me
Promotional-only
Arista #EX-1 Released 5-75

My Father's Song/By The Way
#3-10198 Released 8-75

My Father's Song (stereo/mono versions)
Promotional copy

Shake Me, Wake Me (When It's Over)/ Widescreen
#3-10272 Released 12-75

Shake Me, Wake Me (When Its Over)
(Short & rare long version)
Promotional-only

Evergreen/I Believe In Love
#3-10450 Released 11-76

Evergreen (stereo/mono versions)
Promotional copy

My Heart Belongs To Me/Answer Me
#3-10555 Released 5-77

My Heart Belongs To Me
(Stereo/mono versions)
Promotional copy

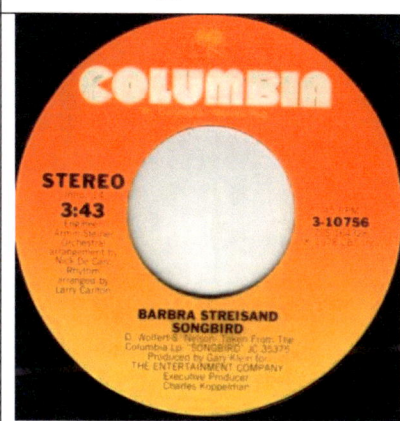
Songbird/Honey Can I Put On Your Clothes
#3-10756 Released 5-78

Songbird (stereo/mono versions)
Promotional copy

Love Theme From Eyes Of Laura Mars
(Prisoner)/Instrumental
#3-10777 Released 7-78

Love Theme From Eyes Of Laura Mars
(Prisoner) (stereo/mono versions)
Promotional copy

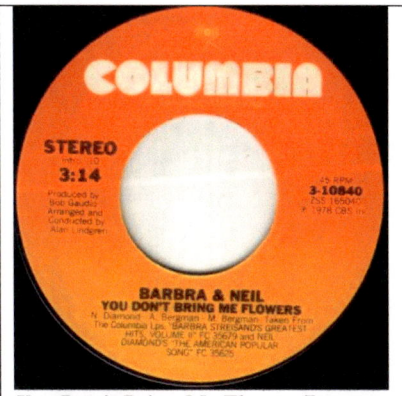
You Don't Bring Me Flowers/Instrumental
(with Neil Diamond)
#3-10840 Released 10-78

You Don't Bring Me Flowers (stereo/
mono versions)
Promotional copy

Superman/A Man I Loved
#3-10931 Released 3-79

Superman (stereo/mono versions)
Promotional copy

The Main Event-Fight/Instrumental
#3-11008 Released 6-79

The Main Event-Fight (long/short versions)
Promotional copy

The Main Event (Ballad/The Main Event-Fight (short version) #AE7 1192
Promotional-only Released 6-79

No More Tears (Enough Is Enough)/Wet (with Donna Summer)
#1-11125 Released 10-79

No More tears (Enough Is Enough) (both sides)
Promotional copy

Kiss Me In The Rain/I Ain't Gonna Cry Tonight
#1-11179 Released 12-79

Kiss Me In The Rain (both sides)
Promotional copy

Woman In Love/Run Wild
#1-11364 Released 8-80

Woman In Love (both sides)
Promotional copy

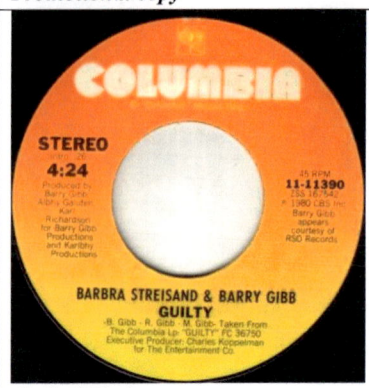
Guilty/Life Story (with Barry Gibb)
#11-11390 Released 10-80

Guilty (both sides)
Promotional copy

What Kind Of Fool (with Barry Gibb)/ The Love Inside #11-11430 Released 1-81	*What Kind Of Fool (both sides)* Promotional copy	*Promises/Make It Like A Memory* #11-02065 Released 4-81
Promises (both sides) Promotional copy	*Comin' In And Out Of Your Life/ Lost Inside Of You* #18-02621 Released 11-81	*Comin' In And Out Of Your Life (both sides)* Promotional copy
Memory/Evergreen #18-02717 Released 2-82	*Memory (both sides)* Promotional copy	*The Way He Makes Me Feel (Studio & Film versions)* #38-04177 Released 10-83
The Way He Makes Me Feel (Studio Versions both sides) white label Promotional copy with rare picture sleeve	*Papa, Can You Hear Me?/Will Someone Ever Look At Me That Way?* #38-04357 Released 1-84	*Papa, Can You Hear Me? (both sides)* Promotional copy

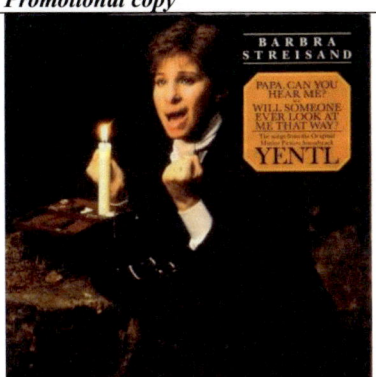

37

Left In The Dark/Here We Are At Last
#38-04605 Released 9-84

Left In The Dark (with/without spoken intro)
Promotional copy (same sleeve)

Make No Mistake, He's Mine (with Kim Carnes)/Clear Sailing
#38-04695 Released 12-84

Make No Mistake, He's Mine (both sides)
Promotional copy with same sleeve

Emotion/Here We Are At Last
#38-04707 Released 3-85

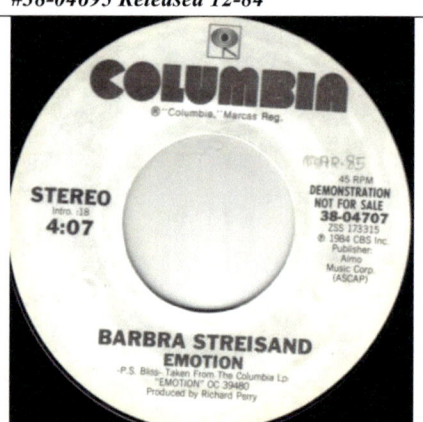

Emotion (both sides)
Promotional copy with same sleeve

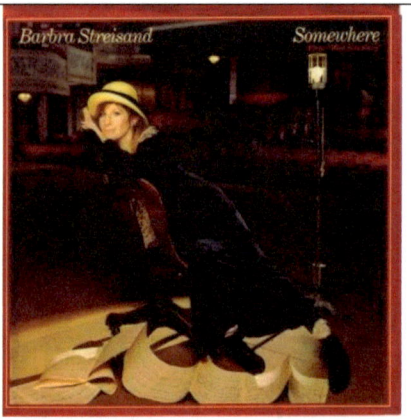

Somewhere/Not While I'm Around
#38-05680 Released 11-85

Somewhere (both sides)
Promotional copy with same sleeve

Send In The Clowns/Being Alive
#38-05837 Released 2-86

Send In The Clowns (both sides)
Promotional copy with same sleeve

Over The Rainbow (with/without spoken intro) #CS7-02727 Released 5-87
Promotional-only release

Till I Loved You (Duet with Don Johnson)/Two People)
#38-08062 Released 10-88

38

Till I Loved You (short & long versions)
Promotional copy with same picture sleeve

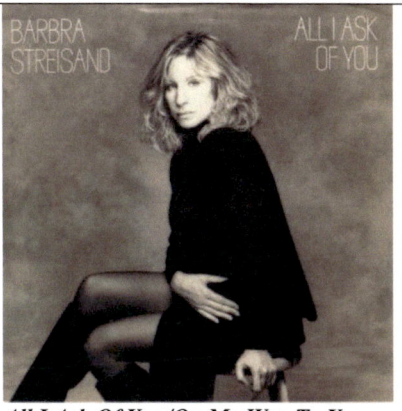

All I Ask Of You/On My Way To You
#38-08026 Released 12-88

All I Ask Of You (both sides)
Promotional copy with same sleeve

What Were We Thinking Of/Why Let It Go?
#38-68691 Released 3-89

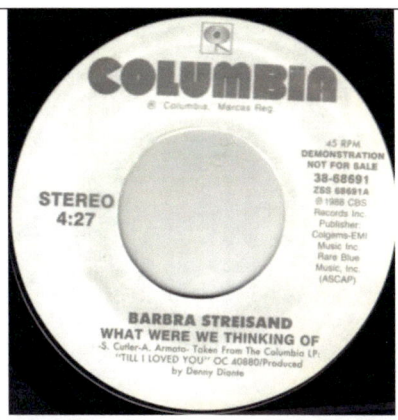

What Were We Thinking Of (both sides)
Promotional copy

We're Not Makin' Love Anymore/Here We Are At Last
#38-73016 Released 9-89

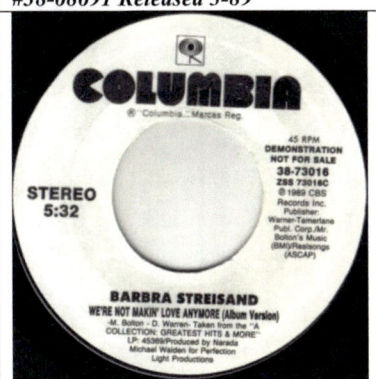

We're Not Makin' Love Anymore (Long & short versions)
Promotional copy

Ordinary Miracles (Live/studio versions)
#38-77533 Released 5-94 (non-LP cuts)

Tell Him (both sides)
#36 78737 Released 10-97

In 1965, Columbia Records released this Promotional only 3-pack that included Why Did I Choose You and singles by Bob Dylan and Andy Williams. Issued in pictured envelope (shown).

People picture sleeve
This is a bootleg sleeve made by a Record Dealer in the 1990's

39

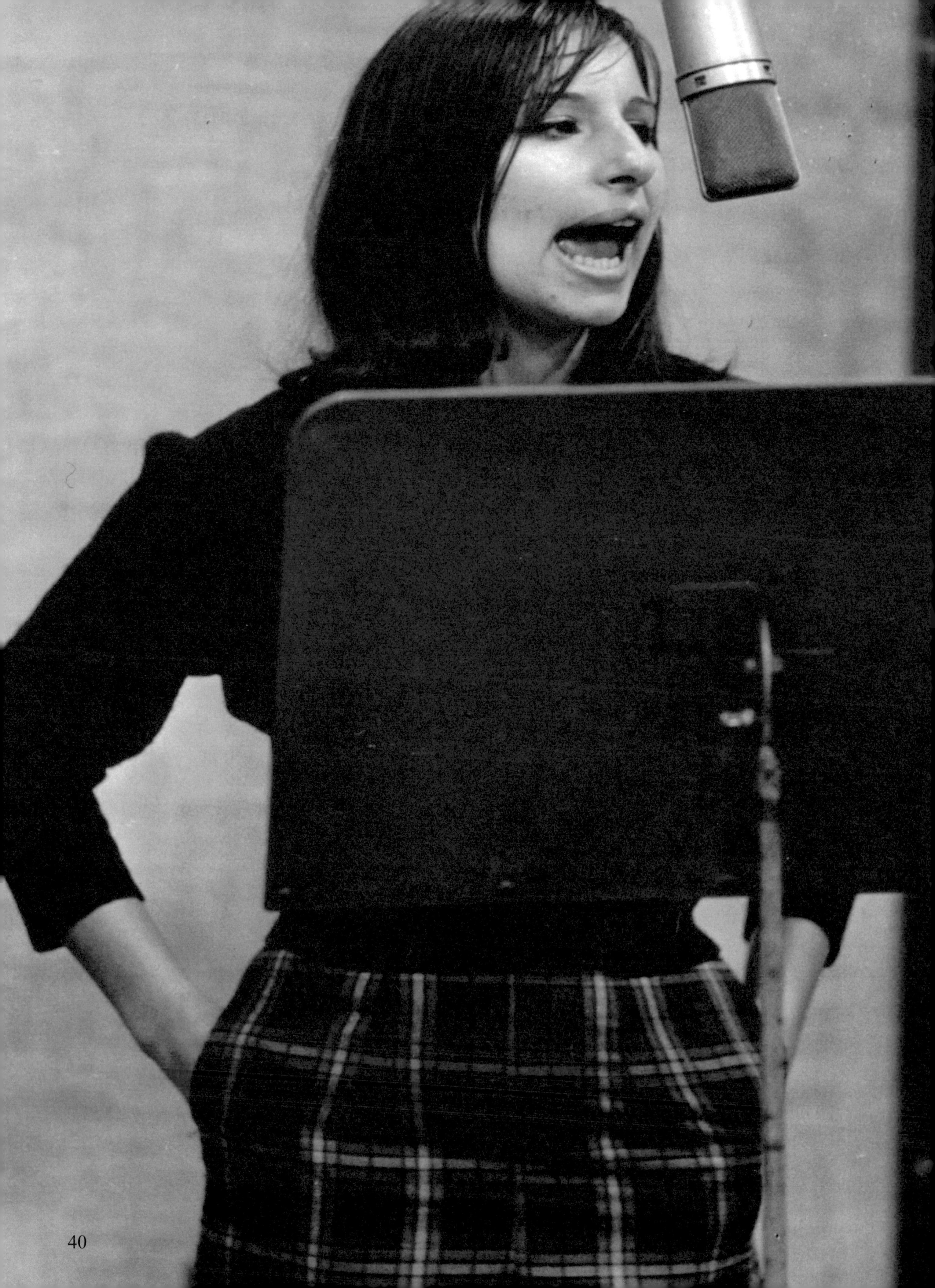

7" EP's US

The following EP's (Extended Plays) were released for jukeboxes and came with jukebox tags and mini covers, all on the Columbia label except where noted.

The Barbra Streisand Album (1963)
#7-8807

(Cry Me A River/A Sleepin' Bee/My Honey's Loving Arms/Much More/A Taste Of Honey)

(Also issued on blue label)
(Cardboard cover)

The Third Album (1964)
#7-8954

(Bewitched/Taking A Chance On Love/My Melancholy Baby/Make Believe/Draw Me A Circle/Never Will I Marry)

(Picture sleeve)

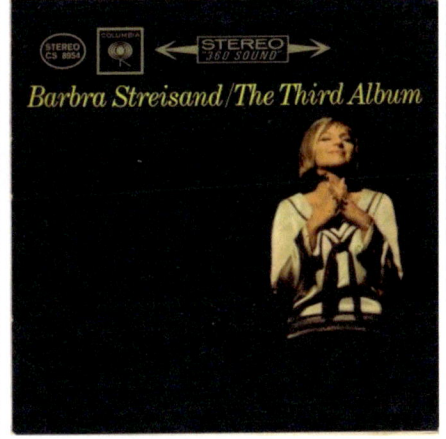

The Third Album (1964)
Same as other release with same catalog number. (Cover is close-up)
(Cardboard cover)

Funny Girl Broadway Cast (1964)
Capital Records #PRO 2622 Promo-only
(Sent to Radio stations)
(Who Are You Now/Coronet Man/Music That Makes Me Dance/Don't Rain On My Parade)

Funny Girl Broadway Cast (1964)
Capital Records #SXA-2059

(You Are Woman/Sadie, Sadie/I'm The Greatest Star/I Want To Be Seen With You Tonight/Don't Rain On My Parade)

(Cardboard cover)

Je m'appelle Barbra (1966)
#7-9347

(Autumn Leaves/What Now My Love/I Wish You Love/Speak To Me Of Love/Ma Premiere Chanson/Free Again)

(Picture sleeve)

Funny Girl Soundtrack Recording (1968)
#7-3220

(Funny Girl/My Man/People/Roller Skate Rag/I'd Rather Be Blue/Don't Rain On My Parade)
(Cardboard cover)

Stoney End (1971)
#7-30378

(Stoney End/Just A Little Lovin' (Early In The Morning)/Maybe/Don't Know Where I Stand/If You Could Read My Mind)
(Cardboard cover)

The Way We Were (1974)
#7Q-32801 (Quadraphonic)

(Being At War With Each Other/Pieces Of Dreams/Something So Right/I've Never Been A Woman Before)
(Cardboard cover)

41

7" Singles International

All CBS unless noted. Unable to confirm People/I Am Woman 1964 Norway & Sweden single releases.*

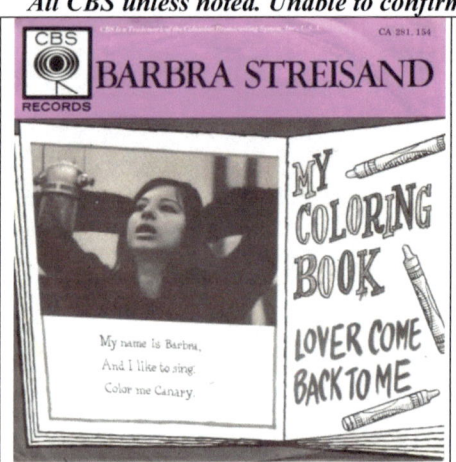

My Coloring Book/Lover Come Back To Me (Holland) 1963
#281154

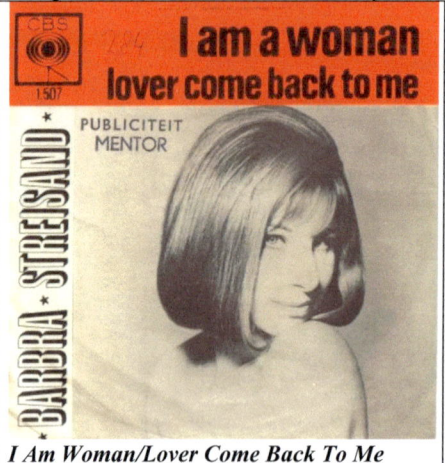

I Am Woman/Lover Come Back To Me (Holland) 1964
#1507
(Misprint showing I Am A Woman on sleeve, later corrected)

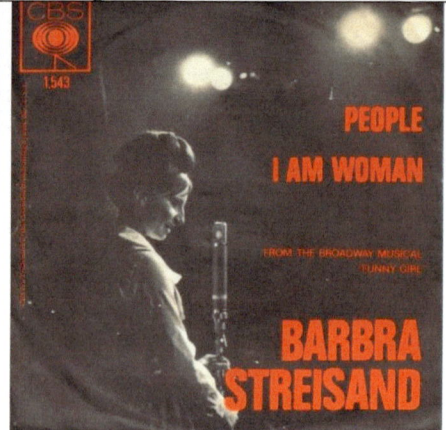

People/I Am Woman (Holland) 1964
#1543

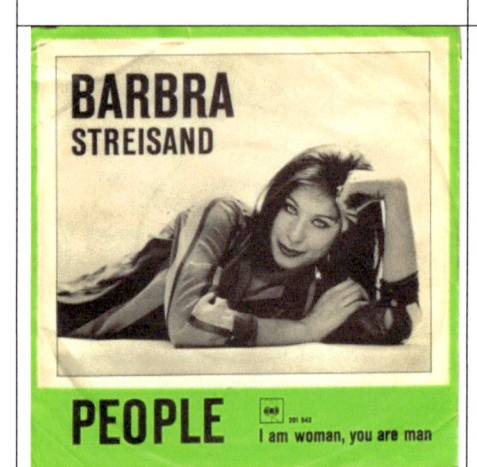

People/I Am Woman (Denmark) 1964
#201543

People/I Am Woman (Mexico) 1964
#5476

People/Lover Come Back To Me (Japan) 1964
#LL-654-C

People/Cry Me A River (England) 1964
AAG223*
This is likely a UK release (not Sweden) based on the catalog #. Unless it's a Norway release.

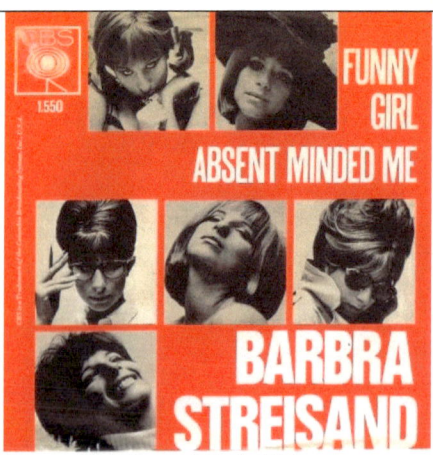

Funny Girl/Absent Minded Me (Holland) 1964
#1550

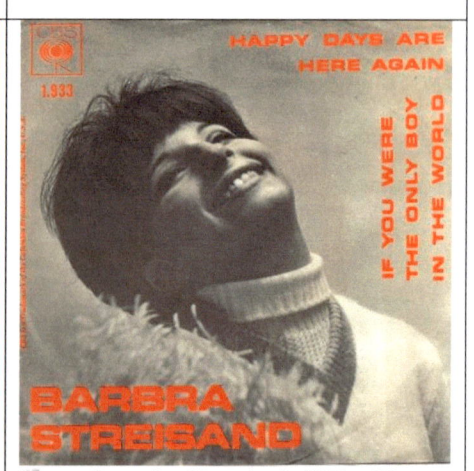

Happy Days Are Here Again/If You Were The Only Boy In The World (Holland) 1965
#1933

Funny Girl/Absent Minded Me
(Japan) 1964
#LL-684-C

People/I Am Woman, You Are Man
(England) 1966 reissue (Streisand was in London playing in Funny Girl)
#201543

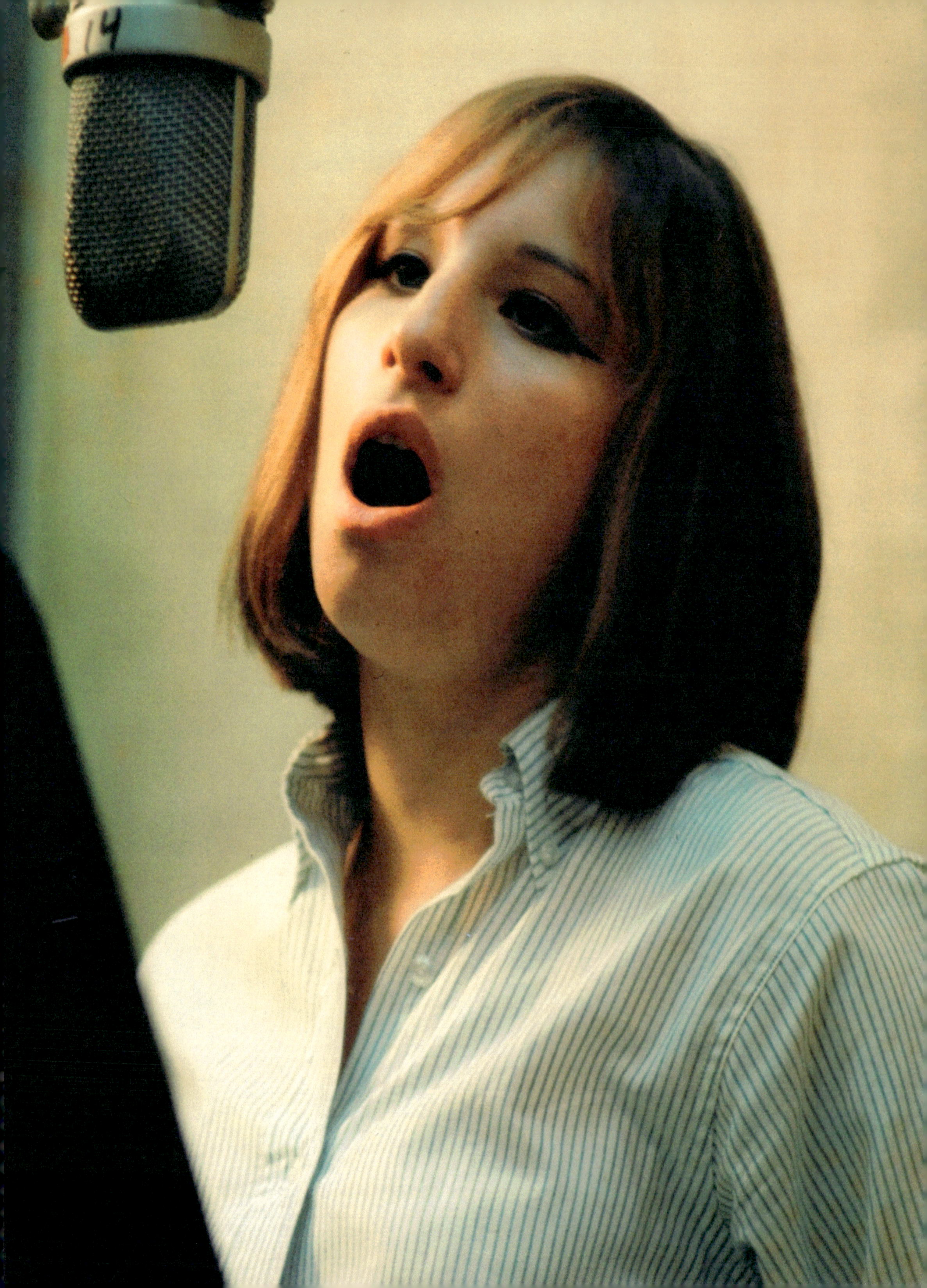

Why Did I Choose You/My Love
(Holland) 1965
#1787

My Man/Where Is The Wonder
(Holland) 1965
#1932

He Touched Me/I Like Him
(Holland) 1965
#1980

Second Hand Rose/The Kind Of Man A Woman Needs
(Holland) 1965
#1984

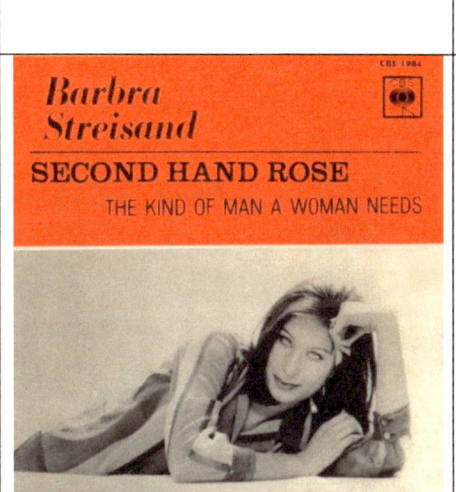

Second Hand Rose/The Kind Of Man A Woman Needs
(Sweden) 1965
#1984

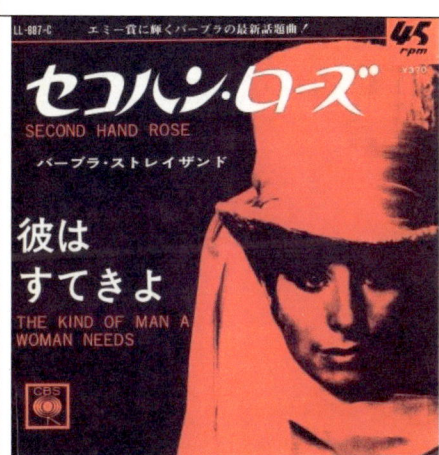

Second Hand Rose/The Kind Of Man A Woman Needs
(Japan) 1965
#LL-887-C

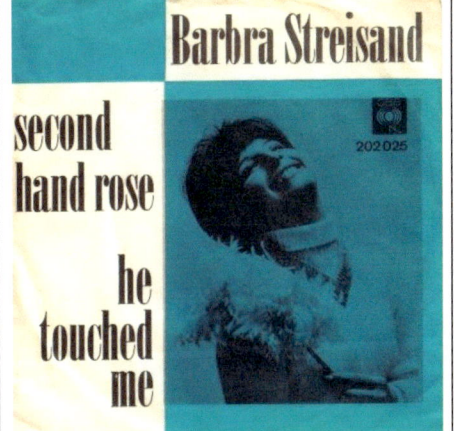

Second Hand Rose/He Touched Me
(Denmark) 1966
#202025

Second Hand Rose/The Kind Of Man A Woman Needs
(Norway) 1966
#1.984

Where Am I Going?/You Wanna Bet
(Holland) 1966
#1998

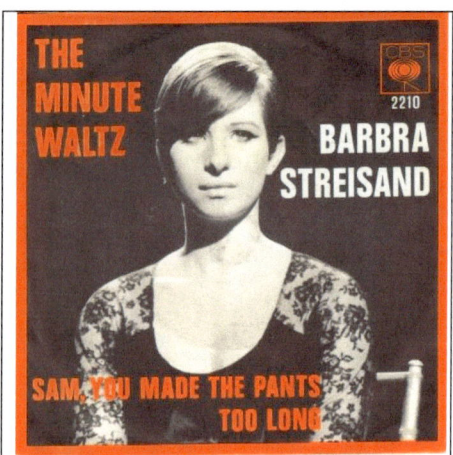

The Minute Waltz/Sam, You Made The Pants Too Long (Holland) 1966 #2210	*The Minute Waltz/Sam You Made The Pants Too Long* (Denmark) 1966 #202210	*The Minute Waltz/C'est Si Bon (It's So Good)* (France) 1966 #2195
Free Again/I've Been Here (Holland) 1966 #2387	*Clopin Clopant/Autumn Leaves* (Holland) 1966 #2558	*Silent Night/Ave Maria* (Germany) 1966 #2417
Silent Night/Ave Maria (France) 1966 #2417	*Silent Night/Ave Maria* (South Africa) 1966 #SSC 732	*Silent Night/Ave Maria* (Holland) 1966 #2417 *Also issued in Italy & Spain in same sleeve*

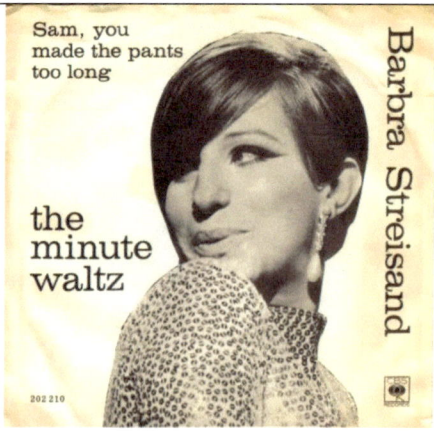

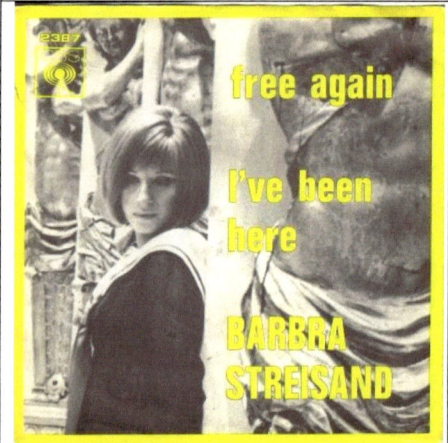

Silent Night/Ave Maria
(Japan) 1966
#LL-2089-C

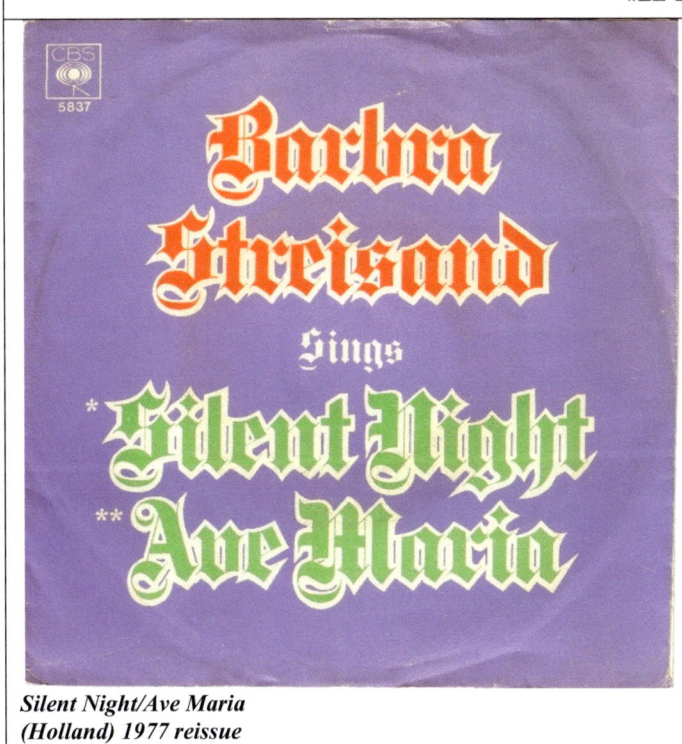

Silent Night/Ave Maria
(Holland) 1977 reissue
#5837

Silent Night/Ave Maria
(England) 1966
#202417

Once Upon A Summertime/Speak To Me Of Love
(France) 1966 Rare Promo-only release #DP 2496

Non…C'est Rien/Les Enfants Qui Pleurent (non-LP cut)
(Italy) 1966
#1885

Non…C'est Rien/Le Mur
(France) 1966
#2155

Stout-Hearted Men/Look
(Holland) 1967
#2989

Stout-Heated Men/People
(South Africa) 1967
#SSC828

Lover Man (Oh, Where Can You Be?)/
My Funny Valentine
(Holland) 1967
#3050

Lover Man (Oh, Where Can You Be?)/
My Funny Valentine
(France) 1967
#3050

White Christmas/Jingle Bells
(Holland) 1967
#3121

My Favorite Things/The Boy Next Door
(Holland)
#3274
Another '68 release Funny Girl/I'd Rather Be Blue (Portugal #3705) was issued, but has unknown showgirl as cover, not Streisand

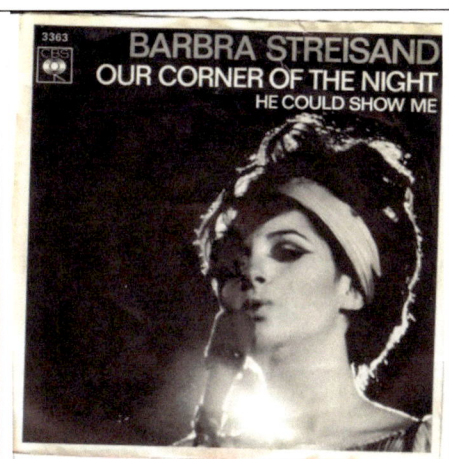

Our Corner Of The Night/He Could Show Me
(Holland) 1968
#3363

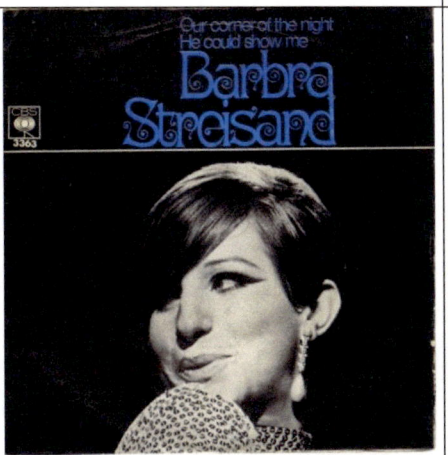

Our Corner Of The Night/He Could Show Me
(Spain) 1968
#3363

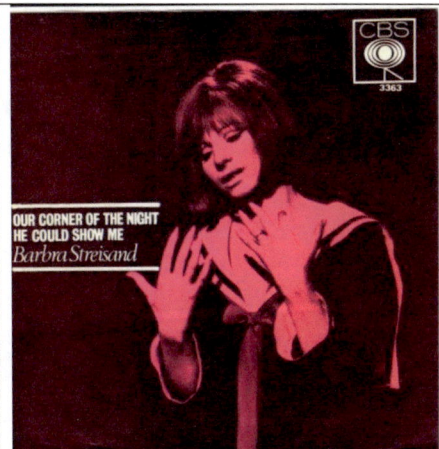

Our Corner Of The Night/He Could Show Me
(Sweden) 1968
#3363

My Man/People
(Argentina) 1969
#22093

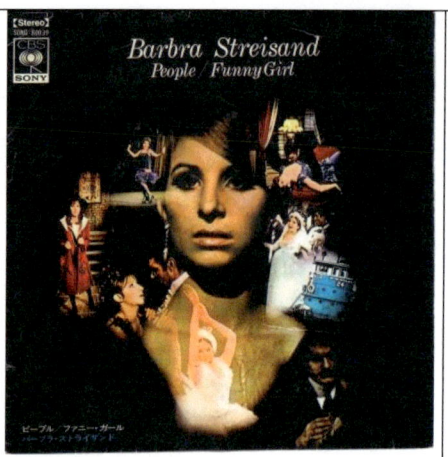

People/Funny Girl
(Japan) 1969
#SONG-80039

People/Funny Girl
(Japan) 1969
Promotional-only with rare sleeve
#SONG-80039

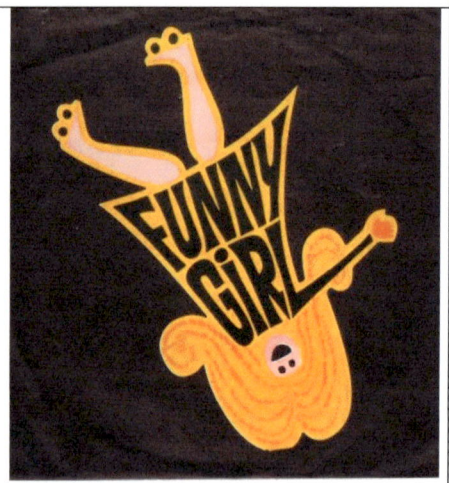

My Man
(Sweden) Promotional-only release 1-sided
1969 (no catalog number)

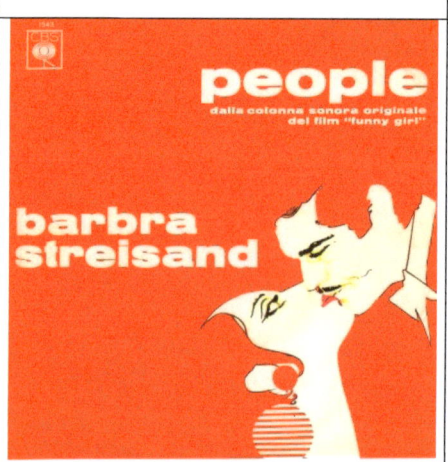

People/I Am Woman, You Are Man
(Italy) 1969
#1543
A People Flexi-disc was issued from Poland in book-style cover with Barbra pictured on back
#33000369021 1968

People (Instrumental) Al Korvin
(No Streisand vocals)
(Italy) 1969
Vedette Records #33167

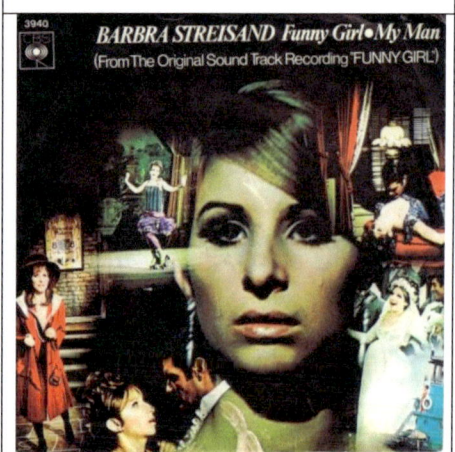

Funny Girl/My Man
(Holland) 1969
#3940

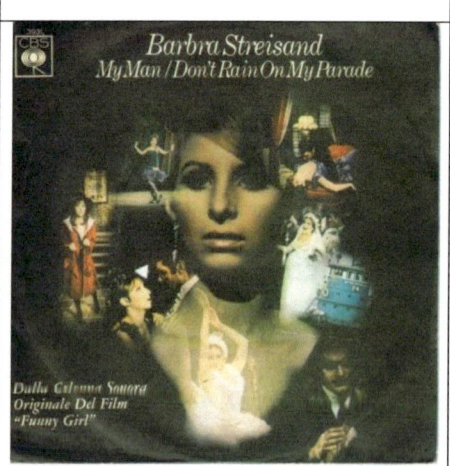

My Man/Don't Rain On My Parade
(Italy) 1969
#3931

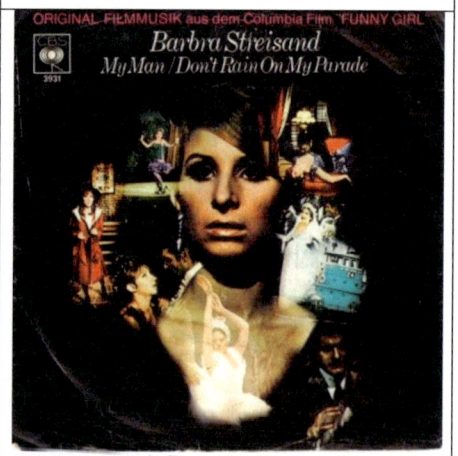

My Man/Don't Rain On My Parade
(Germany) 1969
#3931
(Also issued in France same sleeve)

50

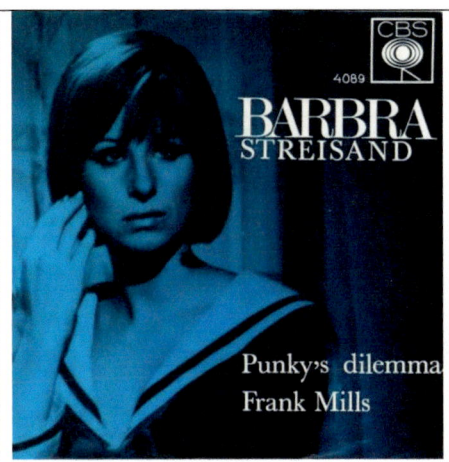

Frank Mills/Punky's Dilemma
(Sweden) 1969
#4089

Frank Mills/Punky's Dilemma
(Holland) 1969
#4089

Les Feuilles Mortes/Non…C'est Rien
(France) 1969
#3960

Les Feuilles Mortes/Non…C'est Rien
(Italy) 1969
#3960

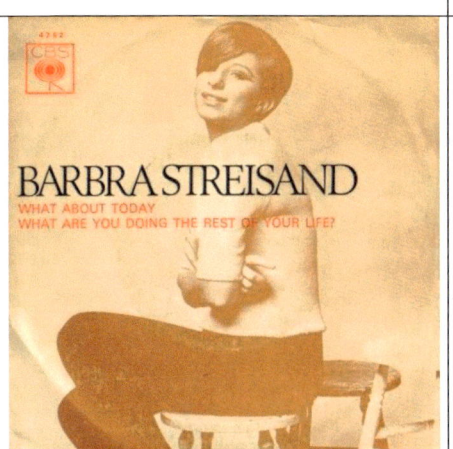

What About Today/What Are You Doing The Rest Of Your Life?
(Portugal) 1970
#4792

Hello Dolly
(Japan) 1970 Promotional-only release 20th Century Fox Records (Catalog number unknown)

Before The Parade Passes By/Love Is Only Love
(France) 1970
#4755

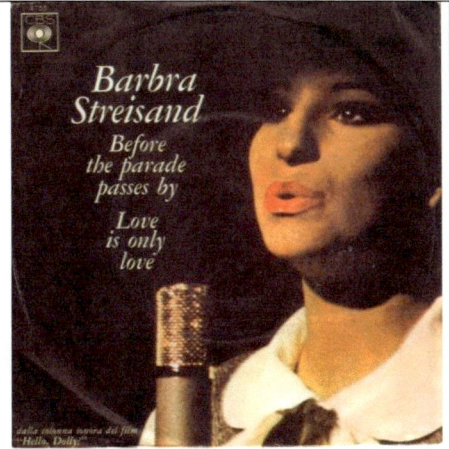

Before The Parade Passes By/Love Is Only Love
(Italy) 1970
#4755

Before The Parade Passes By/Love Is Only Love
(Holland) 1970
#4755

People/My Man
(Spain) 1970
#4945

The Best Thing You've Ever Done/
Summer Me, Winter Me
(Portugal) 1970
#5134

On A Clear Day You Can See Forever
(Soundtrack version Barbra/Montand)
(Japan) 1970 Promo-only release
#SONG 80190

Stoney End/Honey Pie
(Japan) 1970
#CBSA 82091

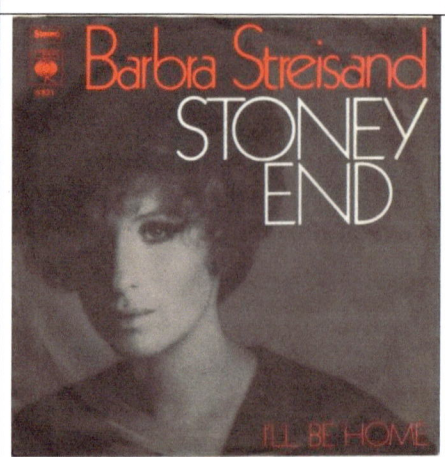

Stoney End/I'll Be Home
(Germany) 1970
#5321

Stoney End/I'll Be Home
(Portugal) 1970
#5321

Stoney End/I'll Be Home
(Sweden) 1970
#5321

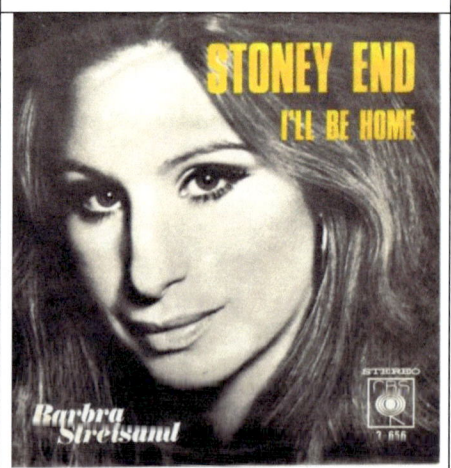

Stoney End/I'll Be Home
(Malaysia) 1970
#2656

Stoney End/I'll Be Home
(Spain) 1970
#5321

Stoney End/I'll Be Home
(Holland) 1970
#5321

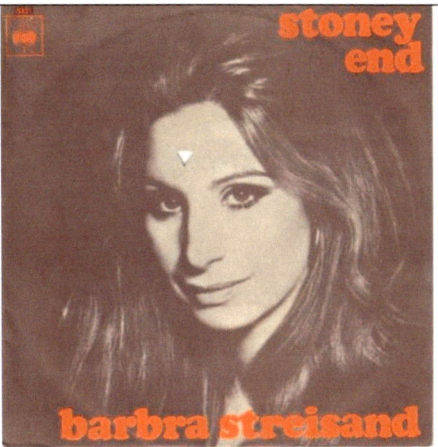

Stoney End/I'll Be Home
(Italy) 1971
#5321

Time And Love/No Easy Way Down
(Japan) 1971
#CBSA 82106

Time And Love/No Easy Way Down
(Spain) 1971
#7123

Time And Love/No Easy Way Down
(Germany) 1971
#7123

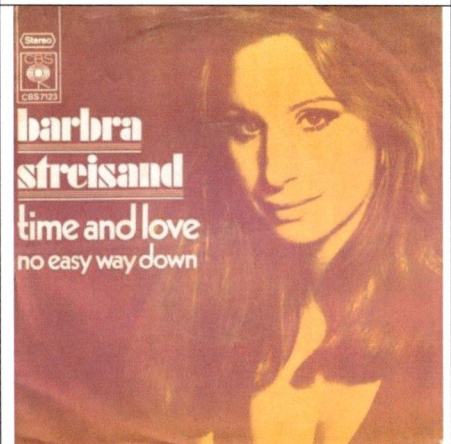

Time And Love/No Easy Way Down
(Holland) 1971
#7123

Time And Love/No Easy Way Down
(Sweden) 1971
#7123

Flim Flam Man/Maybe
(Holland) 1971
#7284

Free The People/Flim Flam Man
(Sweden) 1971
#7277

53

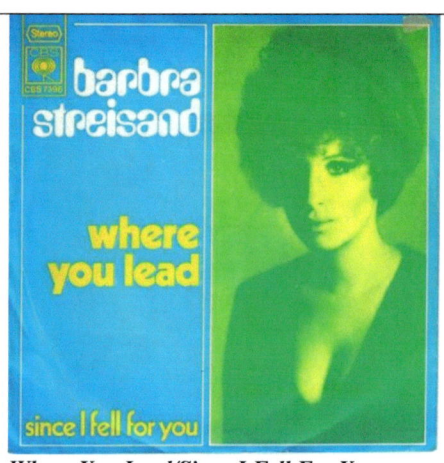

Where You Lead/Since I Fell For You
(Holland) 1971
#7396

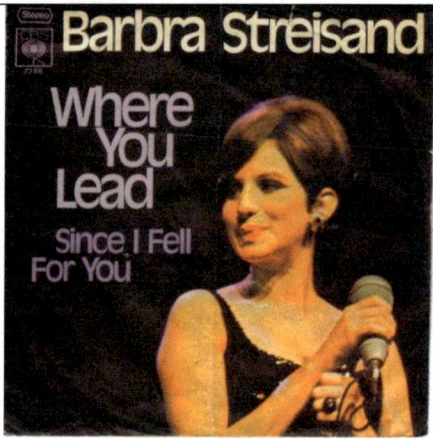

Where You Lead/Since I Fell For You
(Germany) 1971
#7396

Where You Lead/Since I Fell For You
(Portugal) 1971
#7393

Where You Lead/Just A Little Lovin'
(Argentina) 1971
#22390

Mother/The Summer Knows
(Holland) 1971
#7584

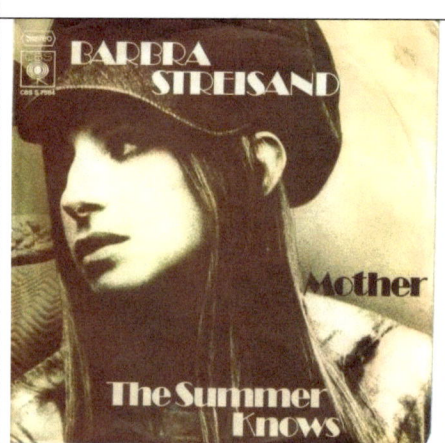

Mother/The Summer Knows
(Germany) 1971
#7584

Mother/You've Got A Friend
(Spain) 1971
#7516

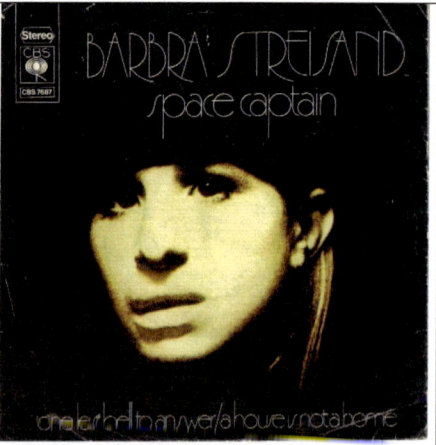

Space Captain/One Less Bell To Answer-
A House Is Not A Home
(Holland) 1971
#7687

Space Captain/One Less Bell To Answer-
A House Is Not A Home
(France) 1971
#7687

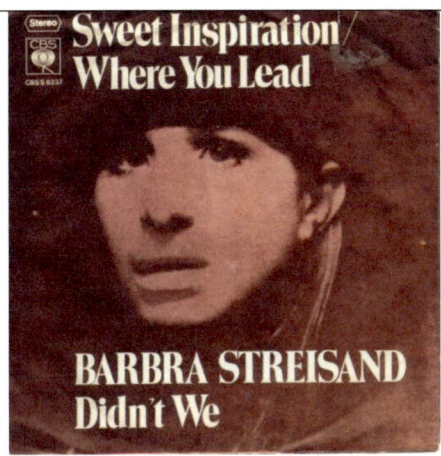

*Sweet Inspiration-Where You Lead/
Didn't We
(Germany) 1972
#8237*

*Sweet Inspiration-Where You Lead/
Didn't We
(Italy) 1972
#8237*

*Sweet Inspiration-Where You Lead/
Didn't We
(Spain) 1972
#8237*

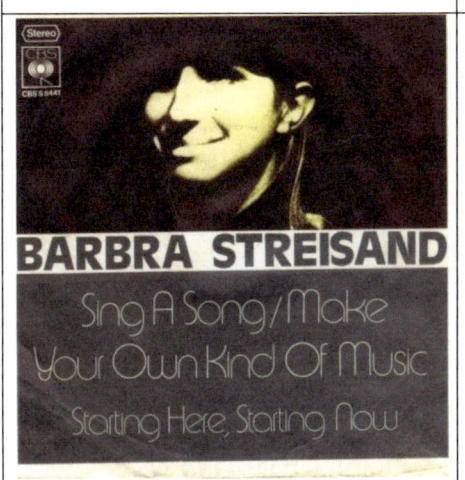

*Sing A Song-Make Your Own Kind Of
Music/Starting Here, Starting Now
(Germany) 1972
#8441*

*Mother/The Summer Knows
(Yugoslavia) 1973
#7584*

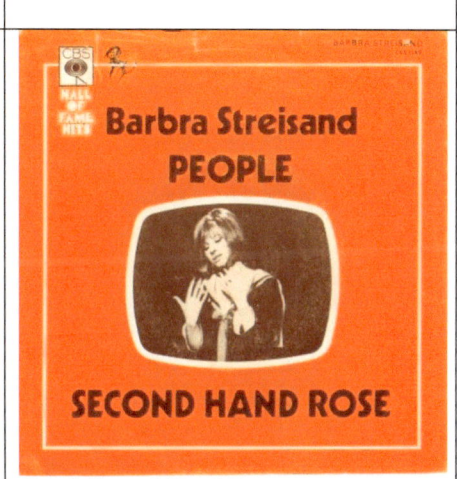

*People/Second Hand Rose
(England) 1973
Hall Of Fame series
#1149*

*Yesterdays/(Leslie Uggams- Smoke Gets In)
(Italy) Issued as part of a Music magazine
Series 1973
Le Canzoni piu Belle #CPB-20*

*All The Things You Are/Aretha
Franklin- Over The Rainbow)
(Italy) Music magazine series 1973
Le Canzoni piu Belle #CPB-37*

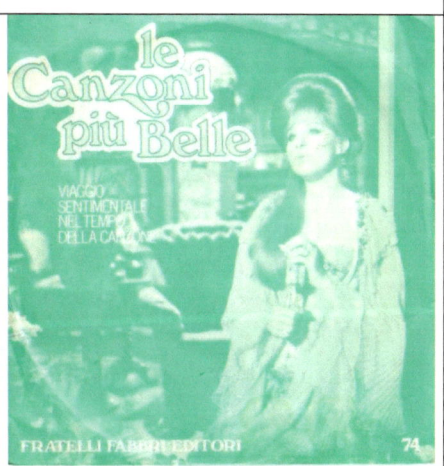

*(Alfie/Shirley Bassey- Goldfinger)
(Italy) Music magazine series 1974
Le Canzoni piu Belle #CPB-74*

Cry Me A River/Nat King Cole-Love A Splendored Thing (Italy) Music Magazine Series 1974 Le Canzoni piu Belle #CPB-59	Hello Dolly/Hello Dolly Finale (Japan) 1974 reissue 20th Century Fox Records #FM-2025	The Way We Were/What Are You Doing The Rest Of Your Life? (Japan) 1974 #SOPB 266
The Way We Were/What Are You Doing The Rest Of Your Life? (Portugal) 1974 #1915	The Way We Were/What Are You Doing The Rest Of Your Life? (Malaysia) 1974 #2-748	The Way We Were/Instrumental (Mexico) 1974 #45-7244
The Way We Were/What Are You Doing The Rest Of Your Life? (Holland) 1974 #1915 (Also issued in Germany as same sleeve)	The Way We Were/What Are You Doing The Rest Of Your Life? (Italy) 1974 #1915	The Way We Were/What Are You Doing The Rest Of Your Life? (Spain) 1974 #1915

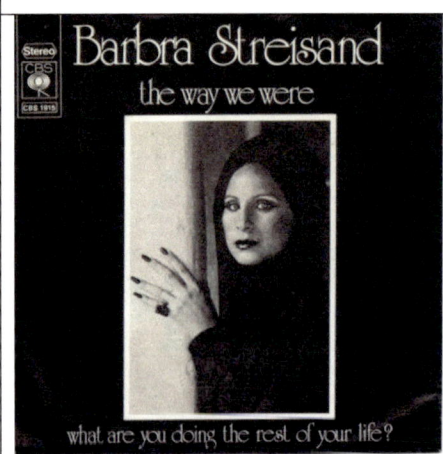

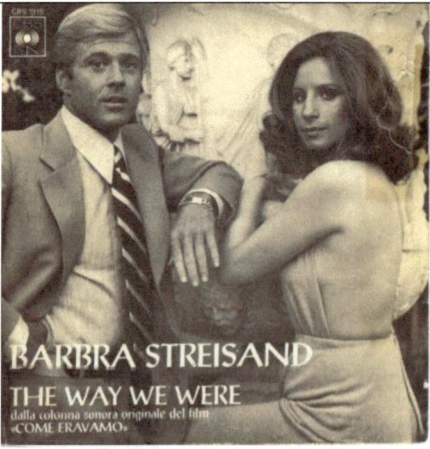

Guava Jelly/Love In The Afternoon
(Spain) 1975
#3008

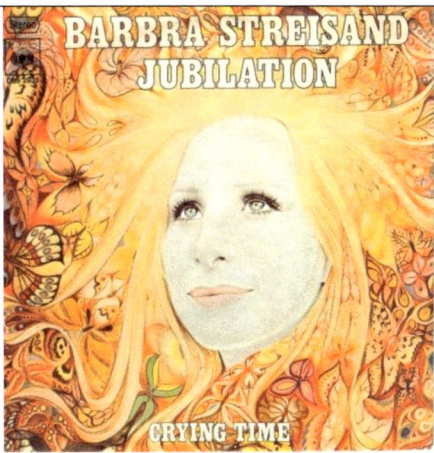

Jubilation/Crying Time
(Germany) 1975
#2933

How Lucky Can You Get/More Than You Know
(Italy) 1975
Arista Records #3C 00696705

How Lucky Can You Get/More Than You Know
(Japan) 1975
Arista Records #BLPB 243-AR

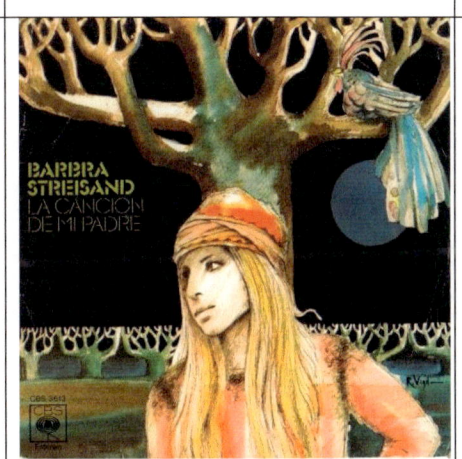

My Father's Song/By The Way
(Spain) 1975
#3613

The Way We Were/People
(England) 1976
Hall Of Fame Series
#3955

The Way We Were/People
(Japan) 1976
#06SP 64

Evergreen/I Believe In Love
(Japan) 1977
#06SP 135

Evergreen/I Believe In Love
(Australia) 1977
#BA 222272

57

Evergreen/I Believe In Love
(Germany) 1977 White label promo
#4855
(Also issued in UK as same sleeve)

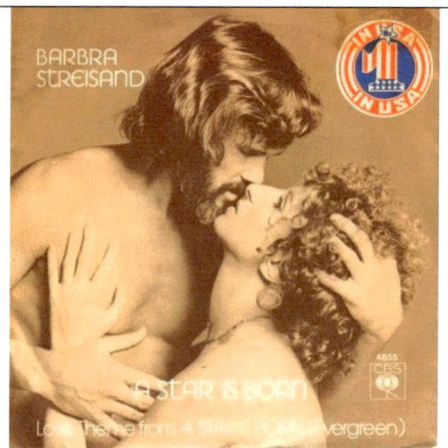

Evergreen/I Believe In Love
(Holland) 1977
#4855

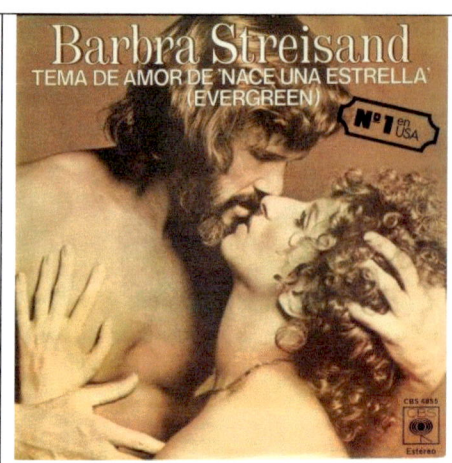

Evergreen/I Believe In Love
(Spain) 1977
#4855

Evergreen/I Believe In Love
(Portugal) 1977
#4855

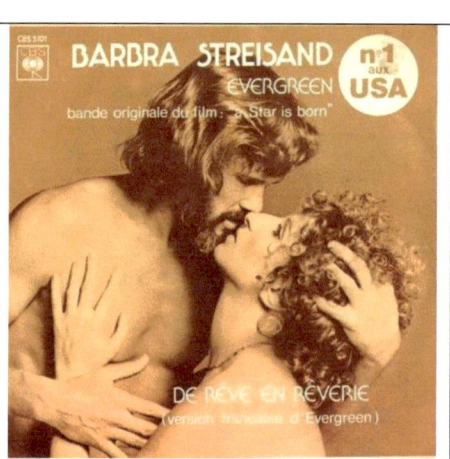

Evergreen (sung in French)/English version
(France) 1977
#5101

Evergreen (sung in Italian)/English version
(Italy) 1977
#5062

Evergreen (sung in Spanish)/English version
(Argentina) 1977
#122888

Evergreen (sung in Spanish)/I Believe In Love
(Spain) 1977
#5866

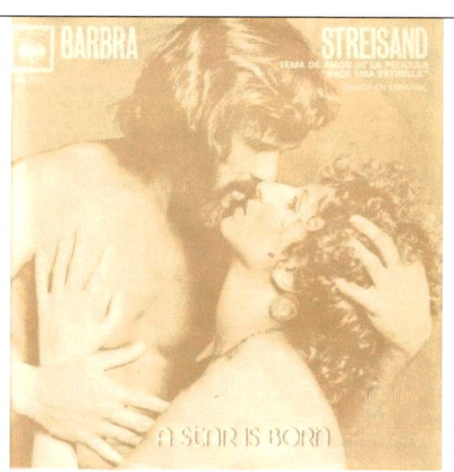

Evergreen (sung in Spanish)/English version
(Mexico) 1977
#7912

Evergreen (sung in Spanish)/English version
(Colombia) 1977
#43280

My Heart Belongs To Me/Answer Me
(Holland) 1977
#5392
(Also issued in Germany & Yugoslavia with same sleeve)

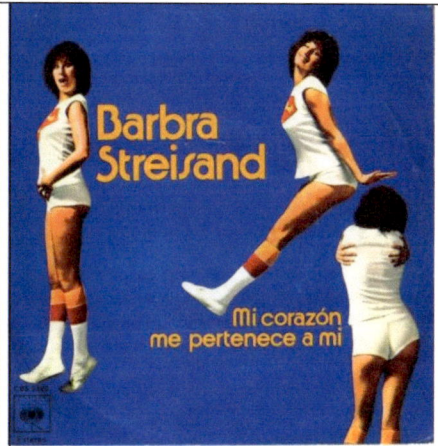

My Heart Belongs To Me/Answer Me
(Spain) 1977
#5392

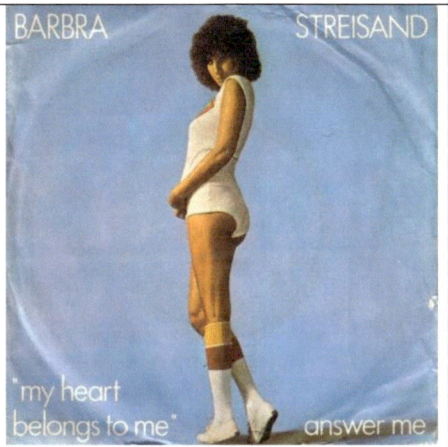

My Heart Belongs To Me/Answer Me
(Italy) 1977
#5392

My Heart Belongs To Me/Answer Me
(Japan) 1977
#06SP 170

Hello Dolly/Finale
(Japan) 1978 reissue
20th Century Fox Records #FMS-1098

Songbird/Honey Can I Put On Your Clothes
(Japan) 1978
#06SP 247

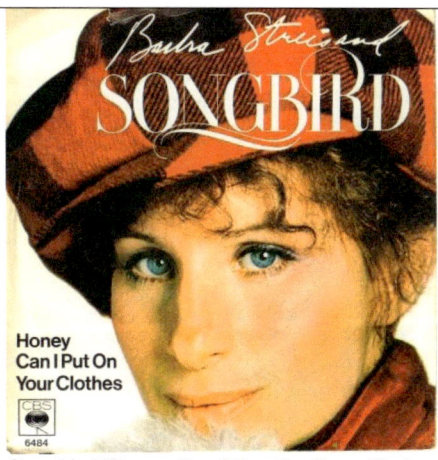

Songbird/Honey Can I Put On Your Clothes
(Holland) 1978
#6484

Songbird/Honey Can I Put On Your Clothes
(Spain) 1978
#6484

Prisoner/Instrumental
(Spain) 1978
#6657

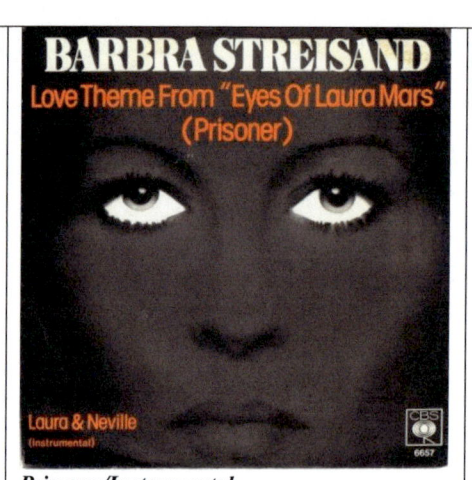

Prisoner/Instrumental
(Holland) 1978
#6657
(Also issued in Germany as same sleeve)

Prisoner/Instrumental
(Italy) 1978
#6657

Prisoner/Instrumental
(Portugal) 1978
#6657
(Front sleeve is Faye Dunaway, back sleeve shown)

Prisoner/Instrumental
(Japan) 1978
#06SP 255

You Don't Bring Me Flowers (with Neil Diamond)/Instrumental
(Japan) 1978
#06SP 279

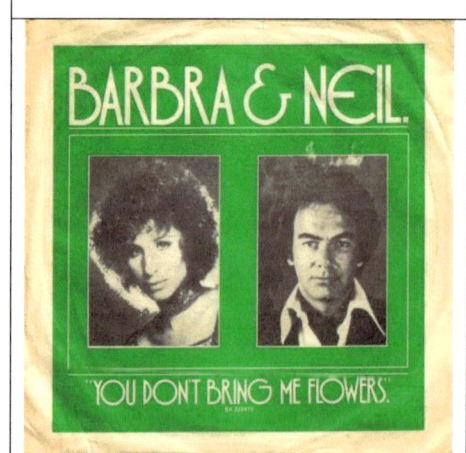

You Don't Bring Me Flowers/Instrumental
(Australia) 1978
#BA 222473

You Don't Bring Me Flowers/Instrumental
(Germany) 1978
#6803
(Also issued in Holland & Portugal in same sleeve)

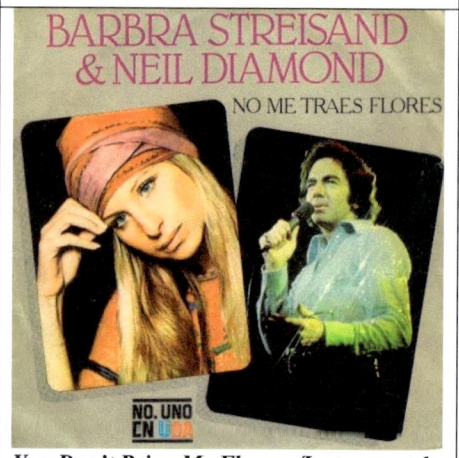

You Don't Bring Me Flowers/Instrumental
(Spain) 1978
#6803

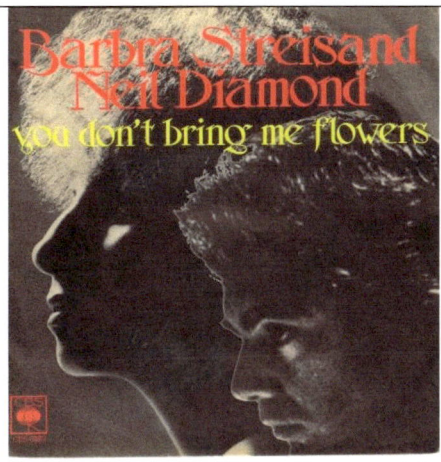

You Don't Bring Me Flowers/Instrumental
(Italy) 1979
#6803
Italy also reissued the single with just Neil Diamond on sleeve #A1297

Superman/Lullaby For Myself
(France) 1979
#6169

Superman/A Man I Loved
(Japan) 1979
#06SP 314

The Main Event-Fight/Instrumental
(Japan) 1979
#06SP 341

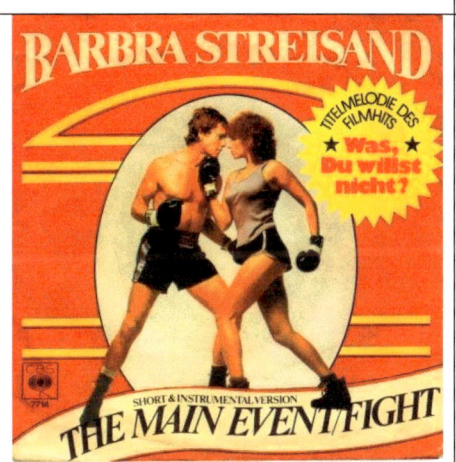

The Main Event-Fight/Instrumental
(Germany) 1979
#7714

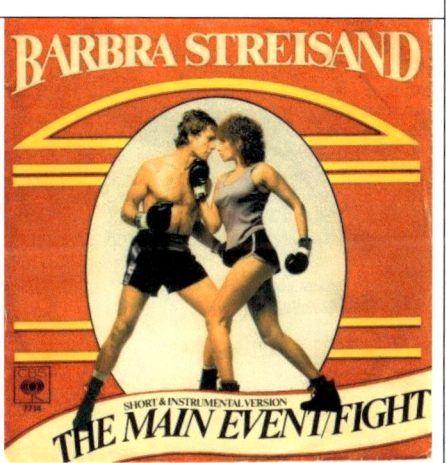

The Main Event-Fight/Instrumental
(Holland) 1979
#7714

The Main Event-Fight/Instrumental
(Portugal) 1979
#7714

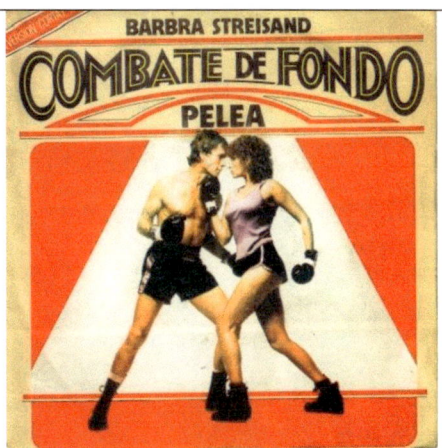

The Main Event-Fight/Instrumental
(Spain) 1979
#7714

The Main Event-Fight/Instrumental
(Italy) 1979
#7714

No More Tears/My Baby Understands
(Donna Summer)
(Holland) 1979
Philips #6175024

No More Tears/My Baby Understands
(Donna Summer)
(Spain) 1979
Casablanca #6175024

No More Tears (Enough Is Enough listed as side A & No More Tears as side B)
(Germany) 1979
Casablanca #BF 18700

No More Tears/My Baby Understands
(Donna Summer)
(Portugal) 1979
Casablanca #6175024

No More Tears/Lucky (Donna Summer)
(Japan) 1979
Casablanca #VIP--2794

No More Tears/My Baby Understands
(Donna Summer)
(Mexico) 1979
Casablanca #1091

No More Tears/My Baby Understands
(Donna Summer)
(Mexico) 1979
Casablanca #1091

No More Tears/My Baby Understands
(Donna Summer)
(France) 1979
Casablanca #101240

No More Tears (long/short versions)
(Sweden) 1979
Casablanca #6198336

No More Tears/My Baby Understands
(Summer)
(Italy) 1979
Casablanca #CA 530
Hungary also released a title sleeve single
#SPSK 70481

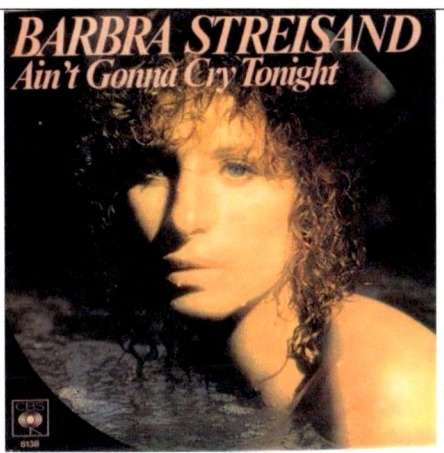

Ain't Gonna Cry Tonight/I Found You Love
(Holland) 1980
#8138

I Ain't Gonna Cry Tonight/I Found You Love
(Spain) 1980
#8138

Splish Splash/I Found You Love
(Germany) 1980
#8344

Woman In Love/Run Wild
(Holland) 1980
#8966
(Single also issued in Italy, Germany, UK, France, & Hungry with same sleeve)

Woman In Love/Run Wild
(Spain) 1980
#8966

Woman In Love/Run Wild
(Brazil) 1980
#43034

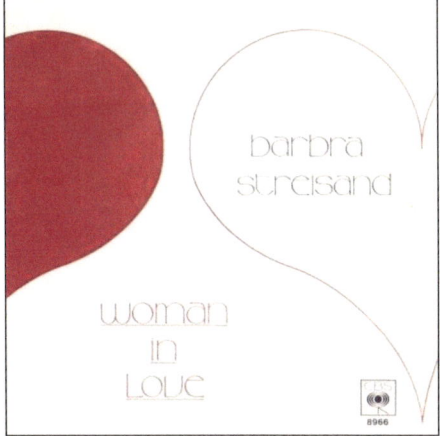

Woman In Love/Run Wild
(Holland) 1980
#8966

Woman In Love/Run Wild
(Japan) 1980
#07SP 506

Guilty Flexi-Discs (1980)
Poland issued several flexi-discs that were 1-sided and do not have Streisand pictured. There's also a few of Woman In Love.

Guilty/Life Story
(Holland) 1980
#9315
(Also issued in Germany as same sleeve)

Guilty/Life Story
(Italy) 1980
#9315

Guilty/Life Story
(Spain) 1980
#9315

Guilty/Life Story
(Australia) 1980
#BA 222766

Guilty/Life Story
(Portugal)
#9315

Guilty/Life Story
(France) 1980
#9315
(Also issued in UK same sleeve)

Guilty/Never Give Up
(France) 1981
#9550

What Kind Of Fool/Make It Like A Memory
(Holland) 1981
#9517

Guilty/Life Story
(Japan) 1980
#07SP 520

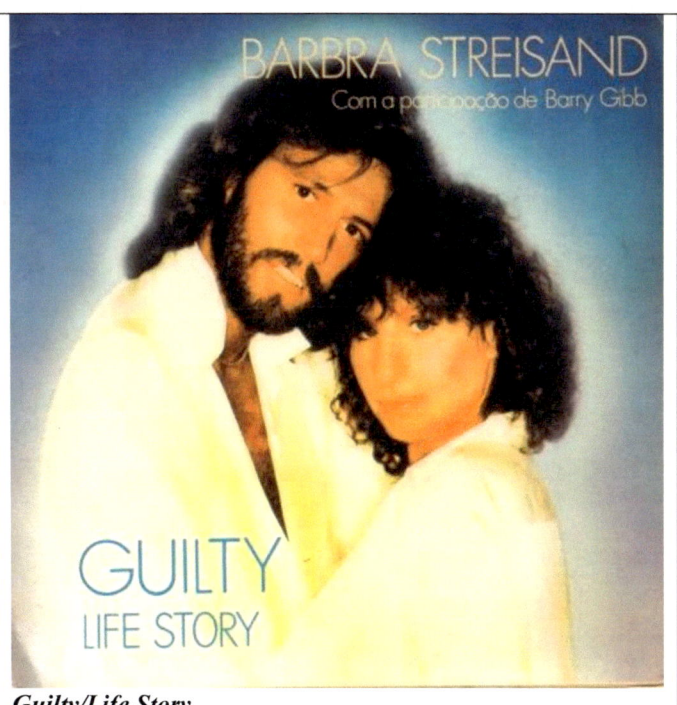

Guilty/Life Story
(Brazil) 1980
#43042

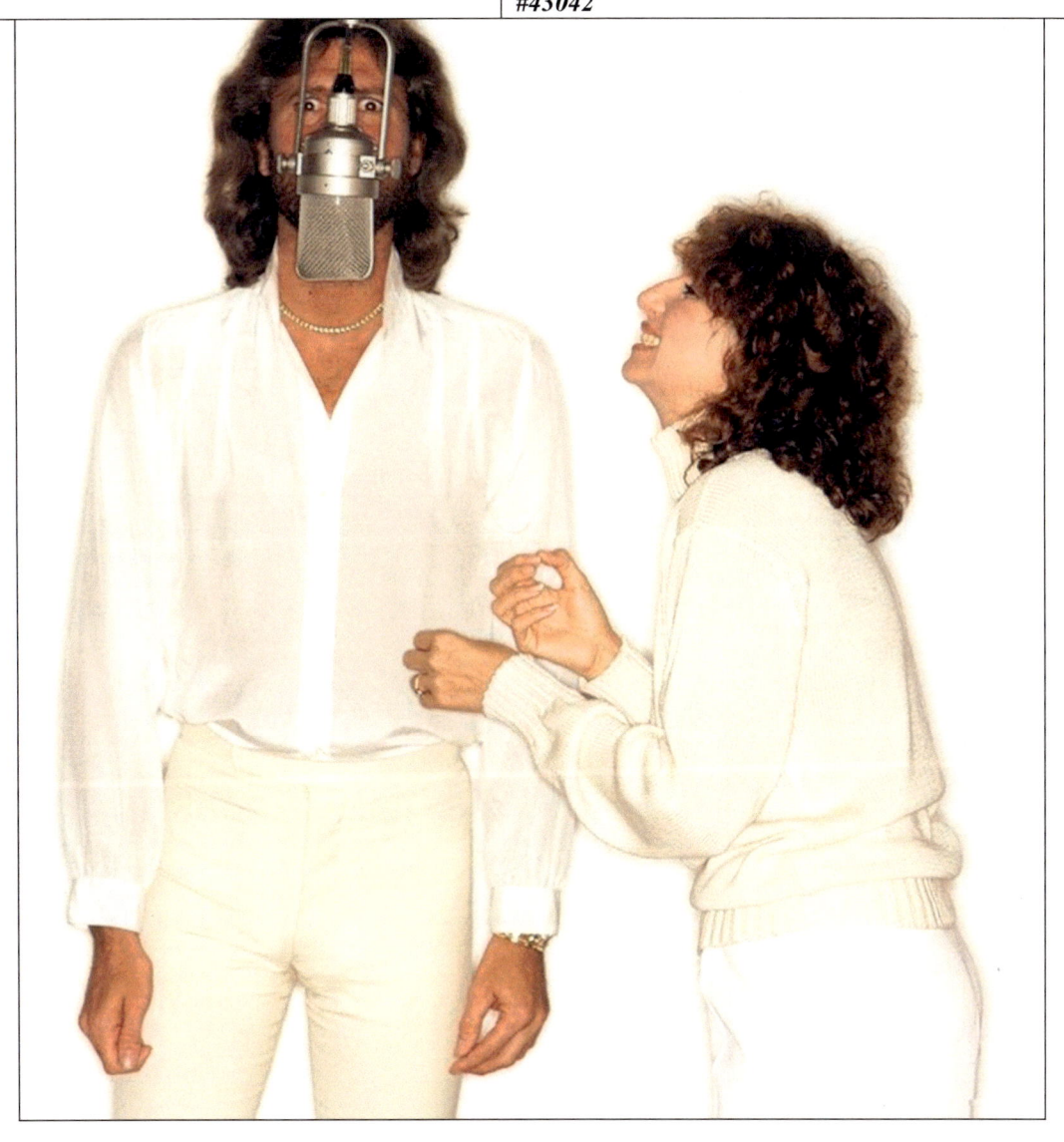

What Kind Of Fool/The Love Inside
(Spain) 1981
#A-1142

Promises/Make It Like A Memory
(Holland) 1981
#A-1203

Promises/Make It Like A Memory
(Japan) 1981
#07SP 547

Promises/Make It Like A Memory
(Brazil) 1981
#43506

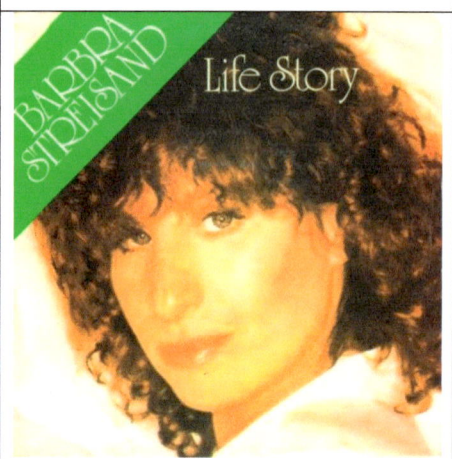

Life Story/Make It Like A Memory
(Holland) 1981
#A-1209

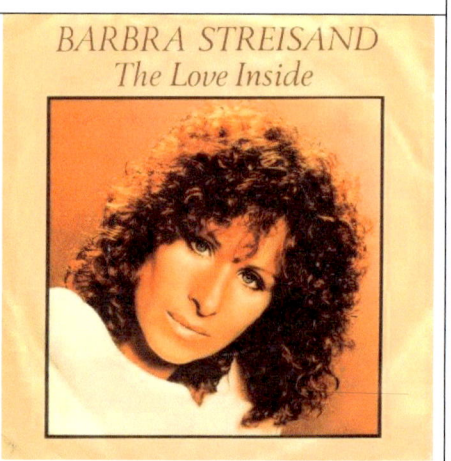

The Love Inside/Never Give Up
(England) 1981
#A1660

Guava Jelly/Life On Mars
(Holland) 1981
#A-1490

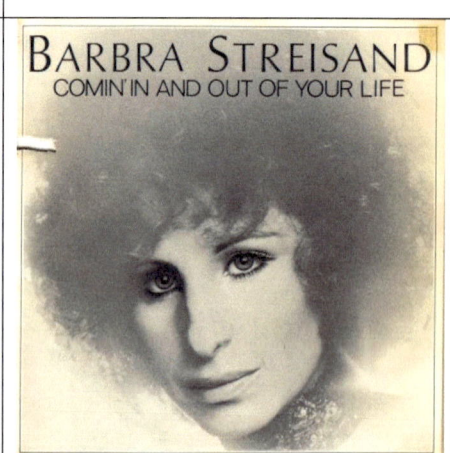

Comin' In And Out Of Your Life/Lost Inside Of You
(Brazil) 1981
#43518

Comin' In And Out Of Your Life/Lost Inside Of You
(Japan) 1981
#07SP 581

Comin' In And Out Of Your Life/Lost Inside Of You
(Spain) 1981
#A-1789

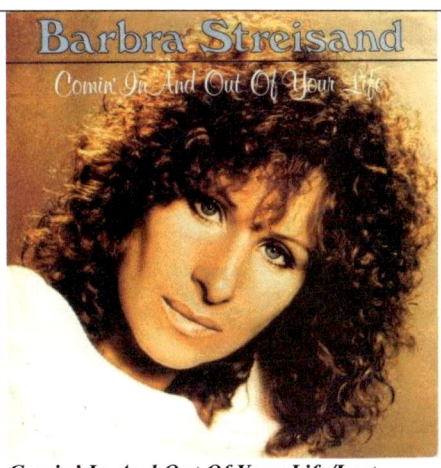

Comin' In And Out Of Your Life/Lost Inside Of You
(Holland) 1981
#A-1789

Comin' In And Out Of Your Life/Lost Inside Of You
(England) 1981
#A-1789

Memory/Lost Inside Of You
(South Africa) 1981
#SSC 5279

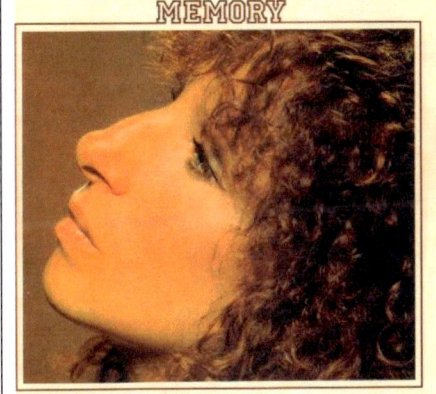

Memory/Evergreen
(Holland) 1982
#A-1983
Also issued in France same sleeve

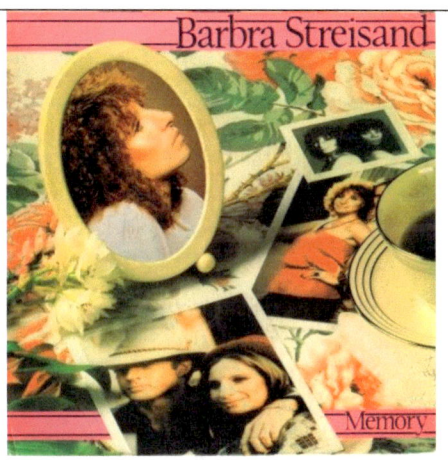

Memory/Evergreen
(Spain) 1982
#A-1983

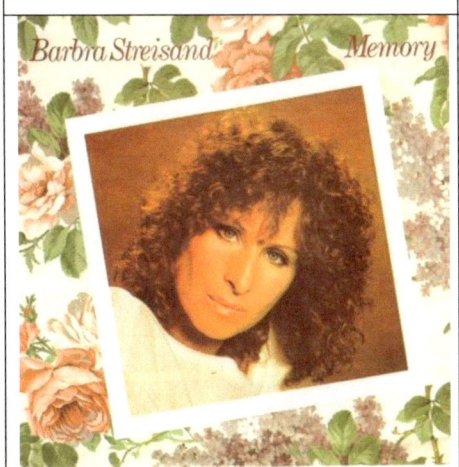

Memory/Evergreen
(England) 1982
#A-1983

Memory/Evergreen
(England) Promotional copy 1982
#BARB1

The Way He Makes Me Feel (Studio/Film versions)
(Japan) 1983
#07SP 768

67

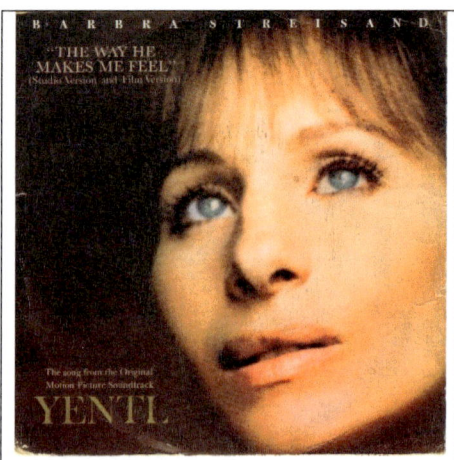

The Way He Makes Me Feel (Studio/Film versions)
(Spain) 1983
#A-3888
Also issued in UK, Holland, Brazil, & France same sleeve.

Papa, Can You Hear Me?/Will Someone Ever Look At Me That Way?
(Spain) 1984
#A-4366
Also issued in Holland, same sleeve.

No Matter What Happens (Studio/Film versions)
(England) 1984
Promotional-only release #A4125

Left In The Dark/Here We Are At Last
(Japan) 1984
#07SP 848

Left In The Dark/Here We Are At Last
(Brazil) 1984
#43592
Also issued in UK, Holland, Portugal, Australia, & Italy in same sleeve.

Left In The Dark (1-sided)
(Spain) 1984 white label promo
#A-4754

Mother/The Summer Knows
(Brazil) 1984
#43600

Make No Mistake, He's Mine/Clear Sailing
(Brazil) 1984
#43598 with insert sheet with lyrics

Make No Mistake, He's Mine/Clear Sailing
(Holland) 1984
#A-4994
Also issued in UK & Spain, same sleeve.

Emotion/Here We Are At Last
(Spain) 1985
#A-6085
Also Holland release with same sleeve as US single

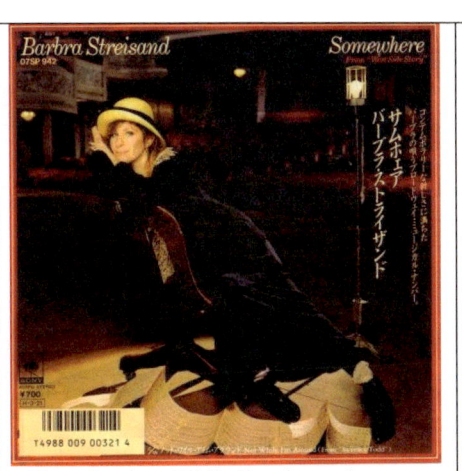

Somewhere/Not While I'm Around
(Japan) 1985
#07SP 942

Somewhere/Not While I'm Around
(Holland) 1985
#A-6707
Also issued in UK, Australia, & Spain in same sleeve.

Send In The Clowns/Being Alive
(England) 1986
#A-6988
Also released in Holland same sleeve

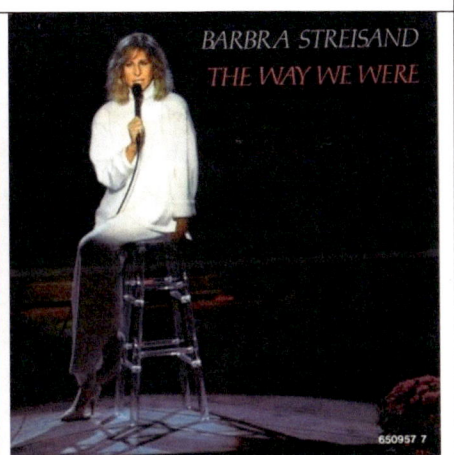

The Way We Were/Evergreen
(Holland) 1987
#6509577

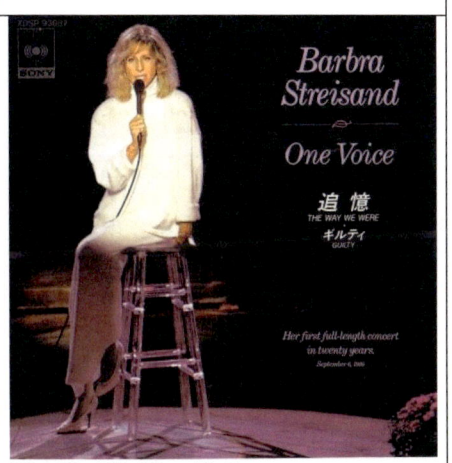

The Way We Were/Guilty
(Japan) 1987
#XDSP 93087 Promotional-only release

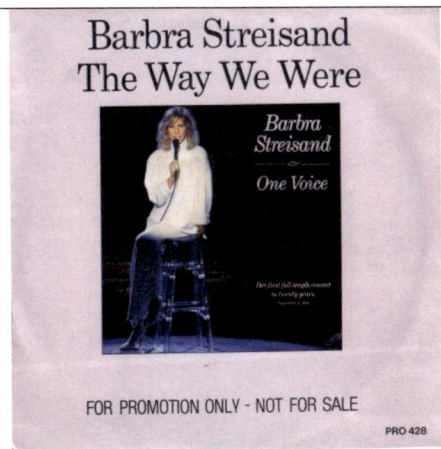

The Way We Were/People
(Holland) 1987
#PRO 428 Promotional-only release

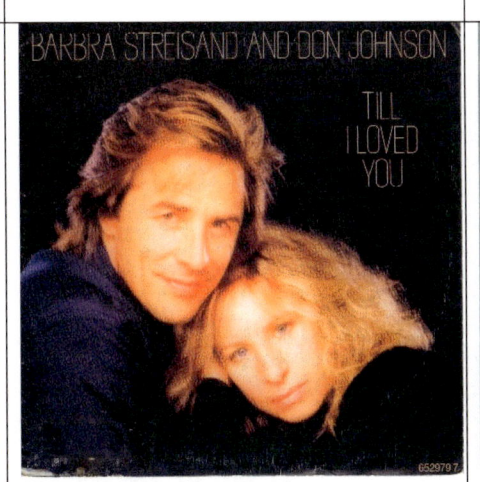

Till I Loved You/Two People
(Spain) 1988
#6529797
Also issued in UK & Holland in same sleeve

All I Ask Of You (1-sided)
(Spain) 1988
#653011-7 Promotional release
Also issued in UK & Holland, same sleeve as US release

69

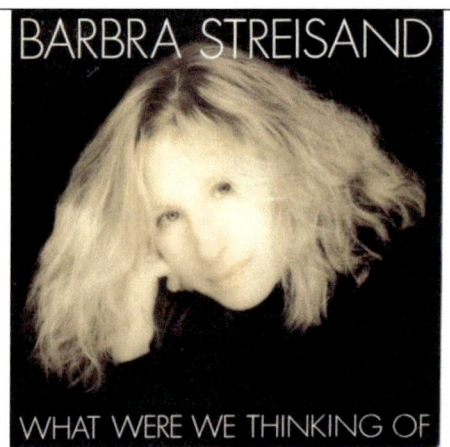

What Were We Thinking Of
(Spain) 1989 1-sided Promotional-only
#ARIC 2147

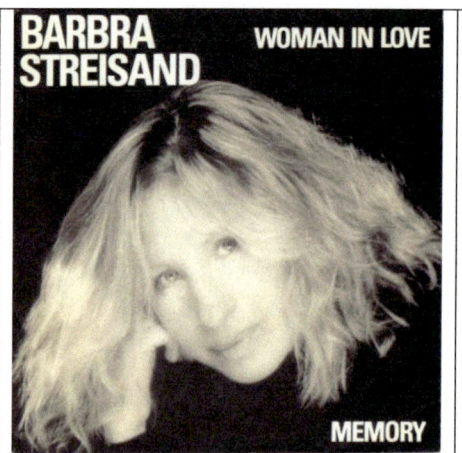

Woman In Love/Memory
(Holland) 1989 Promotional-only release
#PRO 547

We're Not Makin' Love Anymore
(Spain) 1989 1-sided Promotional release
#ARIC 2293

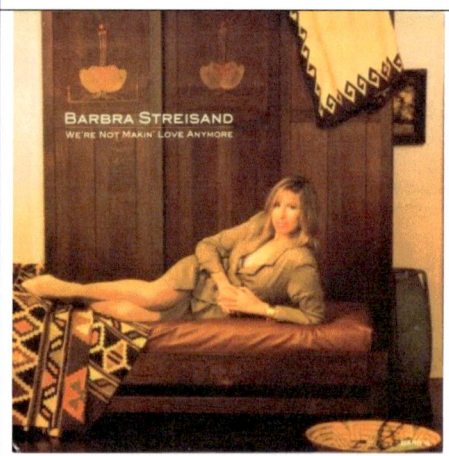

We're Not Makin' Love Anymore/Here We Are At Last
(England) 1989
#BARB 4
Also released in Holland same sleeve
#6553347

Someone That I Used To Love/What Kind Of Fool
(Holland) 1990
#6556447

Places That Belong To You/For All We Know
(England) 1991
#6577947
Also released in Holland same sleeve

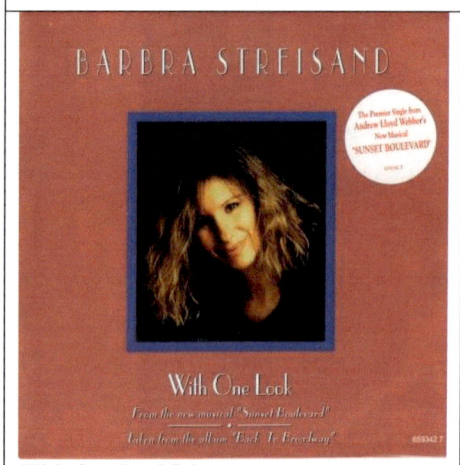

With One Look/Memory
(England) 1993
#6593427
Also issued Spain 1-track promo in same sleeve #ARIC- 222

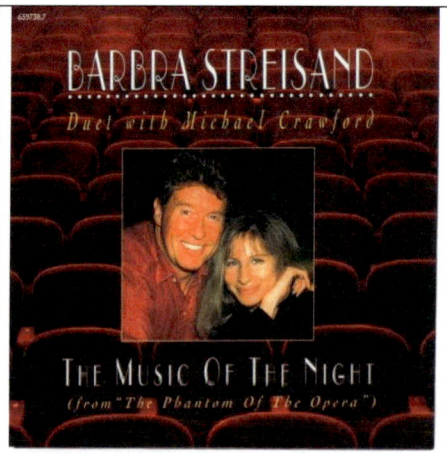

The Music Of The Night/Children Will Listen
(England) 1993
#6597387
Also same release in Holland

As If We Never Said Goodbye/Guilty
(England) 1994
#6603577
Also same release in Holland

71

7" EP's International

(All CBS Records unless noted)

Who Will Buy?/Cry Me A River/My Coloring Book/Come To The Supermarket (In Old Peking)
(England) 1963
#AGG20054

Lover Come Back To Me/Gotta Move/Who's Afraid Of The Big Bad Wolf?/I Don't Care Much/A Taste Of Honey
(England) 1963
#AGG320042

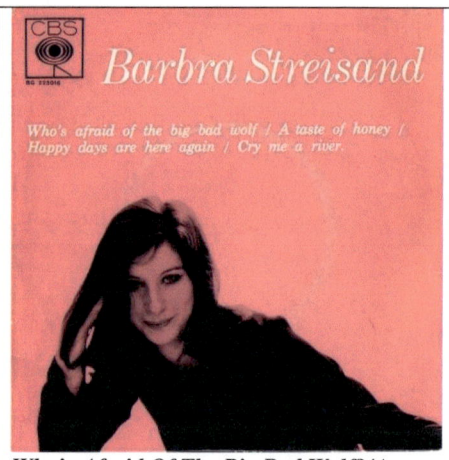

Who's Afraid Of The Big Bad Wolf?/A Taste Of Honey/Happy Days Are Here Again/Cry Me A River
(Australia) 1964
#BG225016

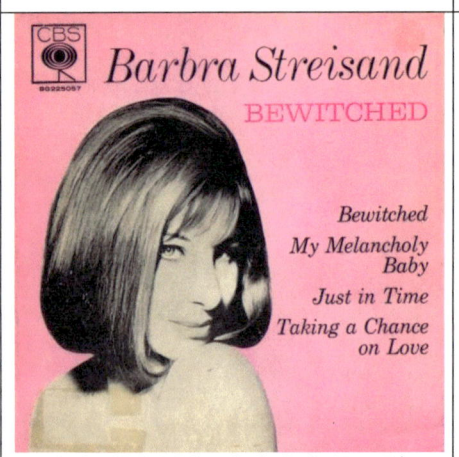

Bewitched/My Melancholy Baby/Just In Time/Taking A Chance On Love
(Australia) 1964
#BG225057

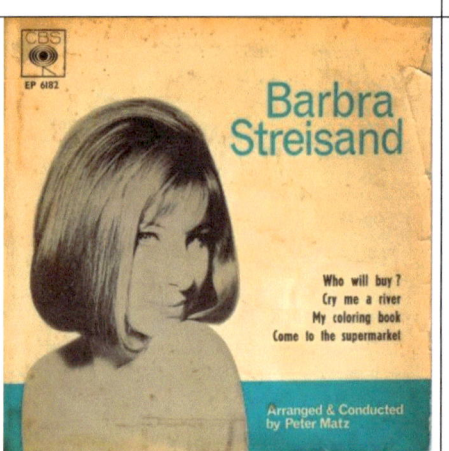

Who Will Buy?/Cry Me A River/My Coloring Book/Come To The Supermarket
(Israel) 1964
#6182

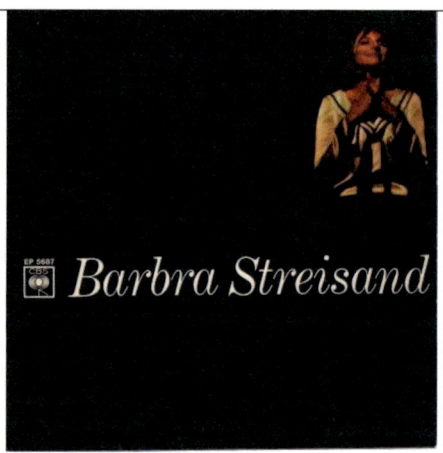

My Melancholy Baby/Taking A Chance On Love/Bewitched/Make Believe
(France) 1964
#5687

Cry Me A River/As Time Goes By/My Melancholy Baby/Just In Time
(Japan) 1964
#LSS-207-C

People/Funny Girl/A Taste Of Honey/As Time Goes By
(Spain) 1964
#5898

People/I Am Woman/Funny Girl/Absent Minded Me
(Portugal) 1964
#5952

72

People/Fine And Dandy/Supper Time/When In Rome
(Holland) 1964
#5716

People/When In Rome/Autumn/Love Is A Bore
(Australia) 1964
#BG225079

People/When In Rome/The Shadow Of Your Smile/Second Hand Rose
(Japan) 1965
#SONE 70012

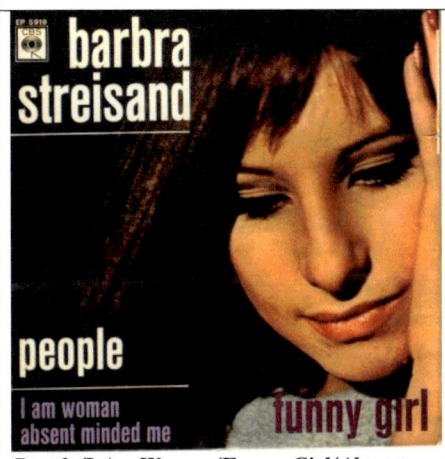

People/I Am Woman/Funny Girl/Absent Minded Me
(Holland) 1965
#5919
(Also issued in France with same cover)

My Man/Happy Days Are Here Again/Why Did I Choose You/People
(England) 1965
#6068
(Also issued in Spain same cover)

My Man/I've Got No Strings/Someone To Watch Over Me/I Can See It
(France) 1965
#6103

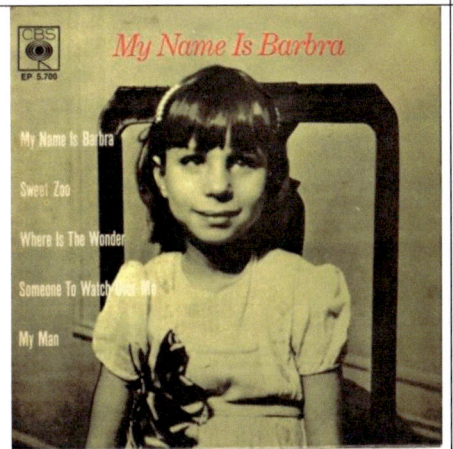

My Name Is Barbra/Sweet Zoo/Where Is The Wonder/Someone To Watch Over Me/My Man
(Holland) 1965
#5700

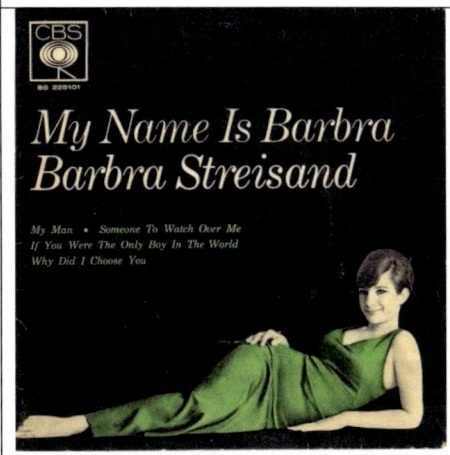

My Man/Someone To Watch Over Me/If You Were The Only Boy In The World/Why Did I Choose You
(Australia) 1965
#BG 225101

People/Someone To Watch Over Me/My Man/My Lord And Master
(Japan) 1965
#LSS-386-C

73

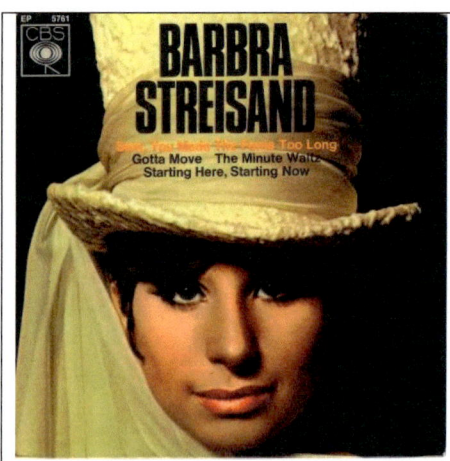

Sam, You Made The Pants To Long/Gotta Move/The Minute Waltz/Starting Here, Starting Now
(Germany) 1965
#5761

The Shadow Of Your Smile/How Much Of The Dream Comes True?/I Got Plenty Of Nothin'/Where's That Rainbow?
(Holland) 1965
#5724

Second Hand Rose/He Touched Me/I Got Plenty Of Nothin'/The Shadow Of Your Smile
(Australia) 1965
#BG 225112

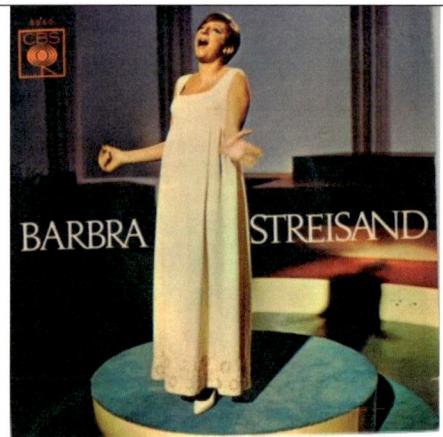

Second Hand Rose/Sam, You Made The Pants Too Long/The Minute Waltz/The Kind Of Man A Woman Needs
(Portugal) 1966
#5640

People/Second Hand Rose/A Taste Of Honey/My Melancholy Baby
(South Africa) 1966 Promotional-only
(No catalog number)

South Africa 1966 Rare second edition of same EP with special four-page sleeve sent to record store dealers.
Promotional-only (no catalog number)

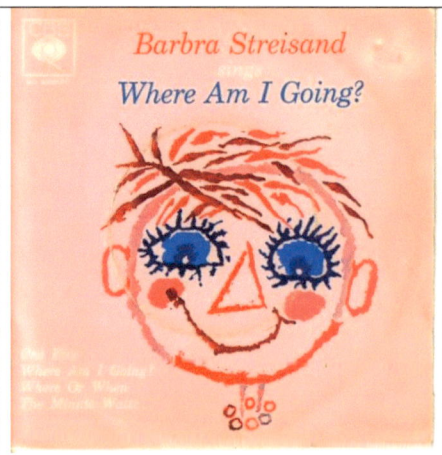

One Kiss/Where Am I Going?/Where Or When/The Minute Waltz
(Australia) 1966
#BG 225130

Non…C'est Rien/The Shadow Of Your Smile/Second Hand Rose/People
(Argentina) 1966
#33391

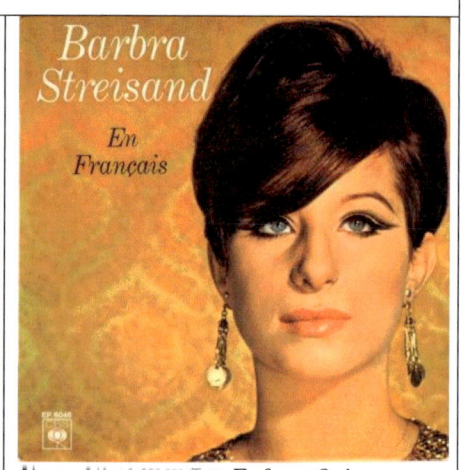

Non…C'est Rien/Les Enfants Qui Pleurent/Et La Mer/Le Mur
(France) 1966
#6048
(Also released in UK & Holland same sleeve & catalog #)

74

En Francais (same tracks as French release)
(Israel) 1966
#6048

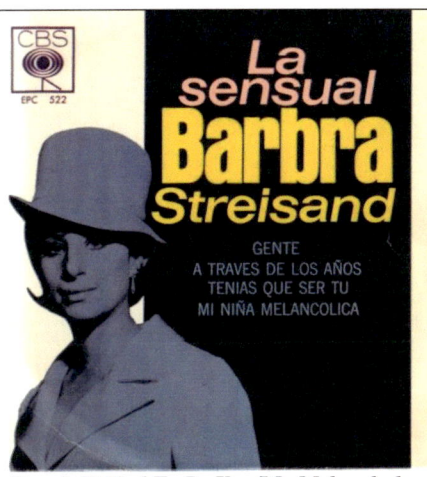

People/It Had To Be You/My Melancholy Baby/As Time Goes By
(Mexico) 1966
#EPC 522

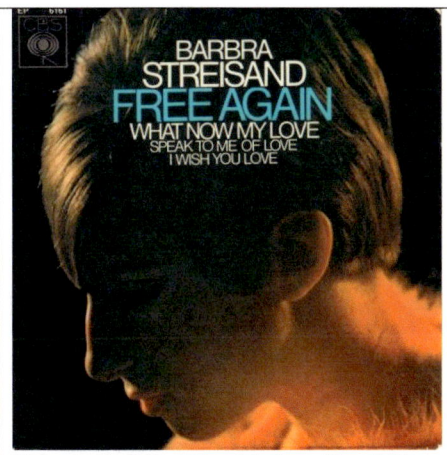

Free Again/What Now My Love/Speak To Me Of Love/I Wish You Love
(Germany) 1966
#6161

Second Hand Rose/Sam, You Made The Pants Too Long/The Minute Waltz/Brother Can You Spare A Dime/I'm Five/Sweet Zoo
(England) 1966
#6150

Second Hand Rose/He Touched Me/Yesterdays/Where Am I Going?
(Germany) 1966
#6003

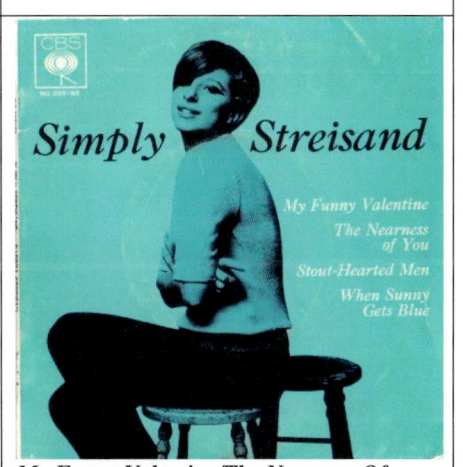

My Funny Valentine/The Nearness Of You/Stout-Hearted Men/When Sunny Gets Blue
(Australia) 1967
#BG 225163

The Shadow Of Your Smile/Yesterdays/A Taste Of Honey/C'est Si Bon (It's So Good)
(Japan) 1967
#LSS-592-C

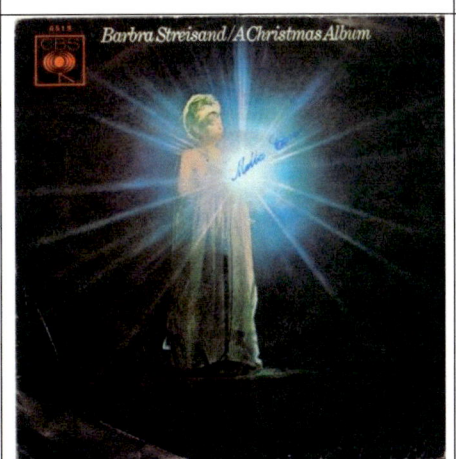

Jingle Bells/Sleep In Heavenly Peace/Gounod's Ave Maria/The Lord's Prayer
(Portugal) 1967
#6519

Free Again/What Now My Love/I Wish You Love/Le Mur
(Mexico) 1968
#EPC 898

I'm The Greatest Star/Funny Girl/People/The Swan
(Iran) 1969
Playboy label #2048

People/My Man/Don't Rain On My Parade/Funny Girl
(Mexico) 1969
#EPC 937

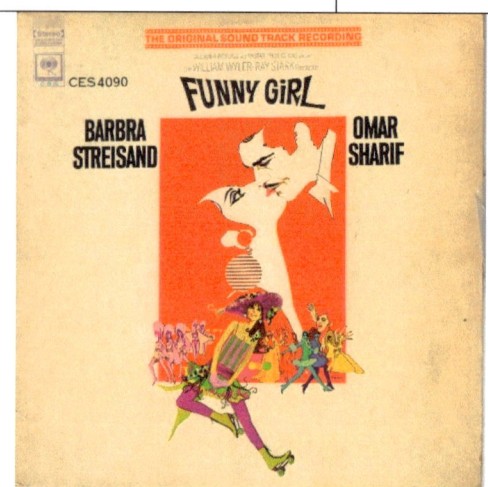

People/Funny Girl/My Man/Don't Rain On My Parade
(Singapore) 1969
#CES 4090

Funny Girl/The Swan/People/You Are Woman-I Am Man
(Thailand) 1969
Coliseum #1089

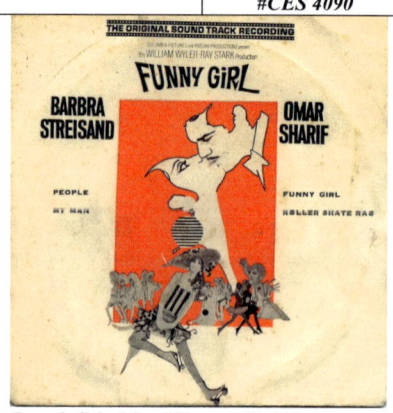

People/My Man/Funny Girl/Roller Skate Rag
(Thailand) 1969 (Unknown catalog #)

People/My Man/ I'd Rather Be Blue Over You/Funny Girl/Roller Skate Rag/You Are Woman-You Are Man
(Thailand) 1969
#030

The Morning After/Where Is The Wonder/Our Corner Of The Night/He Could Show Me
(Portugal) 1968
#6518

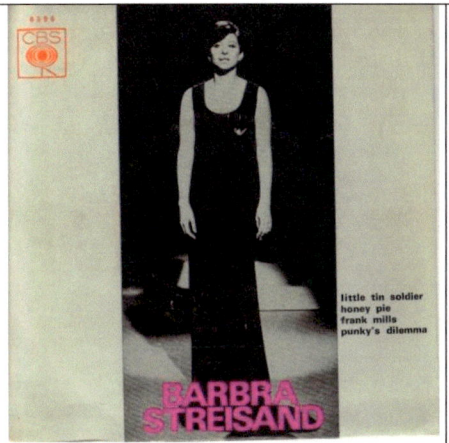

Little Tin Soldier/Honey Pie/Frank Mills/Punky's Dilemma
(Portugal) 1969
#6596

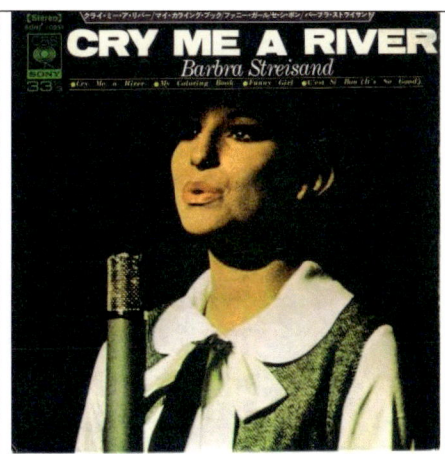

Cry Me A River/My Coloring Book/Funny Girl/C'est Si Bon (Its So Good)
(Japan) 1969
#SONE 70054

People/Cry Me A River/A Taste Of Honey/As Time Goes By
(Brazil) 1970
#56372

Hello Dolly/It Takes A Woman/Just Leave Everything To Me
(Mexico) 1970
20th Century Fox Records #GX 07-641
(Also Thailand EP #MTR 385 same cover)

Hello Dolly-Andy Williams/Before The Parade Passes By/Love Is Only Love
(Mexico) 1970
#EPC 1004
(Williams pictured on front sleeve, back sleeve shown)

The Best Thing You've Ever Done/Ask Yourself Why/Summer Me, Winter Me/Alfie
(Brazil) 1970
#56384

The Summer Knows/You've Got A Friend/Mother/Space Captain
(Australia) 1971
#SBG 225261

Mother/Beautiful/Love
(Mexico) 1971
#EPC 1103

77

Guava Jelly/Simple Man/Let The Good Times Roll
(Mexico) 1975
#EPC 1380

How Lucky Can You Get/More Than You Know/It's Only A Paper Moon-I Like Him/I Like Her/Me And My Shadow
(Japan) 1975 Arista Records
#BLPD 17-AR

Evergreen/People/Stoney End/The Way We Were
(Japan) 1977
#08EP 24

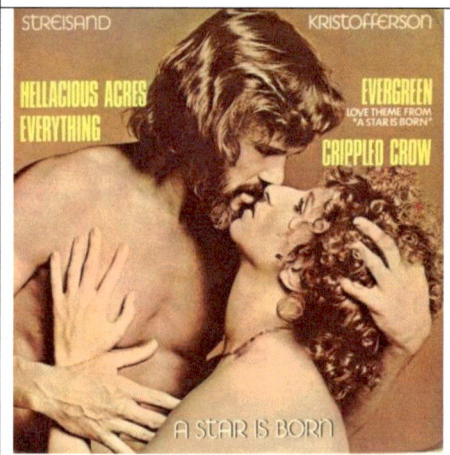

Evergreen/Hellacious Acres/Crippled Crow/Everything
(Brazil) 1978
#56520

Woman In Love/Guilty/Promises/Never Give Up
(Bolivia) 1980
#10325

Woman In Love/What Kind Of Fool/Guilty/Run Wild
(Brazil) 1980
#56552

Woman In Love/Never Give Up/Mother/Love
(Mexico) 1980
#EPC 1626

Till I Loved You/Two People/You Don't Bring Me Flowers/What Kind Of Fool
(England) 1988
#BARB EP2

All I Ask Of You/Somewhere/Memory/Send In The Clowns
(England) 1988
#BARB EP3

79

12" Singles US & International
(All CBS/Columbia Records unless noted)

Shake Me, Wake Me (When It's Over)
(Stereo/mono) Rare 4:55 Disco version
Promotional-only 1975
#AS 217

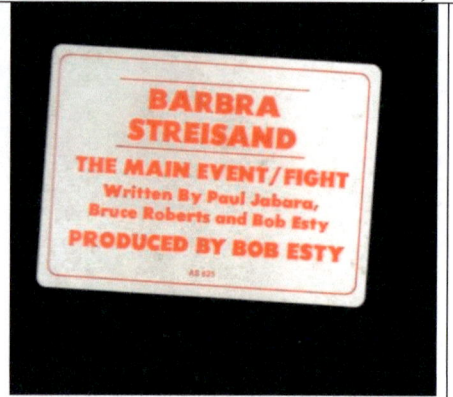

The Main Event/Fight (both sides)
11:42 Disco Mix
Promotional-only 1979
#AS 625

The Main Event (long version/instrumental)
(England) with picture label 1979
#12-7714

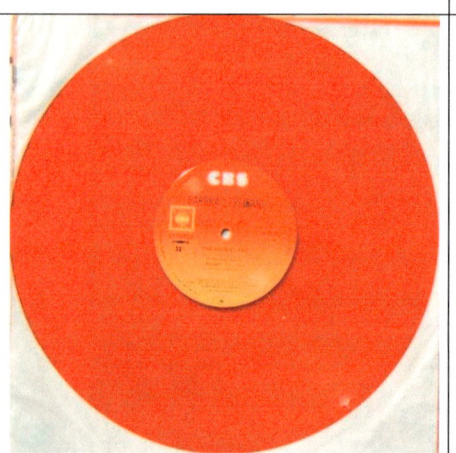

The Main Event/Fight (long/short versions)
(Mexico) 1979 Red vinyl
#BS-35017

The Main Event/Fight (long/short versions)
(Colombia) 1979 Light Yellow vinyl
#442-1006

No More Tears (1-sided) 11:40
Casablanca 1979 Extended Disco version
#NBD 20199

No More Tears (1-sided) 11:40
Promotional copy with same cover
Columbia/Casablanca (same catalog #)

No More Tears/Wet
(Japan) 1979 with OBI and sticker
#25AP 1724

No More Tears/Wet
(Brazil) 1979
#34077

80

No More Tears/Wet
(Colombia) 1979 Yellow vinyl
#442-1015

No More Tears/Wet
(Colombia) 1979 Blue vinyl
#442-1015

Also released as regular vinyl with same cover in UK, Spain, Holland, & Argentina

No More Tears/Wet
(Colombia) 1979 Pink vinyl
#442-1015

No More Tears/Wet
(Mexico) Red vinyl
#BS 35,016

Woman In Love/Guilty
(Colombia) 1980 Yellow vinyl
#442-1098

Woman In Love/Guilty
(Colombia) 1980 Green vinyl
#442-1098

Guilty/Make It Like A Memory
(Mexico) 1980 Red vinyl
#BS 35024

Guilty/Life Story
(Holland) 1980
#12.9315

Promises (5:55)/Make It Like A Memory
1981 Extended version picture label
#43-02089
Also same release in Holland #12-1332

81

Woman In Love 12" Picture Disc-Rare International Bootleg Test Pressing (1-sided)
Obtained by an International Record Dealer, there's no country listed or catalog number. Streisand's original recording is on the disc.
Note: There's a few 12" and 7" International bootleg picture discs that feature Streisand pictured on the disc, but without her recordings, just piano music or other artists. I believe a Record Dealer made them. Some have Amnesty International listed on the disc.

Woman In Love/Run Wild
(Holland) 1980 #12.8966

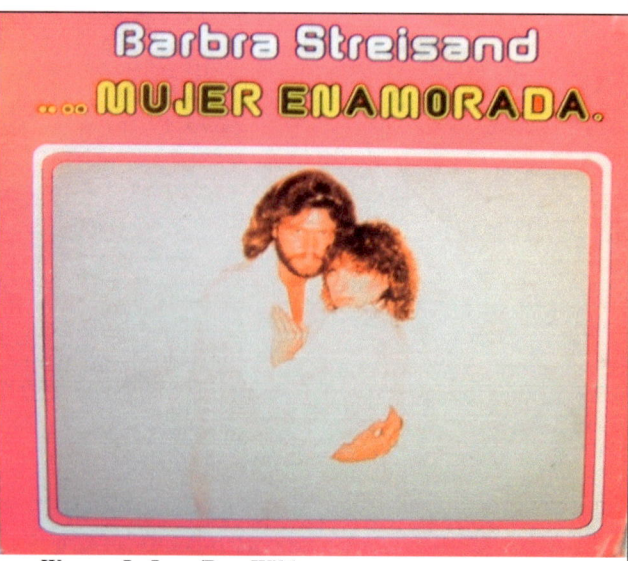

Woman In Love/Run Wild
(Venezuela) 1980 #MS 4029

Promises (both sides)
1981 Promotional copy
#43-02089

Memory (both sides)
1982 Promotional-only release
#AS 1610
Also issued Comin' In And Out Of Your Life/The Way We Were/The Love Inside (Italy)
1981 Promotional #12 PRM 035 (no picture sleeve).

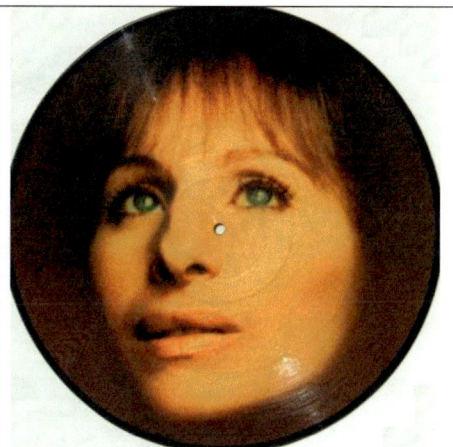

The Way He Makes Me Feel (Studio/Film versions)
1983 Promotional-only picture disc
#AS 991791

Left In The Dark (with/without spoken intro)
1984 Promotional-only release
#AS 1929

Left In The Dark/Here We Are At Last/ Woman In Love/Guilty/Memory (England) 1984
#TA 4754

Emotion (6:34)/Instrumental
1985 Extended version
#44-05167

Heart Don't Change Me Mind (both sides)
1985 Test Pressing (plain label)
#AV-2

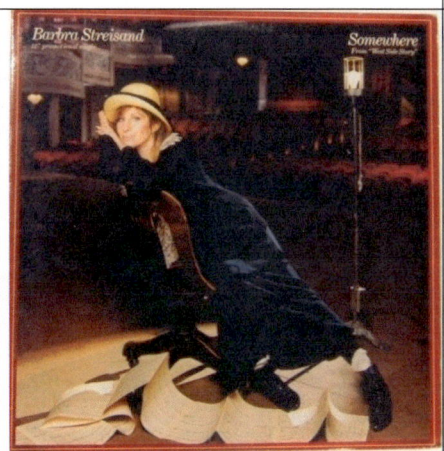

Somewhere (both sides)
1985 Promotional-only release
#CAS 2220

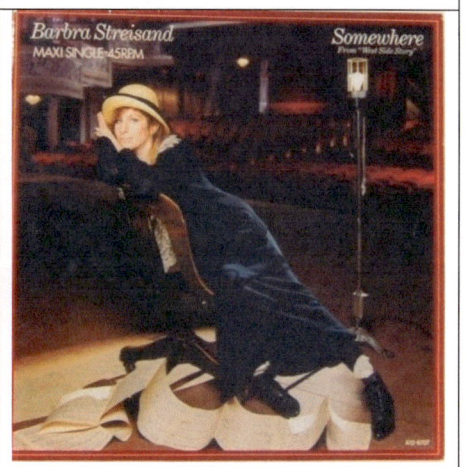

Somewhere/Not While I'm Around (England) 1986
#A126707

83

The Main Event-Fight/Promises
1987 Reissue Extended versions
Mixed Masters #44H 06920

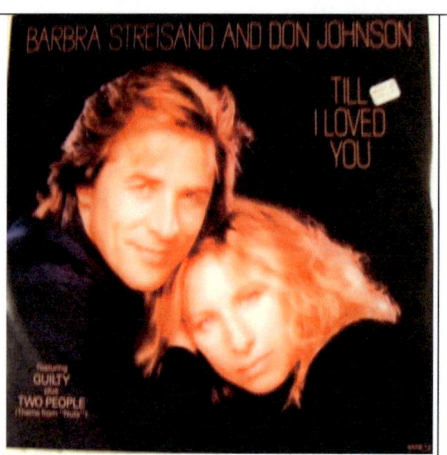

Till I Loved You/Guilty/Two People
(England) 1988
#BARB T2
Also released in Holland same cover
#6529796

All I Ask Of You/On My Way To You/Life Story/Emotion
(Spain) 1988
#653011-6
(Also same release in Holland)

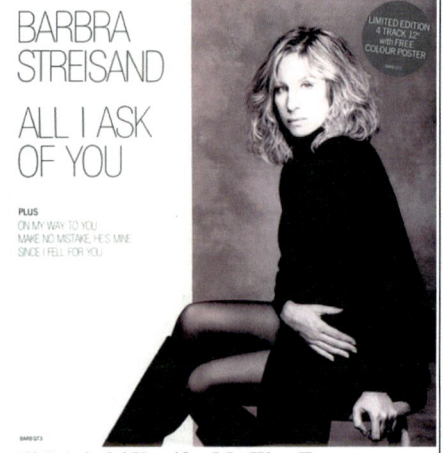

All I Ask Of You/On My Way To You/Make No Mistake, He's Mine/Since I Fell For You
(England) 1988 (issued with color poster)
#BARB QT3

All I Ask Of You/On My Way To You/Life Story/Emotion
(England) 1988
#BARB T3

We're Not Makin' Love Anymore/Here We Are At Last/Till I Loved You/The Love Inside
(England) 1989 (same release in Holland)
#BARB T4
(Also UK release with No More Tears/Wet #BARB QT4 same cover)

Tell Him (radio edit)/Everything Must Change/Tell Him (album version)/Where Is The Love (Dion)
(Holland) 1997
#665205-6

Night Of My Life (4 different Dance Remixes)
2005
#44-080392

Night Of My Life (2 mixes)
(England) 2005 Promo-only release
#BS01

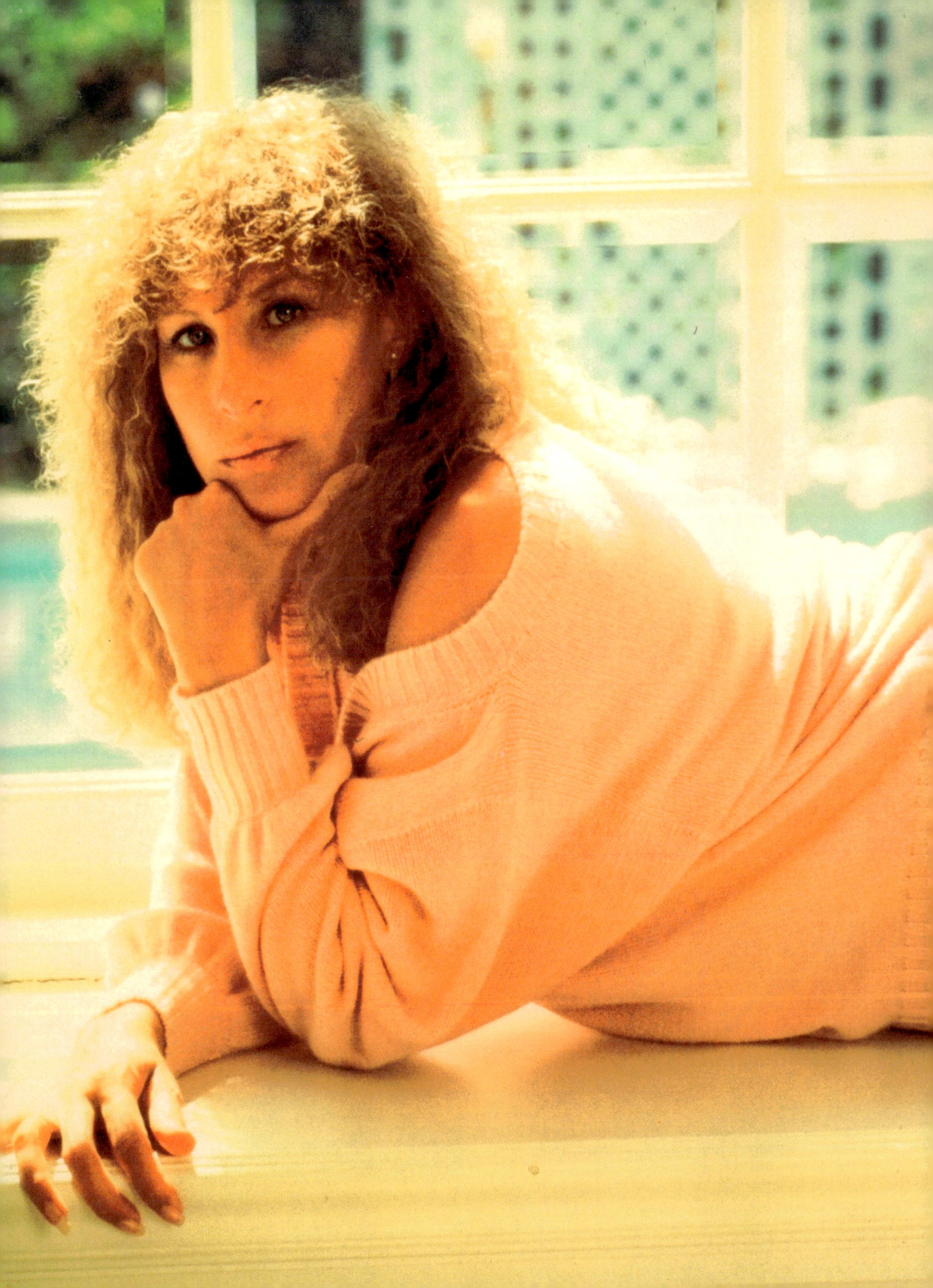

Cassette Singles

Columbia released the following singles, issued with covers:

Till I Loved You #38T 08062
All I Ask Of You #38T 08026
What Were We Thinking Of #38T 68691
We're Not Makin' Love Anymore
#38T 73016
Ordinary Miracles #38T 77533
I Finally Found Someone #38T 78480

UK Releases:
We're Not Makin' Love Anymore #BARBM4
Places That Belong To You #657794-4
With One Look #659342-4
Music Of The Night #659738-4
As If We Never Said Goodbye #660357-4
I Finally Found Someone #5820834
Tell Him #6653054

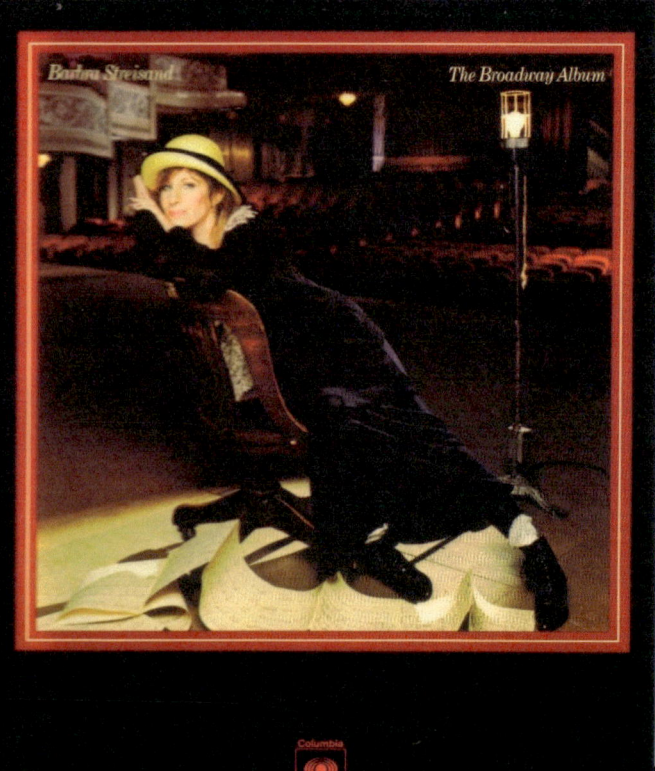

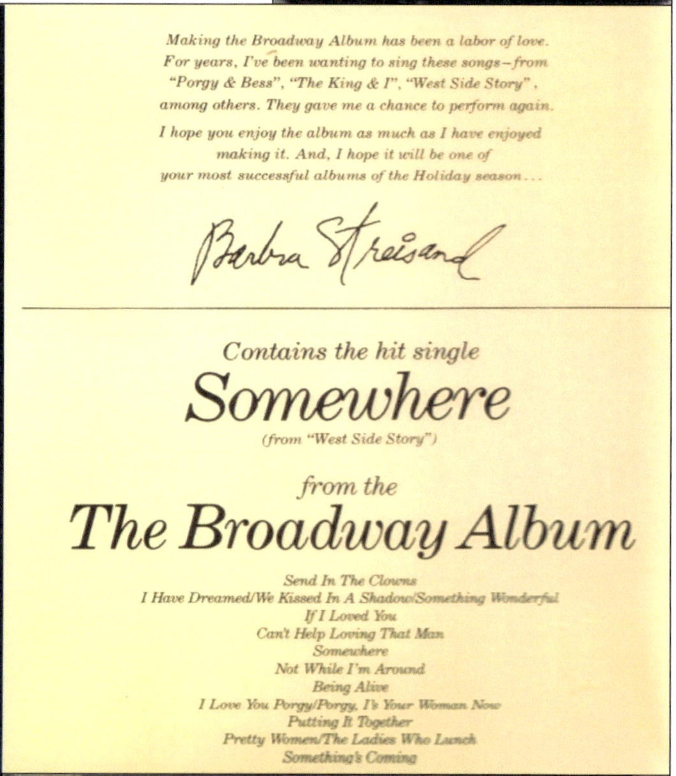

Somewhere 1985 Promotional-only cassette single issued in thick black plastic case and note card with message from Barbra. (Back cover shown)
#OC-40092 Columbia records

Canadian edition released as two promotional-only cassettes of The Broadway Album & A Christmas Album. Issued in thick white plastic case. CBS 1985

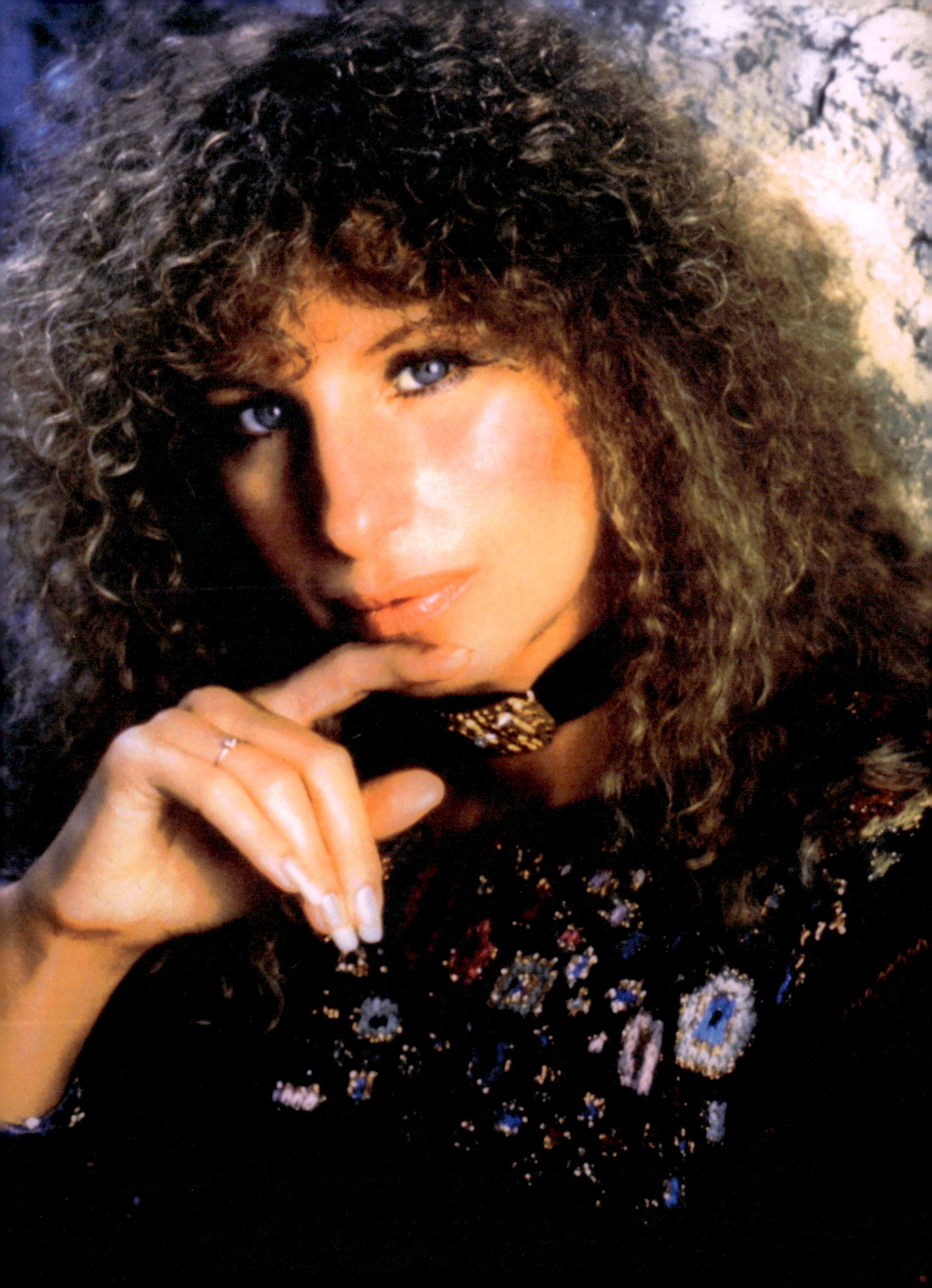

CD Singles US & International
(All CBS/Columbia unless noted)

Till I Loved You/Two People
1988 3"CD single
#38K-08062

Till I Loved You (regular/edited versions)
1988 Promotional-only
#CSK 1312

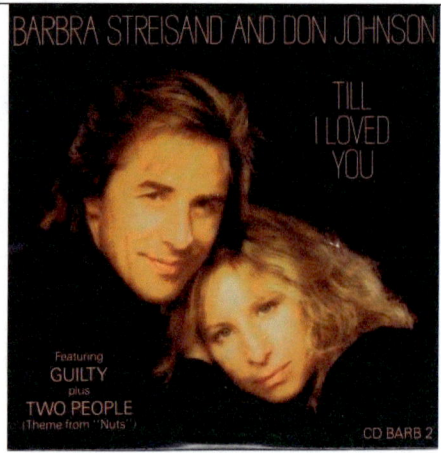

Till I Loved You/Guilty/Left In The Dark/Two People
(England) 1988 (Card sleeve)
#CD BARB2
Also Austria 3" CD single #652979-3

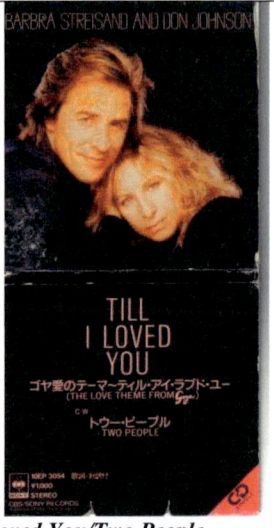

Till I Loved You/Two People
(Japan) 1988 3"CD (with mini poster)
#10EP3054

All I Ask Of You
1988 Promotional-only
#CSK 1258

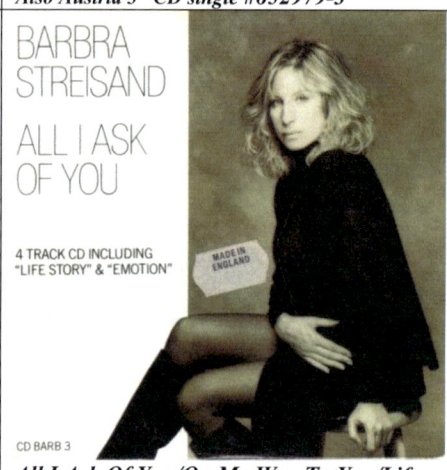

All I Ask Of You/On My Way To You/Life Story/Emotion
(England) 1988 #CD BARB3 (Card sleeve)
(Also 3" Holland #6530113)

All I Ask Of You/Somewhere/Memory/Send In The Clowns
(England) 1988 Rare Picture Disc
#CP BARB 3

We're Not Makin' Love Anymore (single/album versions)
1989 Promotional-only
#CSK 1816

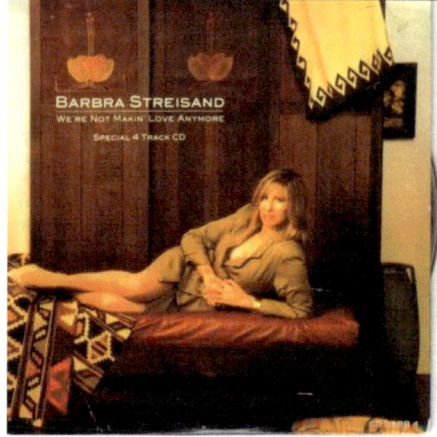

We're Not Makin' Love Anymore/Till I Loved You/Kiss Me In The Rain/The Places You Find Love
(England) 1989 #CD BARB 4 (Card sleeve)
(Also 3" single Austria #6553341)

88

We're Not Makin' Love Anymore/Wet/No More Tears
(England) 1989 Picture Disc
#BARB C4

We're Not Makin' Love Anymore/Here We At Last
(Japan) 1989 3"CD #CSDS 8112

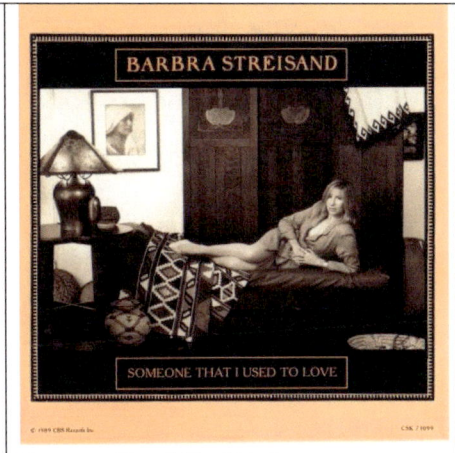

Someone That I Used To Love
1989 Promotional-only
#CSK 73099

Someone That I Used To Love/What Kind Of Fool
(Austria) 1989 3"CD single (Card sleeve)
#6556441

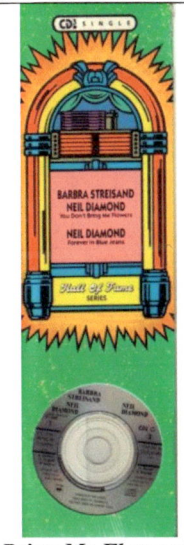

You Don't Bring Me Flowers/Forever In Blue Jeans (Neil Diamond)
1990 3"CD Hall Of Fame #CSIG 000232

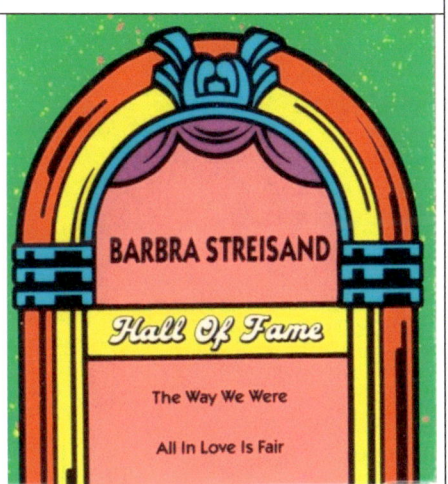

The Way We Were/All In Love Is Fair
1990 3" CD Hall Of Fame
#13K 68660

Woman In Love/Run Wild/The Way We Were
(Austria) 1991
#657686-2 (slim jewel case)

Woman In Love/Run Wild
(Austria) 1991 (Card sleeve)
#664325-1

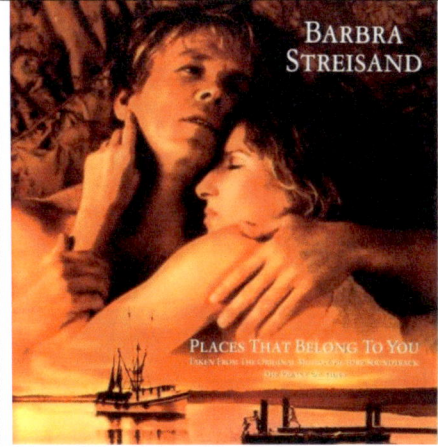

Places That Belong To You
1991 Promotional-only release
#CSK4257

89

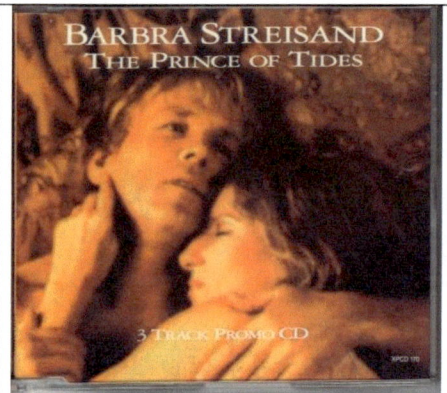

Places That Belong To You/For All We Know/Prince Of Tides (Main Title)
(England) 1992 Promotional-only
#XPCD 170 (slim jewel case)

Places That Belong To You/Warm All Over/I Know Him So Well/You'll Never Know
(England) 1992 Picture Disc
#6577949 (slim jewel case)

Places That Belong To You/For All We Know
(Austria) 1992 Promotional copy
#SAMPCD 1593 (slim jewel case)

Also Austria 3-track in similar sleeve
#6577945

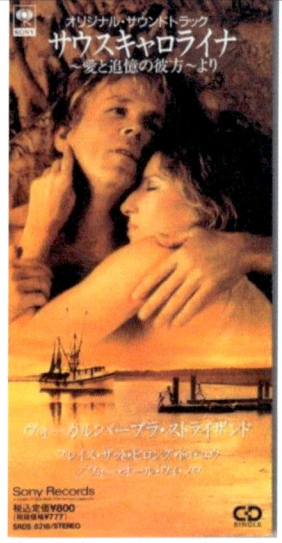

Places That Belong To You/For All We Know
(Japan) 1992 3" single #SPDS 8218

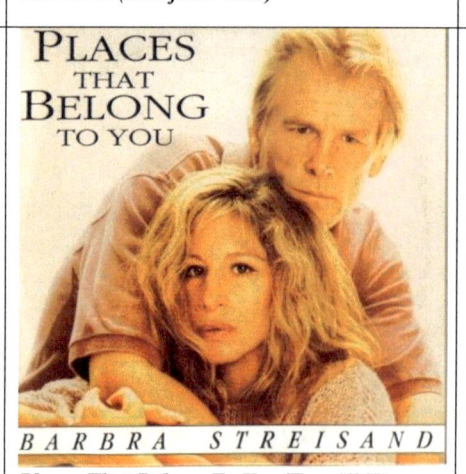

Places That Belong To You/For All We Know
(Australia) 1992
#657794-2 (Card sleeve)

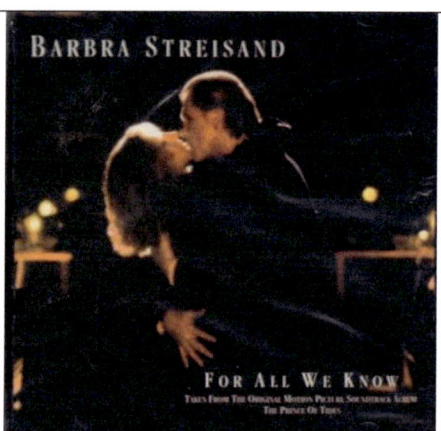

For All We Know
1992 Promotional-only
#CSK 4507

With One Look/Memory/All I Ask Of You
(England) 1993
#6593421 (slim jewel case)
(Also released in Australia)

(Also With One Look/Memory Austria release in card sleeve same catalog #)

Children Will Listen (with spoken intro/album versions)
1993 Promotional-only
#CSK 5288

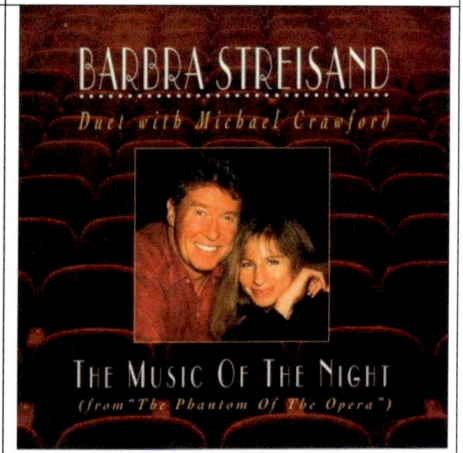

Music Of The Night (edit/album versions)
1993 Promotional-only
#CSK 5429

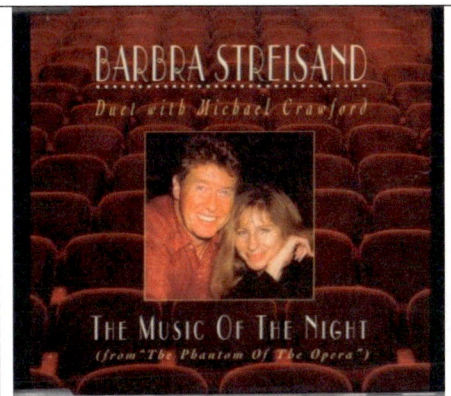

Music Of The Night/Children Will Listen
(with spoken intro)/Move On (alternate)
(Austria) 1993
#659738-2 (slim jewel case)

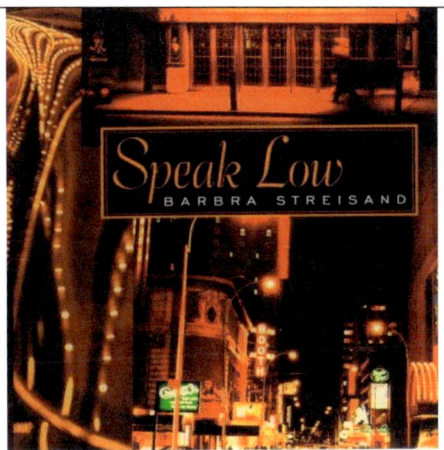

Speak Low
1993 Promotional-only
#CSK 5580

I've Got A Crush On You (edit/album versions)
1993 Capital Records Promotional-only
#DPRO-79316

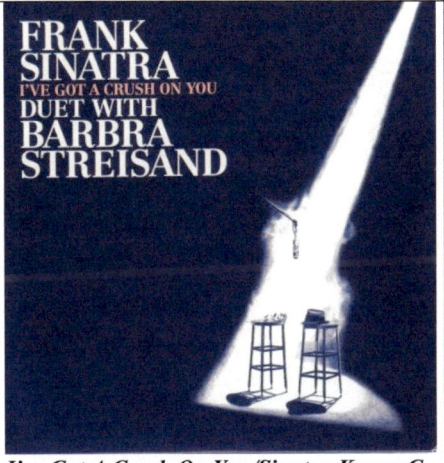

I've Got A Crush On You/Sinatra-Kenny G One More For My Baby
(Holland) 1993 (Card sleeve)
Capitol #C2 7243-8-8811372
Same release in Australia #724388113922

I've Got A Crush On You/One More For My Baby (Sinatra & Kenny G)
(Japan) 1993 3"CD single
Capital #TODP 2443

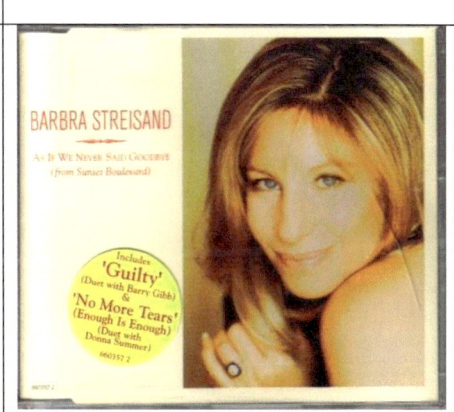

As If We Never Said Goodbye/Guilty/No More Tears
(England) 1994
#660357-2 (slim jewel case)
(Also same release in Austria)

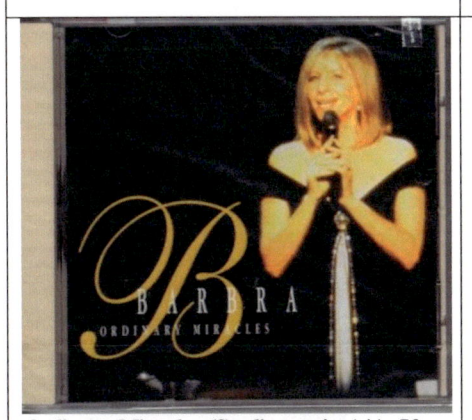

Ordinary Miracles (Studio version)/As If We Never Said Goodbye/Evergreen/ Ordinary Miracles (Live version)
1994
#44K77534

Also card sleeve Australian single #660842-2

Evergreen
1994 Promotional-only
#CSK 6602

Also Austria promo card sleeve #SAMPCD 2416

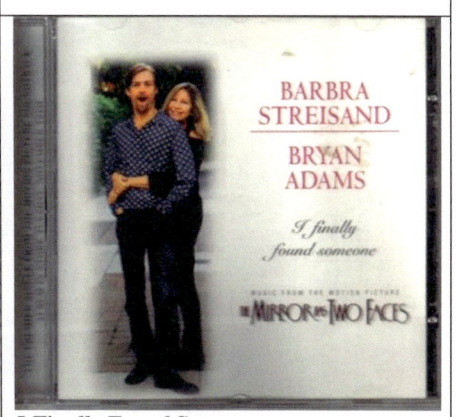

I Finally Found Someone
1996 Promotional copy
#CSK 9157

(Also UK Promotional copy issued same cover slim jewel case #588 507-2)

91

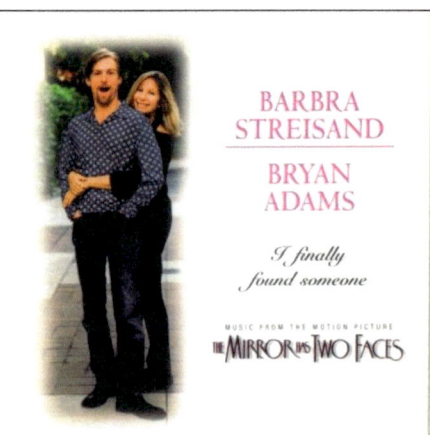

I Finally Found Someone/Let's Make A Night To Remember (Bryan Adams)/ Evergreen (Spanish version)
1996 (issued in card sleeve)
#38K 78480

I Finally Found Someone/Star (Bryan Adams)
(Japan) 1996 3" CD
A & M Records #PODM-1068

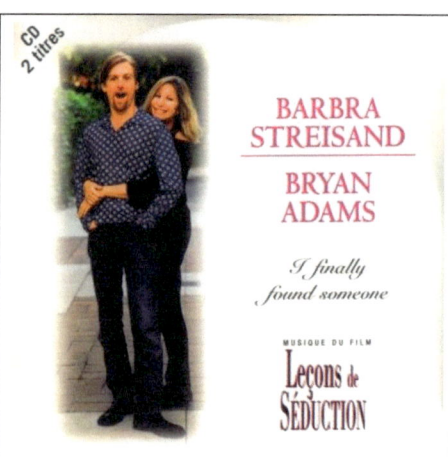

I Finally Found Someone/I Think About You (Bryan Adams)
(France) 1996 (Card sleeve)
A & M Records #582088-2

Also issued with 2 Bryan Adams tracks #582088-2)

I Finally Found Someone (with 3 Bryan Adams tracks)
(Australia) 1996 (slim jewel case)
A & M Records #582083-2

(Also issued as same cover in Germany, UK, and Mexico)

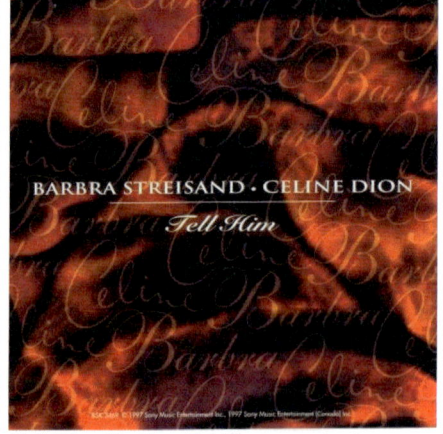

Tell Him (Radio edit/Album version)
1997 Promotional copy
#BSK 3469
Also 1-track promo issued in Austria #SAMPCS4718 (slim jewel case)
(Same cover) Same promo in Mexico

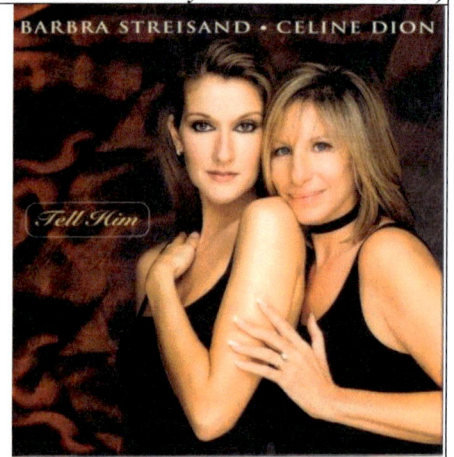

Tell Him/Everything Must Change/Where Is The Love (Celine Dion)
1997 withdrawn US single in card sleeve
#DIDP 094427

Tell Him/Everything Must Change/Where Is The Love (Celine Dion)
(Japan) 1997
#SRCS 8540

Tell Him (Radio edit)/Everything Must Change/Where Is The Love (Celine Dion)
(Austria) 1997 (slim jewel case)
#665205-2

(Same release in Australia, Mexico, South Africa & UK)

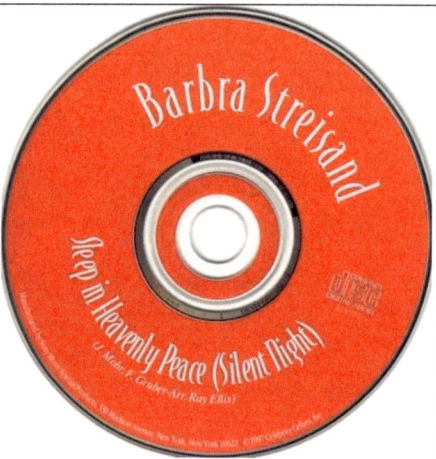

Sleep In Heavenly Peace (Silent Night)
1997 Celebrity Cellars Special Streisand Wine packaged with CD issued in Christmas card sleeve
Sony Music Special Products #A28773

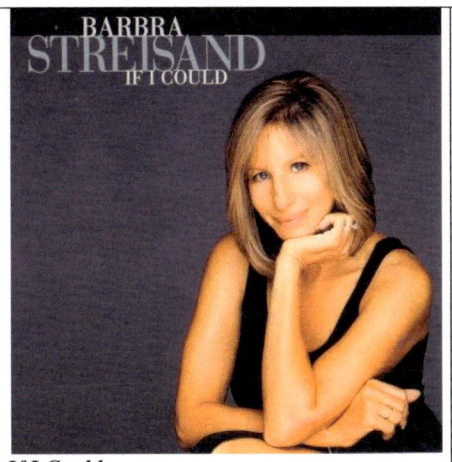

If I Could
1998 Promotional-only release
#CSK 3932
Also Austria 1-track promo #XPCD961 (slim jewel case)

If I Could/At The Same Time/I Believe (Single version)/Evergreen (French version) (Austria) 1998 (slim jewel case)
#665522-2

(Also If I Could/I Believe Austria single in card sleeve #665522-1)

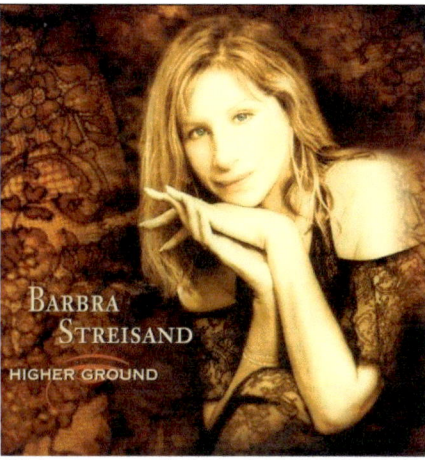

Higher Ground/Call Hook #1/Call Hook #2
1998 Promotional-only
#CSK 41047

I've Dreamed Of You/At The Same Time
1999
#38K 79211
(Also 1-track promotional copy #CSK42424)

I've Dreamed Of You (Austria) 1999 1-track promo copy #SAMPCS 7377 (slim jewel case)

Also 2-track single issued with same cover in Austria, Australia, & South Africa

Let's Start Right Now
1999 (Sold at Sam Goodie with CD A Love Like Ours)
#CK 63981

If You Ever Leave Me
1999 Promotional-only
#CSK 42713

If You Ever Leave Me/Just Because (non-LP cut)/Let's Start Right Now (non-LP cut) (England) 1999
#668124-2 (slim jewel case)
Also same released in Austria & Australia

(Also If You Ever Leave Me/Just Because 2-track in card sleeve UK #667801-1)

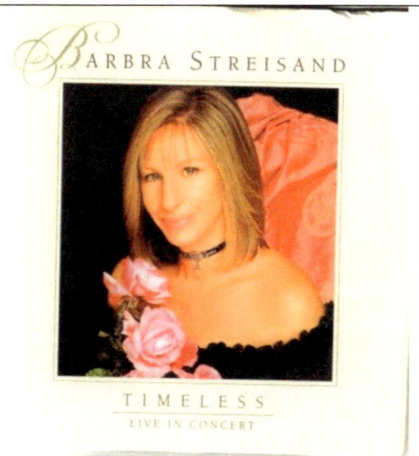

Come Rain Or Come Shine (Live in Australia) 2000
Barnes & Noble bonus disc sold with Timeless CD (Issued in card sleeve)
#DIDP 101288
Also Australian promo #SAMP2289

God Bless America (Live '92)
2001 Target exclusive with Christmas Memories CD
#CSK 54832

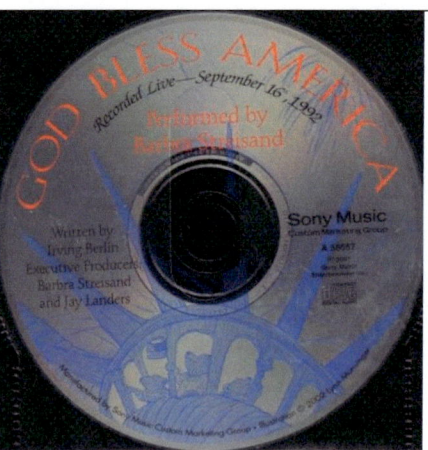

God Bless America (Live '92)
2001 (Sold with children's book God Bless America)
#A 58657

I Won't Be The One To Let Go (Two Radio Edit tracks)
2002 Promotional-only release
#CSK 59450

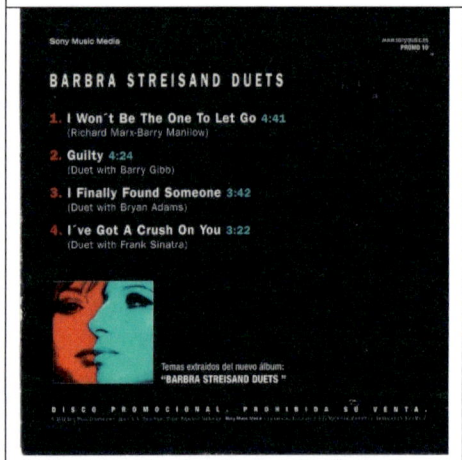

I Won't Be The One To Let Go/Guilty/I Finally Found Someone/I've Got A Crush On You
(Spain) 2002 Promotional-only
#PROMO 10 (Card sleeve) Back cover shown

Smile/Calling You/Moon River
(Austria) 2003 Picture Disc (same cover as US) (slim jewel case)
#SAMP CD 13500-2 Promotional-only

Smile/Calling You/Moon River
2003 Promotional-only release
#CSK 56599 (slim jewel case)
(Disc with blue backing)

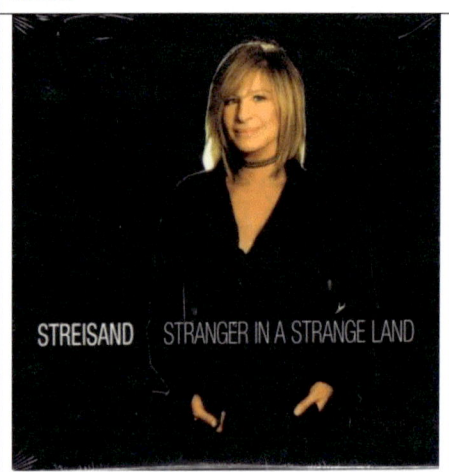

Stranger In A Strange Land
2005 (Card sleeve)
#CSK 17286
Also issued #CSK 17311

Stranger In A Strange Land (Radio edit)
(Sweden/EEC) 2005 Promotional copy
#SAMPCD 150511 (slim jewel case)

Also UK single #82876 748652
(slim jewel case and same sleeve)

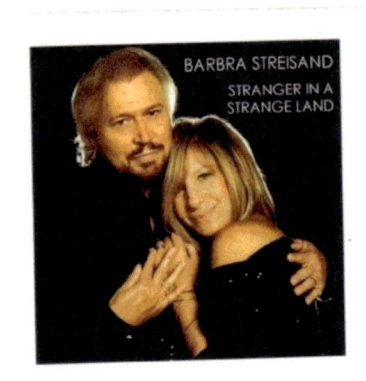

Stranger In A Strange Land
(Australia) 2005 SONY/BMG
Promotional-only in card sleeve
(No catalog #) CD with blue backing

94

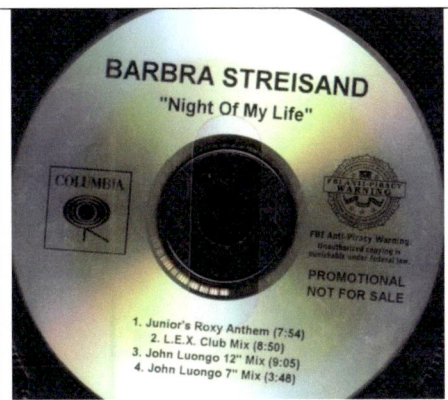

Night Of My Life (4-Tracks Dance Mixes)
2005 Promotional-only release
(No catalog number) (Released in red Columbia card sleeve)
(Also issued as 6-tracks)

Night Of My Life
2005 Special Promotional-only release
#CSK 17288
Rare single with 11 different mixes
(Unable to obtain)

Come Tomorrow/Night Of My Life (Love To Infinity Master Mix)
(England) 2005 (slim jewel case)
#82876 771472

Smoke Gets In Your Eyes/Love Dance/In The Wee Small Hours Of The Morning
2009 Promotional-only (no catalog #)
Acetate type disc with blue backing

That Face
2011 Promotional-only (acetate disc)
(No catalog # or cover)

Also UK released promo acetate single of Solitary Moon, no catalog #

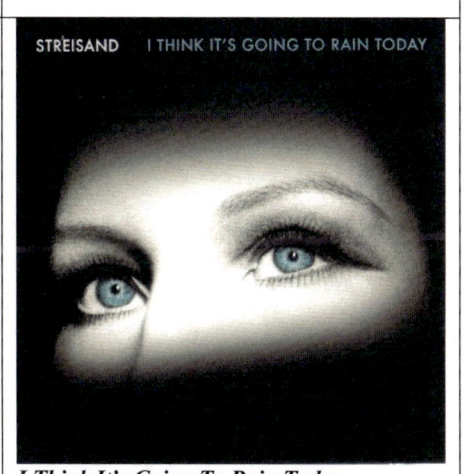

I Think It's Going To Rain Today
2012 Promotional-only
(No catalog number)

Also Holland 1-track promo in same cover
#11204940

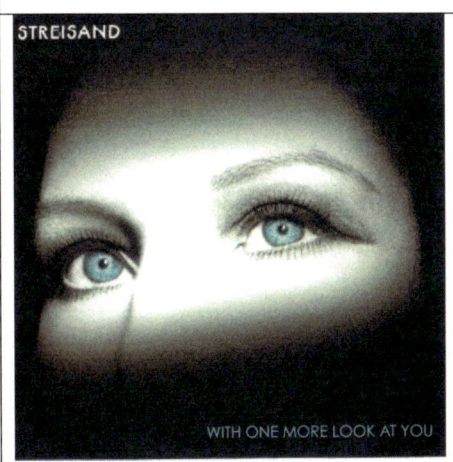

With One More Look At You
(England) 2012
#LC 12723
Issued in plastic wallet

It Had To Be You
(England) 2014 promo acetate single
Issued in plastic wallet with promo sticker
no catalog #

I'd Want It To Be You
(England) 2014 promo acetate single
Issued in plastic wallet, no catalog #

Movie Radio Spots

The following were released on vinyl and sent to Radio Stations for commercial airtime.

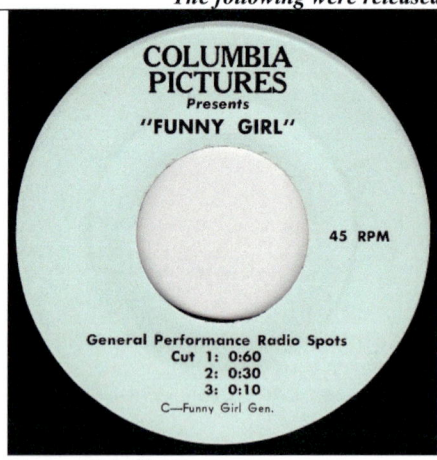

Funny Girl (1968)
(Columbia Pictures)
7" 1-sided
7" reissue Academy Award 1969
(1-sided)

Hello Dolly (1969)
(20th Century Fox)
7" 1-sided

On A Clear Day You Can See Forever (1970) (Paramount Pictures)
12" 1-sided

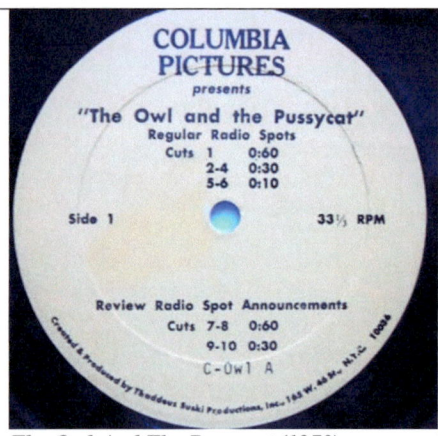

The Owl And The Pussycat (1970)
(Columbia Pictures)
12" 1-sided
Also 7" re-release 1-sided (1971)

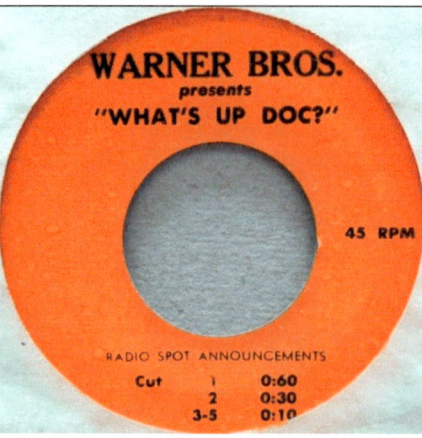

What's Up Doc? (1972)
(Warner Bros.)
7" 1-sided

Up The Sandbox (1972)
(A National General Pictures Release)
7" 1-sided

The Way We Were (1973)
(Columbia Pictures)
7" 2-sided
Also reissue 7" 1-sided (1974)

For Pete's Sake (1974)
(Columbia Pictures)
7" 1-sided

Funny Lady (1975)
(Columbia Pictures)
10" 2-sided (#JB 192)
Also 7" reissue 1-sided (#JB 252)

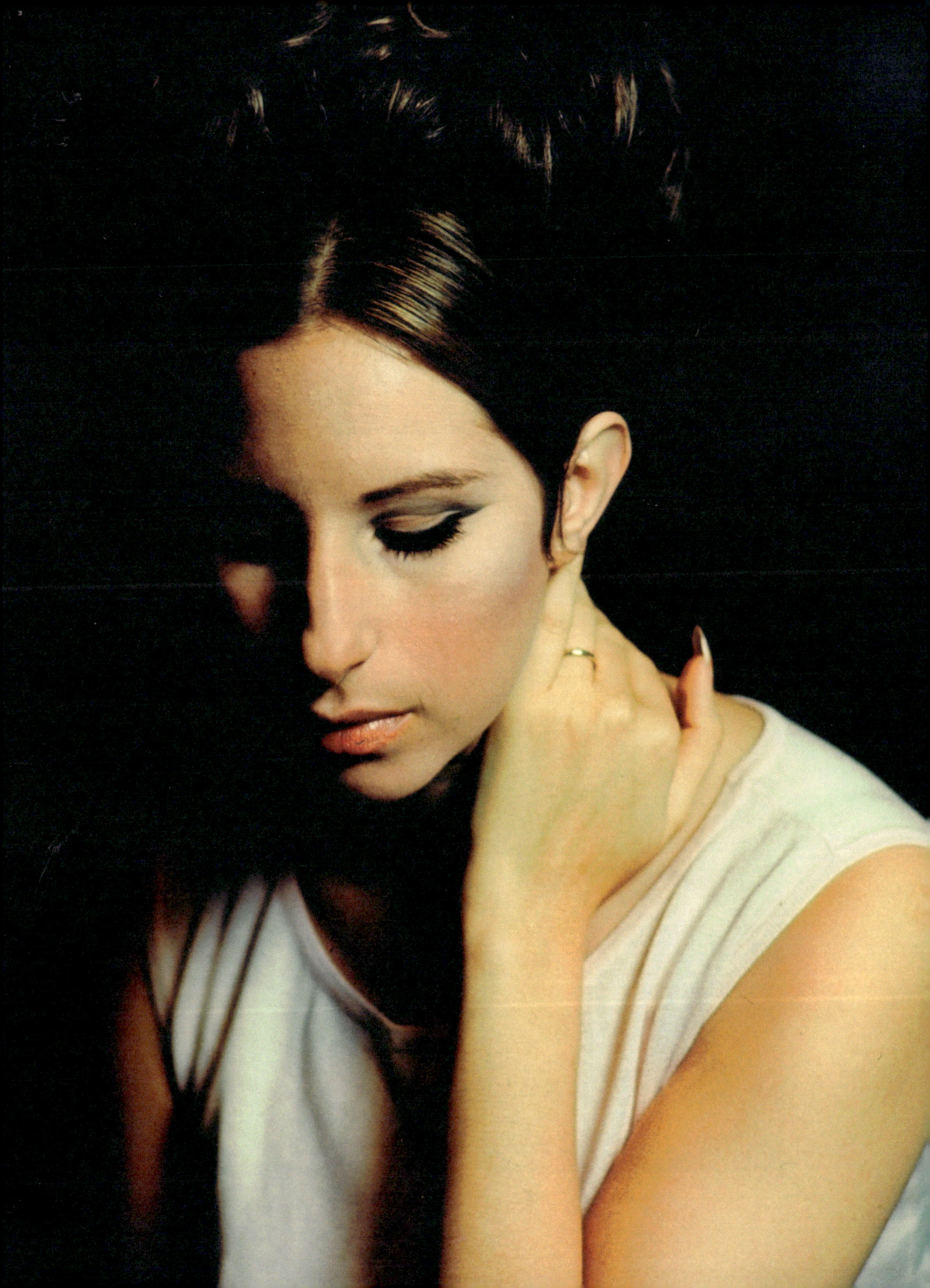

Acetate Records

Acetates are generally used as Demos and as Masters to produce regular vinyl records. Pressed on a heavy thick disc, the singles are 10" and the albums are 12". Streisand's first demo (pictured below) was Come To The Supermarket/Have I Stayed Too Long At The Fair (1961), auctioned in 2007.

One of the rarest acetates (also sold at auction) is the 1962 RCA Demo Recording. Streisand auditioned for RCA in 1962 and this album was produced. (Side 1: A Sleepin' Bee, Have I Stayed Too Long At The Fair, When The Sun Comes Out, A Taste Of Honey, At The Codfish Ball (2 takes). Side 2: Lover, Come Back To Me (2 takes), Bewitched, I Had Myself A True Love, Soon It's Gonna Rain)

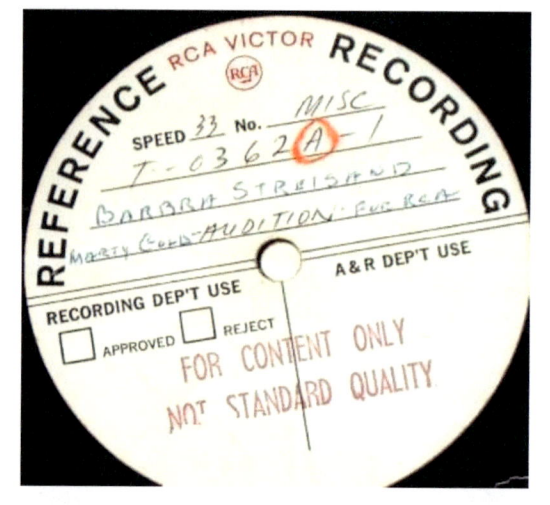

Stoney End 10" single (1-sided) (1970) 　　　　　*My Heart Belongs To Me 10" single (1-sided) (1977)*

98

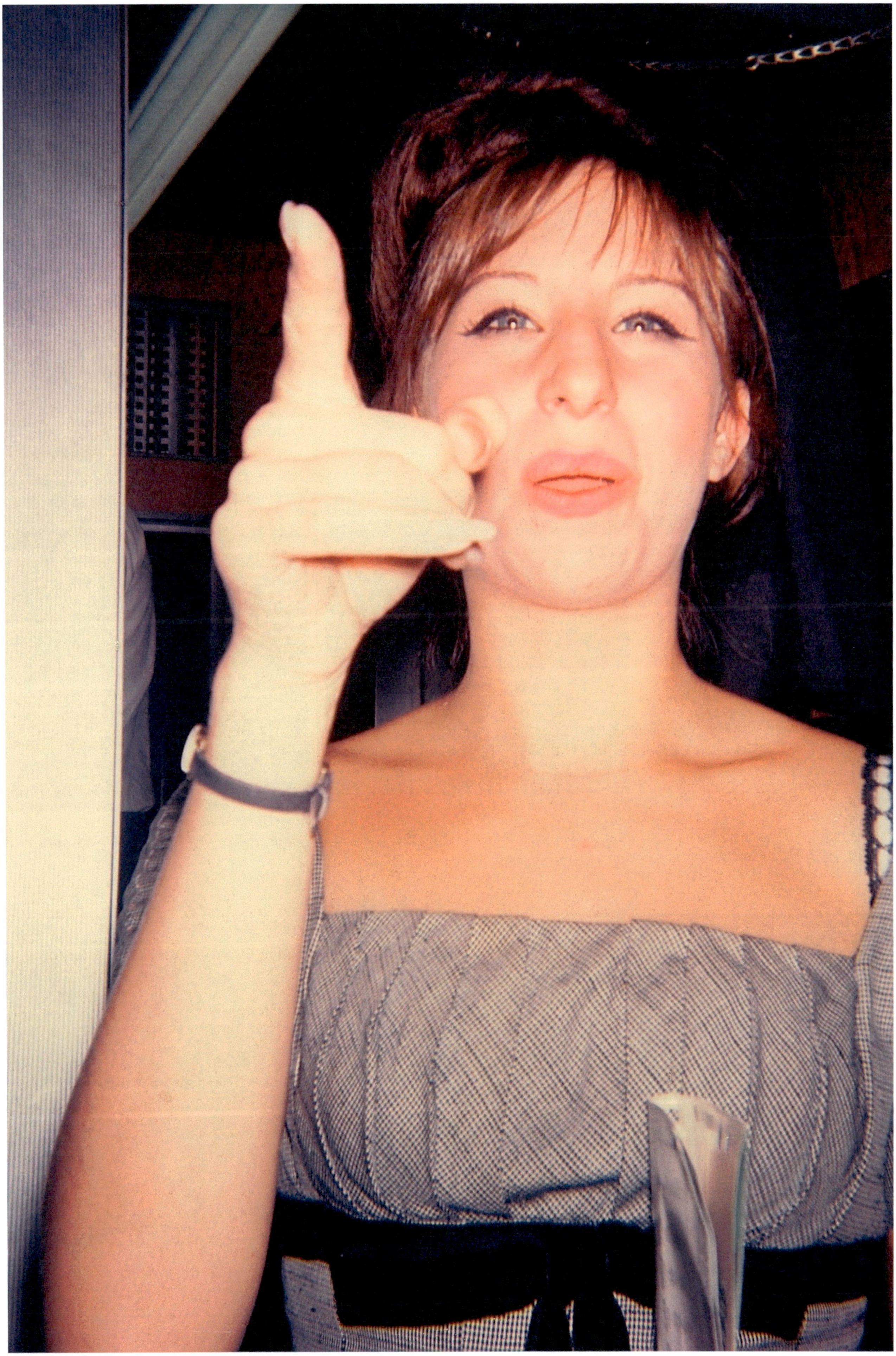

12" LP's US

The albums issued as LP's (Long Plays). All Columbia Records label unless noted.

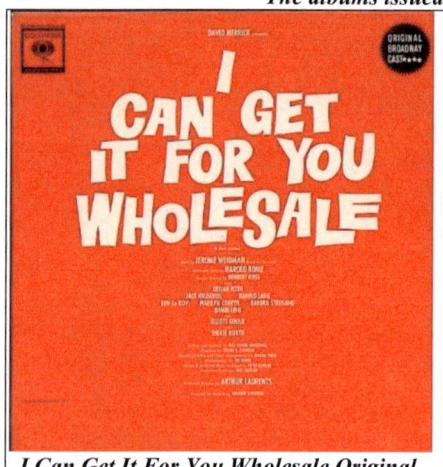

I Can Get It For You Wholesale Original Broadway Cast Recording (1962)
(Gatefold cover)
Stereo KOS 2180 Mono KOL 5780
Reissued AKOS 2180

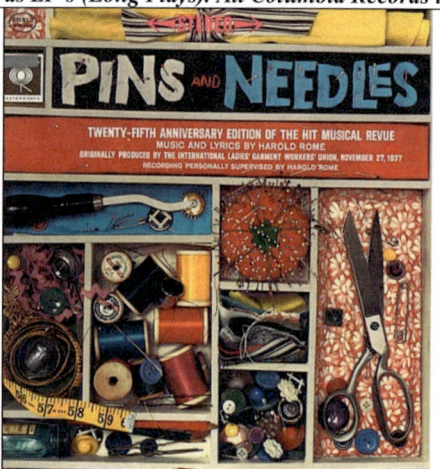

Pins And Needles (1962)
(Gatefold cover)
Stereo OS2210 Mono OL 5810
Reissued AKOS 2210

The Barbra Streisand Album (1963)
Stereo CS 8807
Mono CL 2007
Reissued PC 8807

The Second Album (1963)
Stereo CS 8854
Mono CL 2054
Reissued PC (& KCS) 8854

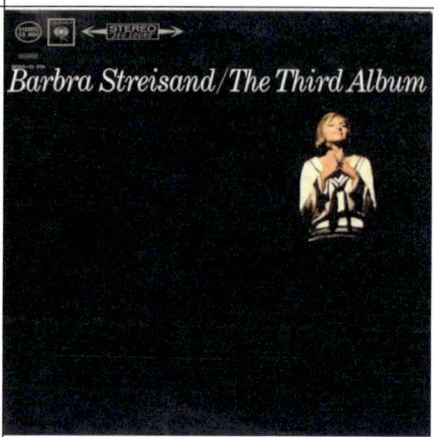

The Third Album (1964)
Stereo CS 8954
Mono CL 2154
Reissued PC 8954

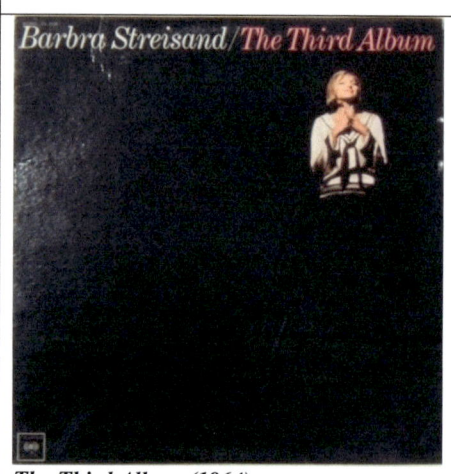

The Third Album (1964)
Some copies were issued with pink titles.

Funny Girl Original Broadway Cast (1964)
(Gatefold cover)
Stereo SVAS 2059
Mono VAS 2059 (Alternate on Cornet Man)
Reissues (3) STAO 1-2059, 2059, 502059

People (1964)
Stereo CS 9015
Mono CL 2215
Reissued 9015

My Name Is Barbra (1965)
Stereo CS 9136
Mono CL 2236
Reissued PC 9136

100

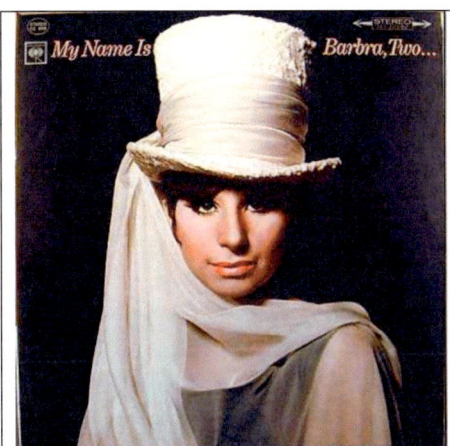

My Name Is Barbra, Two (1965)
Stereo CS 9209
Mono CL 2409
Reissued PC 9209

Color Me Barbra (1966)
Stereo CS 9278 Mono CL 2478
(four-page color insert included)
Reissued PC 9278 cover is darker pink (shown)

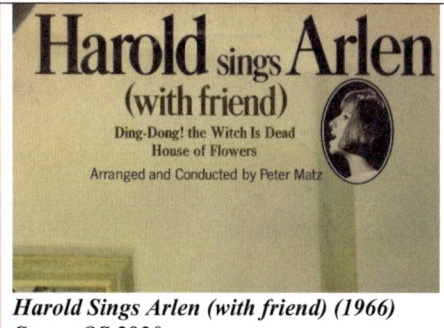

Harold Sings Arlen (with friend) (1966)
Stereo OS 2920
Mono OL 6520
Reissued AOC 2920

Je m'appelle Barbra (1966)
Stereo CS 9347
Mono CL 2547
Reissued PC 9347
Some copies were released with the misprinted Free Again label.

Simply Streisand (1967)
Stereo CS 9482
Mono CL 2682
(Included "Songs By Barbra" booklet)
Reissued PC 9482

Songs By Barbra booklet

A Christmas Album (1967)
Stereo CS 9557
Mono CL 2757 (last of Mono LP's)
(Included "Songs By Barbra" booklet)
Reissued PC 9557

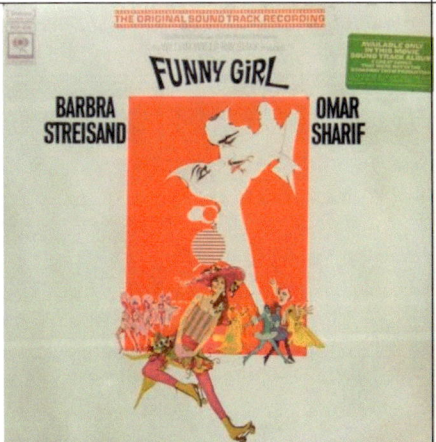

Funny Girl Original Soundtrack (1968)
BOS 3220 (Gatefold cover)
(Included insert sleeve promoting Barbra's LP's)
Reissued 1970's without gatefold cover

A Happening In Central Park (1968)
CS 9710
Reissued KCS 9710

101

What About Today? (1969)
CS 9816
Reissued KCS & PC 9816

Hello Dolly (1969)
20th Century Fox Records
DTCS 5103 (Gatefold cover)
Reissued Casablanca Records ST 102
(Non-gatefold)

Greatest Hits (1970)
KCS 9968
Reissued PC 9968

On A Clear Day You Can See Forever (1970)
S 30086 (Gatefold cover)
Reissued AS 30086

The Owl And The Pussycat Original Soundtrack (1970)
S 30401 Reissued AS 30401

CBS released the music from the film on Blood, Sweat & Tears 2012 CD 'Rare, Rarer & Rarest' #WOU 3040 (Without the film's dialogue.)

Stoney End (1971)
KC 30378
Reissued PC 30378

Barbra Joan Streisand (1971)
KC 30792 (Gatefold cover with Poster)
Reissued PC 30792

Live At The Forum (1972)
KC 31760 (Gatefold cover with Poster)
Reissued PC 31760

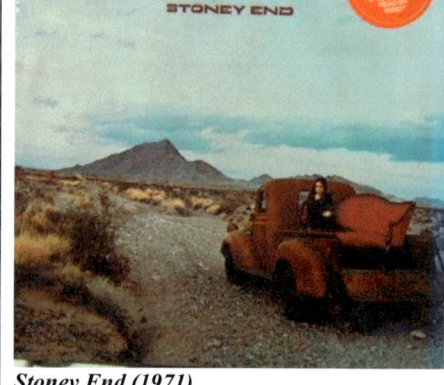

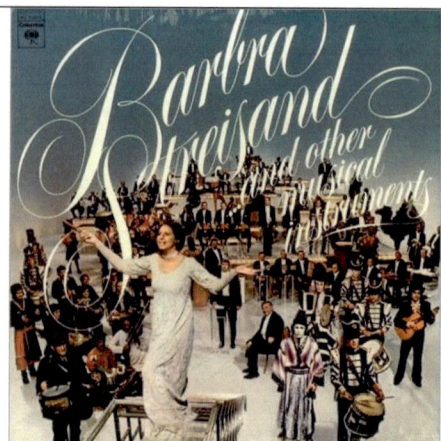

Barbra Streisand And Other Musical Instruments (1973)
PC 32655 (Gatefold cover)

The Way We Were (1974)
PC 32801
First issued with titles on cover, then withdrawn due to The Way We Were Film Producer Ray Stark

Reissued 1974 without titles (Same catalog number) Reissued Half Speed Master HC 42801

The Way We Were Original Soundtrack Recording (1974)
KS 32830

Butterfly (1974)
PC 33005
(Gatefold cover)

Funny Lady (1975)
AL 9007 Arista Records
(Gatefold cover)
Arista also released a compilation LP in 1982 Soundtrack Memories (#ABM 2005) This has another alternate version of How Lucky Can You Get not available elsewhere.

Lazy Afternoon (1975)
PC 33815
(Gatefold cover) Back cover shown

Classical Barbra (1976)
M33452
(with insert sleeve)
Back cover shown

A Star Is Born (1976)
JS 34403
(Gatefold cover with insert sleeve)

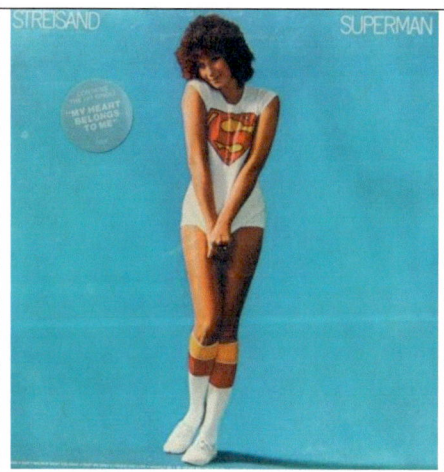

Superman (1977)
JC 34830
(Included four-page insert booklet and insert sleeve)

Songbird (1978)
JC 35375
(with insert sleeve)

Greatest Hits Vol. 2 (1978)
FC 35679
(with insert sleeve)
Reissued Half Speed Mastered HC 45679

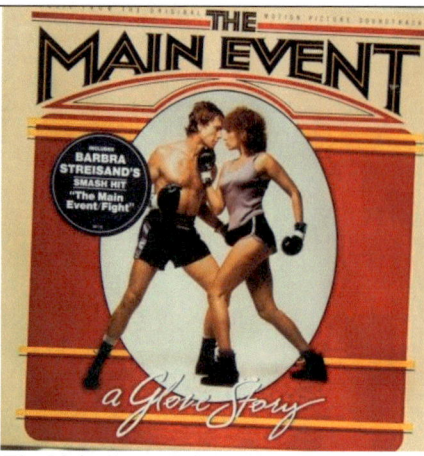

The Main Event Original Soundtrack (1979)
JS 3645
(with insert sleeve)

Wet (1979)
FC 36258
(with insert sleeve)
Donna Summer's On The Radio 1979 LP Contains the 11:40 version of No More Tears.
Also issued on CD #124715
Casablanca label

Guilty (1980)
FC 36750
(Gatefold cover with insert sleeve)
Reissued Half Speed Mastered HC 46750

Memories (1981)
FC 37678
(with insert sleeve)
Reissued Half Speed Mastered HC 47678

Yentl (1983)
JS 39152
(Gatefold cover with insert sleeve)

Emotion (1984)
OC 39480
(with insert sleeve)

The Broadway Album (1985)
OC 40092
(with insert sheet and sleeve)

One Voice (1987)
OC 40788 (with insert sleeve)

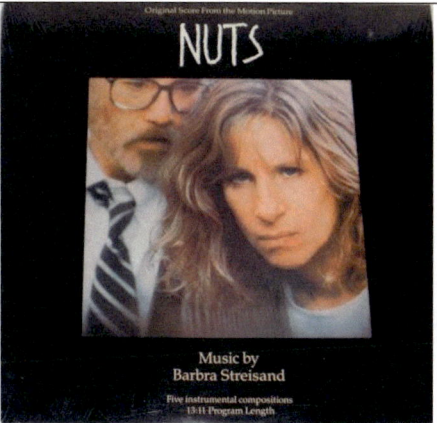

Nuts Original Soundtrack (1987)
4C 40876

Till I Loved You (1988)
OC 40880 (with insert sleeve)
(Streisand also is credited on Don Johnson's Let It Roll LP/CD (Epic #4608762) as background vocal on What If It Takes All Night, but you cannot hear her.)

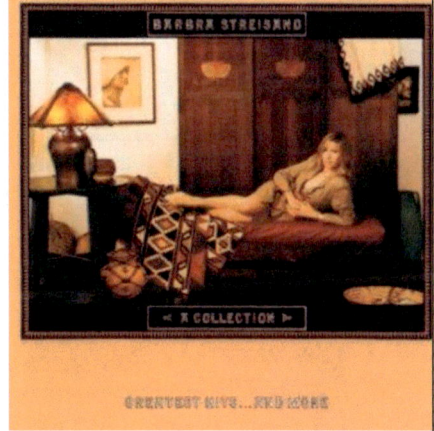

A Collection Greatest Hits…And More (1989)
OC 45369 (with insert sleeve)

Love Is The Answer (2009)
#88697433541
Deluxe Collector's Edition 2-LP set
Gatefold cover with insert sleeves

Release Me
(Released Sept. 25, 2012)
#C 545855
Special Collector's edition with inserts

Partners (2014)
#88843-09114-13
Special Collector's 2-LP edition, with inserts

105

Promotional LP's

The following were issued as white label promos and sent to radio stations. After 1966, the LP's were issued with time strips on the covers and with regular red label LP's until the release of Butterfly in 1974.

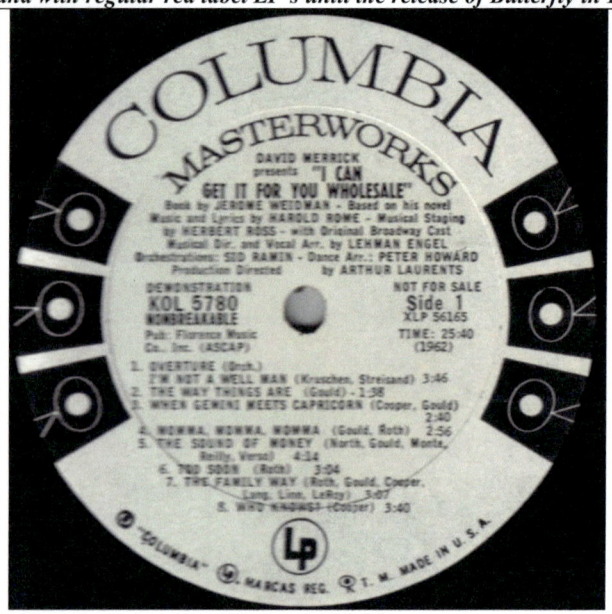

I Can Get It For You Wholesale (1962)
Issued with Demo sticker on back cover and Columbia stationery letter
KOL 5780

Pins And Needles (1962)
Worker's Union promo sticker on back cover   OL 5810

The Barbra Streisand Album (1963)
Time Strip on cover   CL 2007

The Second Barbra Streisand Album (1963)
Rare Blue vinyl pressing with time strip on cover
CL 2054

The Third Album (1964)
Issued with Columbia stationery note and 2-sided page
Magazine cover and article on back
CL 2154

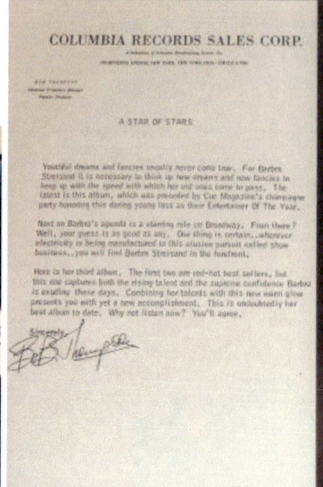

106

People (1964)
Time strip on cover
CL 2215

My Name Is Barbra (1965)
Time strip on cover
CL 2336
There's a special 2nd release Oct. 1965 for the TV Special rebroadcast. Back cover (shown) has text promoting the show.

My Name Is Barbra, Two (1965)
Time strip on cover
CL 2409

Color Me Barbra (1966)
Red vinyl pressing with time strip on cover
CL 2478
Also white label promo issued on black vinyl

Harold Sings Arlen (with friend) (1966)
Time strip on cover
OL 6520

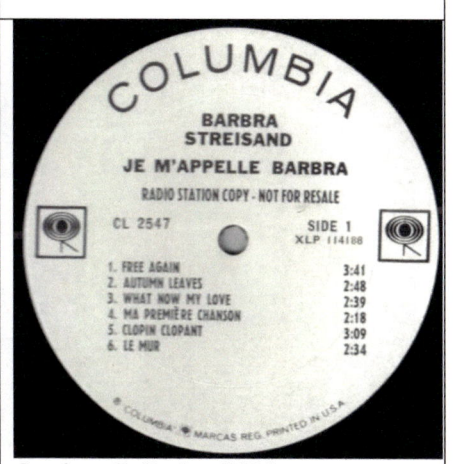

Je m'appelle Barbra (1966)
Time strip on cover
CL 2547

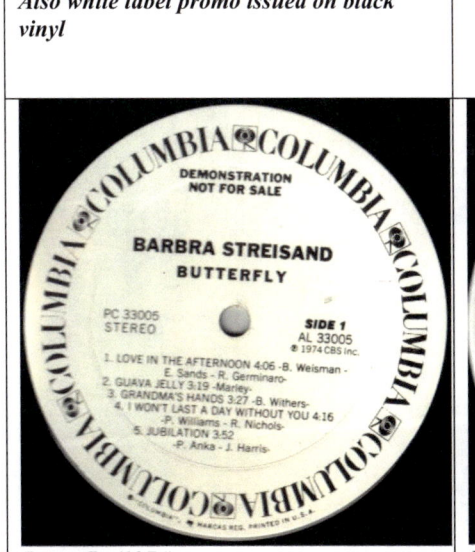

Butterfly (1974)
Time strip on cover
PC 33005

Funny Lady (1975)
Promo sticker on cover
ALDJ-9004
Also white label test pressing issued in plain white cover

Lazy Afternoon (1975)
Time strip on cover
PC 33815

Classical Barbra (1976)
Time strip on cover with gold promo stamp on back cover
M 33452

A Star Is Born (1976)
Time strip with gold promo stamp on back Cover
JS 34403
Also Advanced promo LP (shown)

Streisand Superman (1977)
Time strip with gold promo stamp on back cover
JC 34830

Songbird (1978)
Gold promo stamp on back cover
JC 35375

Greatest Hits Volume II (1978)
Gold promo stamp on back cover
FC 35679

The Main Event (1979)
Gold promo stamp on back cover
JS 36115

Wet (1979)
Gold promo stamp on back cover
FC 36258

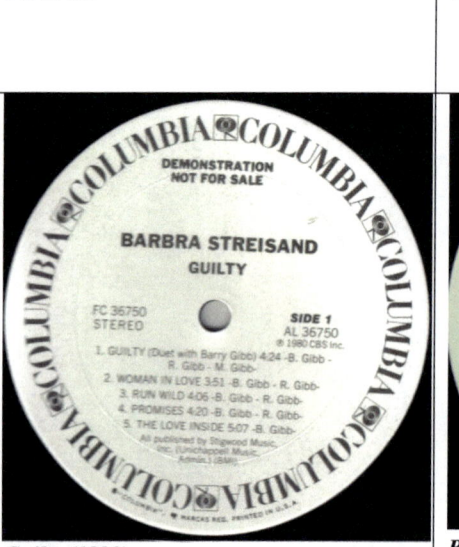

Guilty (1980)
Gold promo stamp on back cover
FC 36750
(The last of the white label promos)

Butterfly (1974)
Rare Advanced Matrix Promotional LP
Issued in plain white cover, plain label

108

Quadraphonic LP's

Introduced in the early 1970's, Quads were a new unique listing format. Several of the LP's contained alternate takes.

Funny Girl (1968)
SQ 30992 (non-gatefold cover)
(Alternate lines on Sadie, Sadie and The Swan)

Stoney End (1971)
CQ 30378
(Alternates takes No Easy Way Down, Stoney End, Time And Love, Free The People)

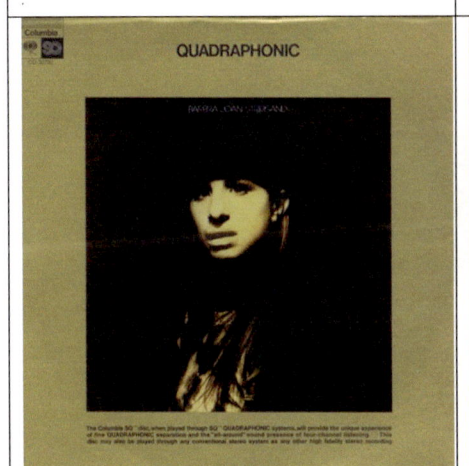

Barbra Joan Streisand (1971)
CQ 30792 (non-gatefold cover)
(Beautiful, Where You Lead, Space Captain, Mother, I Mean To Shine, The Summer Knows alternates)

Live At The Forum (1972)
CQ 31760 (non-gatefold cover)
(Contains only extra monologue line)

The Way We Were (1974)
PCQ 32801
(Being At War With Each Other & The Way We Were alternate takes)

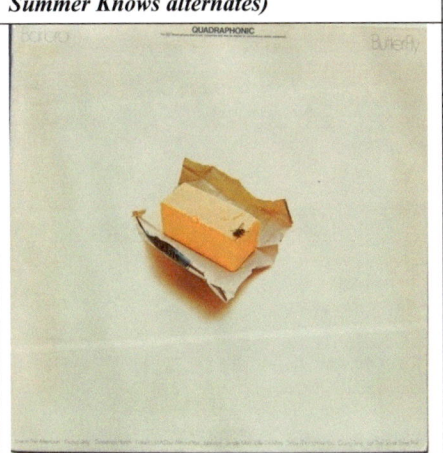

Butterfly (1974)
PCQ 33005 (gatefold cover)
(Love In The Afternoon, Guava Jelly, Jubilation, Simple Man, Life On Mars, Since I Don't Have You, Let The Goodtime Roll alternate takes)

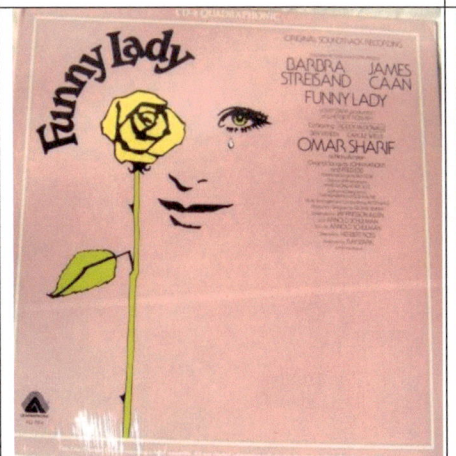

Funny Lady (1975)
AQ 9004 (gatefold cover)
(How Lucky Can You Get, If I Loved Again, Clap Hands, Let's Here It For Me alternate takes)

Lazy Afternoon (1975)
PCQ 33815 (gatefold cover)
(no alternate takes)

Rare & Collectible Vinyl

One of the rarest vinyl records is the My Name Is Barbra LP on green vinyl. The LP has the regular red label, which indicates it's not a promotional release (CL 2336).

Music From On A Clear Day You Can See Forever
Rare advanced promotional-only LP 1969 Paramount EV 2303A
(All alternate takes and non-LP cuts)

*(Main Title/Hurry It's Lovely Up Here/Love With All The Trimmings (2 Versions)
Wait 'Til We're Sixty Five (duet with Larry Blyden)/Melinda/Go To Sleep/He Isn't
You-She Isn't You/Who Is There Among Us Who Knows (Jack Nicholson with
Barbra humming)/What Did I Have Part 1 & 2/Come Back To Me/On A Clear Day/
On A Clear Day Finale)*

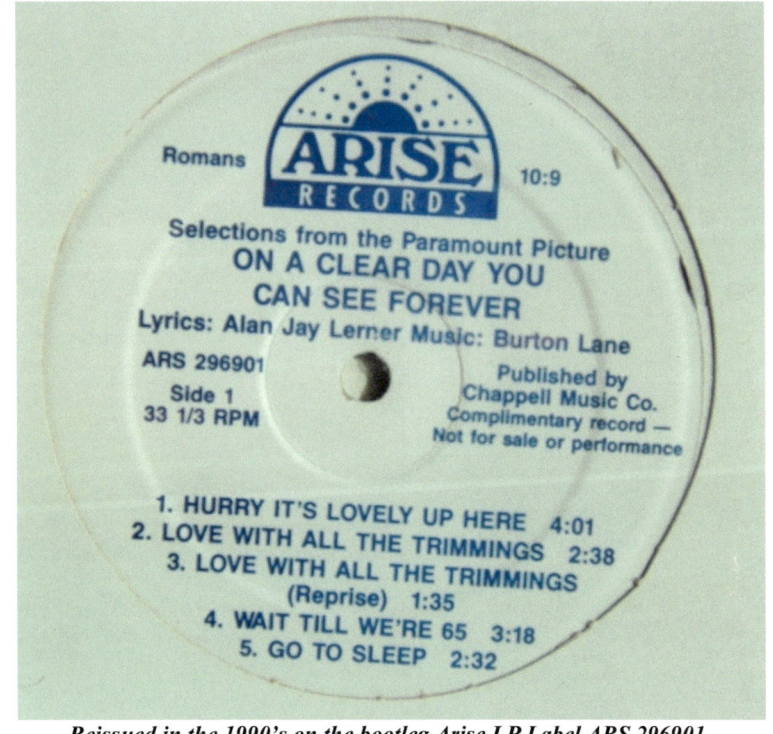

Reissued in the 1990's on the bootleg Arise LP Label ARS 296901

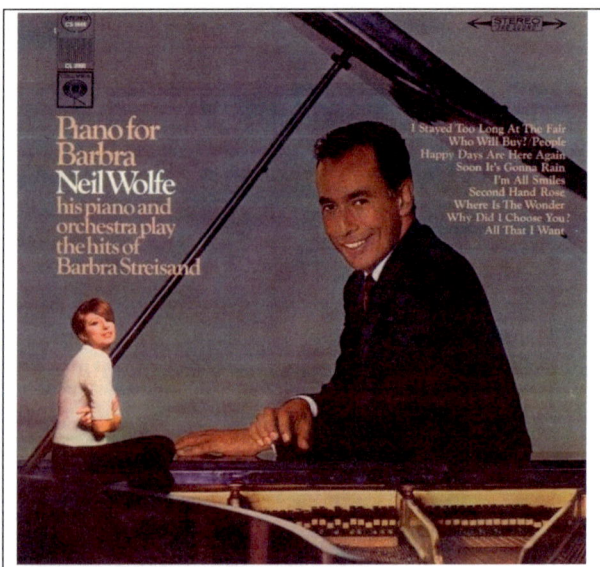

Piano For Barbra Neil Wolfe (1967)
CS 9600 (Instrumental LP of Streisand hits. No vocals.)

Selections From Funny Girl (1968) 1-Sided
DC42268 Published by Chappell-Styne Inc
Rare advanced promotional-only release (Alternate Takes)
(You're A Funny Girl/You Are Woman, I Am Man/Locked In A Pink Velvet Jail (Omar Sharif Non-LP cut)/People/ Sadie, Sadie/You're A Funny Girl)

Season's Greetings From Barbra Streisand…And Friends (1970) Columbia Special Products Maxwell House CSS 1075 (O Little Town Of Bethlehem/Silent Night/Ave Maria/The Christmas Song/The Best Gift) Streisand on Side 1, Jim Nabors, Doris Day & Andre Kostelanetz on Side 2)

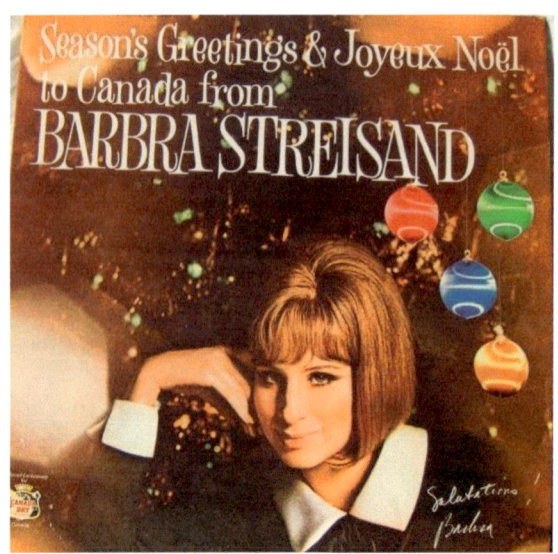

Canadian Edition for Canada Dry   CSPS 444

Funny Lady Theatre Owners Film Exhibit 10" Promotional LP Issued with 11x14 presskit folder (1974).

Great Day/Five And 10 Cent Store/Love Song (Isn't It Better)/ Blind Date/Production Number (All My Life On A Stage) (Non-LP cut)

Eyes Of Laura Mars Soundtrack (1978)
JS 35487 (Contains the single Prisoner)

Free Again (1980)   AIFAM Records AG 3321
(Bootleg LP of Je m'appelle Barbra with unique cover)

Streisand Live 1963 (1980)
Bel Canto 5001 Bootleg LP of the Hungry i Nightclub show
In San Francisco

(Any Place I Hang My Hat Is Home/Keepin' Out Of Mischief Now/Cry Me A River/Lover, Come Back To Me/I Stayed Too Long At The Fair/My Honey's Loving Arms/Soon It's Gonna Rain/When The Sun Comes Out/Much More/Like A Straw In The Wind/Right As The Rain/Down With Love/Bewitched/Happy Days Are Here Again)

The Great Garland Duets (1980)
Paragon 1001 Bootleg LP
Contains two Streisand duets from the 1963 Judy Garland Show.

Emotion Limited Edition Picture Disc (1984)
#9C9-39909

The Kismet Albums

In 1984 and 1985 Karma Productions (run by a group of fans) produced 12 bootleg LP's containing rare and unreleased material. The back covers have Promotional-only stamps. There's a gap in the catalog numbers, no missing LP's.

Memories Are Made Of This (Kismet 1001)

The Burt Bacharach Special 1971/Crying Time (With Ray Charles)/Recording Sessions & Rehearsals for The Way We Were

Lookin' Back (Kismet 1002)

Ed Sullivan 1962 My Coloring Book & Lover Come Back To Me/Ed Sullivan 1969 Hello Dolly Medley & 1970 Clear Day live from Vegas/1963 Judy Garland Show/For Pete's Sake (Don't Let Him Down)

Moments To Remember (Kismet 1003)

If I Close My Eyes/Who Among Us Who Knows (with Jack Nicholson)/Wait Til We're 65 (with Larry Blyden)/Best Thing You've Ever Done (Recording Session)/Let's Here It For Me (Alternate)/Everything Must Change/It's A Funky Type Thing/On Broadway/1968 NY Funny Girl Premiere Interview/Dinah Shore Special 1963-Cry Me A River/Happy Days/Brotherhood Of Man/1968 LA Funny Girl Premiere Interview

Flashback (Kismet 1004)

The Promise/A Quiet Thing-There Won't Be Trumpets/PM East 1962-Right As The Rain/Soon It's Gonna Rain/I Stayed Too Long At The Fair/Gary Moore Show 1962 When The Sun Comes Out & Happy Days/1965 My Name Is Barbra Commercial/You're The Top (with Ryan O'Neal)/Bob Hope Show 1963/Amercia (I Love Liberty 1982)/1983 British Awards/Carelessly Tossed/Tonight Show A Sleepin' Bee '61/1964 What's My Line/I Don't Care/Put Your Arms Around Me, Honey

SRO (Kismet 1005)

1966 PA JFK Stadium Concert
Overture/Any Place I Hang My Hat Is Home/My Honey's Loving Arms/I Hate Music/I'll Tell The Man In The Street/Cry Me A River/Folk Monologue/Value/Gotta Move/Why Did I Choose You/Where Am I Going?/Who Will Buy?

Memory Lane (Kismet 1007)

Nat. Assoc for Retarded Children Commercial/Recording Sessions: How Lucky Can You Get & Let's Hear It For Me/
Funny Girl Alternates-Funny Girl/You Are Woman, I Am Man/Don't Rain On My Parade/Pink Velvet Jail/People/Sadie, Sadie/JFK '66 When The Sun Comes Out/I Can See It/He Touched Me

Magic Moments (Kismet 1008)

Woman In The Moon Recording Sessions and Live 1963 Hungry i Night Club show:
Any Place I Hang My Hat Is Home/Keepin' Out Of Mischief/My Honey's Loving Arms/Right As The Rain/When The Sun Comes Out/Who's Afraid Of The Big Bad Wolf?/Down With Love

Lost In Time (Kismet 1009)

Wholesale 1962 Interview/Zing Went The String Of My Heart (short clip only)/1977 LA Radio Call-In/Evergreen in Spanish, French, & Italian/Et la mer/Les enfants qui Pleurent/No More Tears Outtake/1963 Bob Hope-Folk song/Any Place I Hang My Hat Is Home/Gotta Move/Yentl Outtakes The Moon & I/Several Sins A Day

Beginnings (Kismet 1010)

Tonight Show 2-1-63 A Sleepin' Bee/Tonight Show 10-4-62 Right As The Rain/Tonight Show 11-2-62 Happy Days

After Hours (Kismet 1012)

No More Tears & The Main Event Recording Sessions

Good Times (Kismet 1013)

1965 Christmas Seals Radio Show/ When The Sun Comes Out/Don't Rain On My Parade/My Coloring Book/People/ Jack Park Tonight Show 5-22-61- Much More/Hungry i 1963 Monologue/Soon It's Gonna Rain/Happy Days/Hollywood Bowl 1967 Natural Sounds & Marty The Martian

On Broadway (Kismet 1016)

Butterfly Recording Sessions-You Light Up My Life (The Promise)/Funky Type Thing/On Broadway/Everything Must Change

117

Public Service Announcements on LP

Christmas Seal Campaign 1965
Program (14:47) Decca Records #MG 200536 (1965) Streisand talking with When The Sun Comes Out, Don't Rain On My Parade, My Coloring Book, & People. The Wayfarers are on the other side.

Christmas Seal Campaign 1965
Decca Records #MG 200545
The Barbra Streisand Show
Contains a 5:29 program Streisand talking with My Honey's Loving Arms & I'll Tell The Man In The Street.
Other Celebrities included are Andy Williams, Peter Paul & Mary, and Al Hirt.

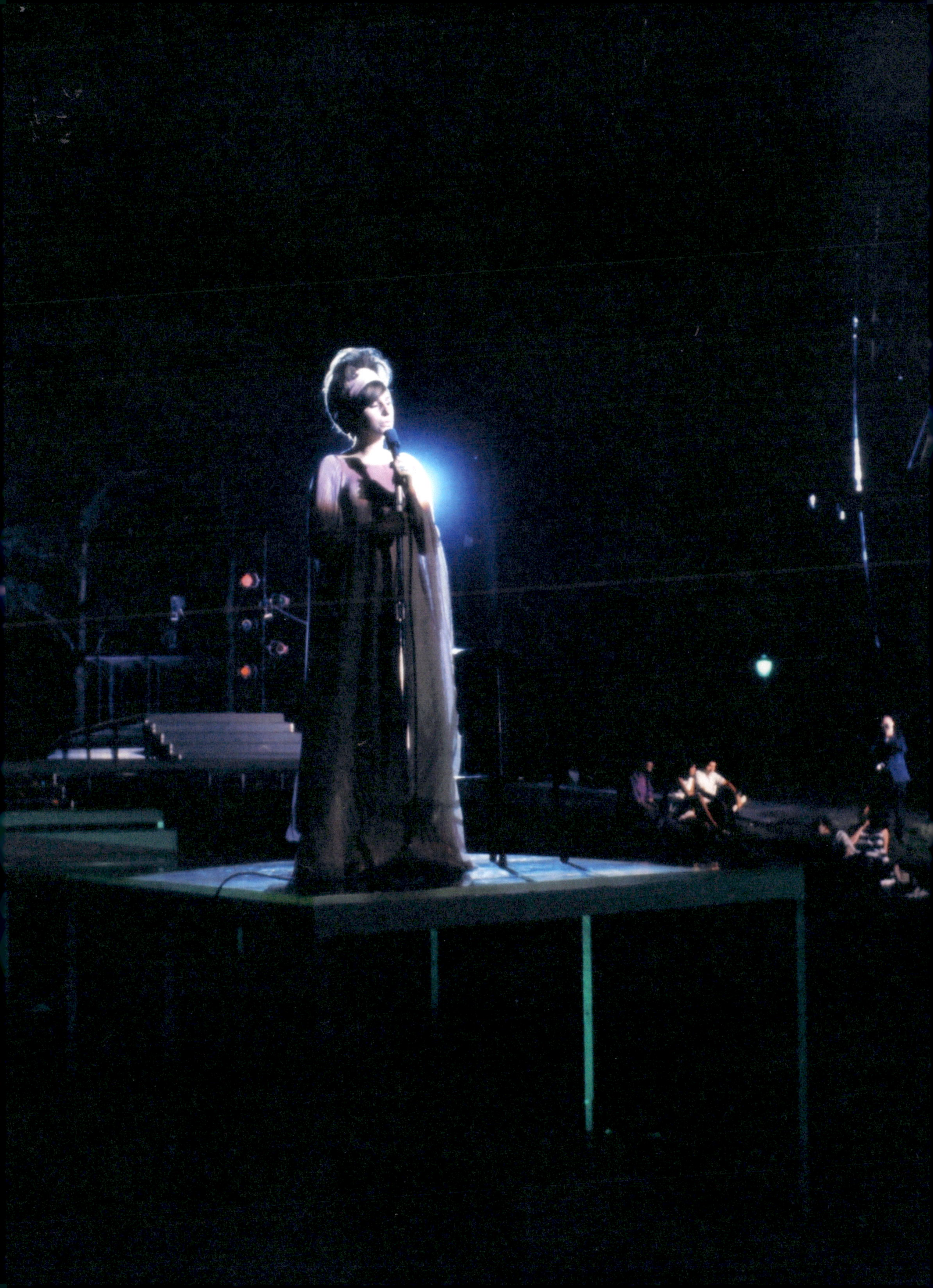

United Way 1965
United Community Funds & Councils Of America, Inc
#UCF-9216C
Side 2 contains 10 announcements from Streisand. The Brothers Four are on Side 1.

In The Fight Against MS Multiple Sclerosis
1969 Celebrity Spot Announcements
Decca Records #MG 201893
Contains two (0:55 & 0:25) spots from Streisand

Also 1970 MS Celebrity Spot Announcement LP that contains two spots from Streisand.

American Heart Association 1972 Heart Fund
GR-1278 (Contains a 30 second spot from Streisand)

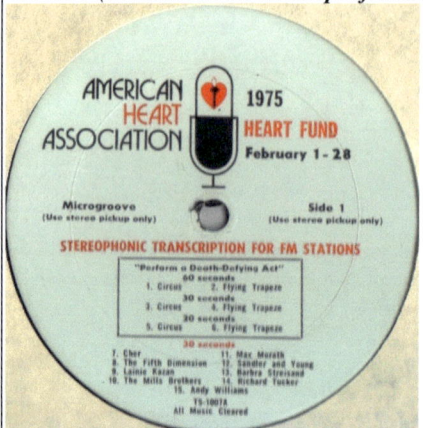

1975 Heart Fund LP
Contains a 30 second spot from Streisand Same as '72 version except People music in background.
#T5-1001/1.

The National Association for Retarded Children

1971 Celebrity Spot Announcements   NARC 71-1
Contains 30 and 60 second spots from Streisand.

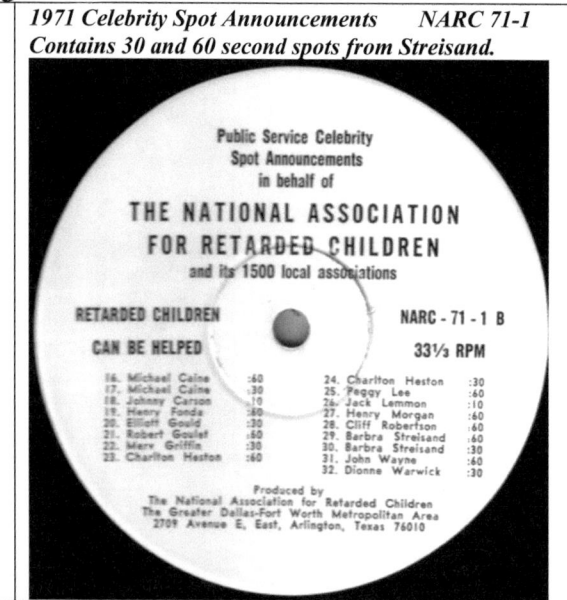

1972 Celebrity Spot Announcements   NARC 72-1
Contains three spots from Streisand 60, 30, & 20 seconds.

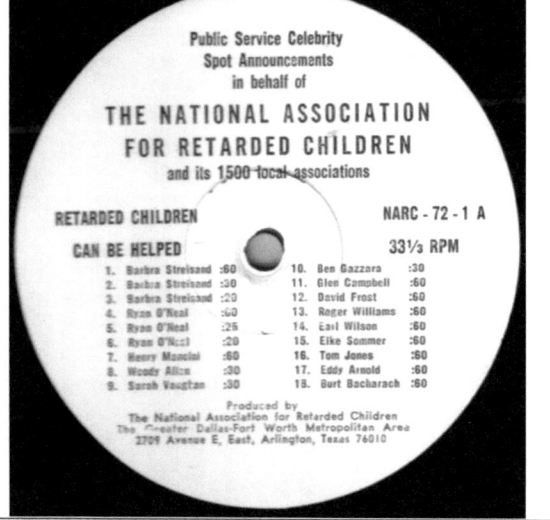

1973 Celebrity Spot Announcements   NARC-1973
Contains three spots from Streisand 60, 30, & 20 seconds.

121

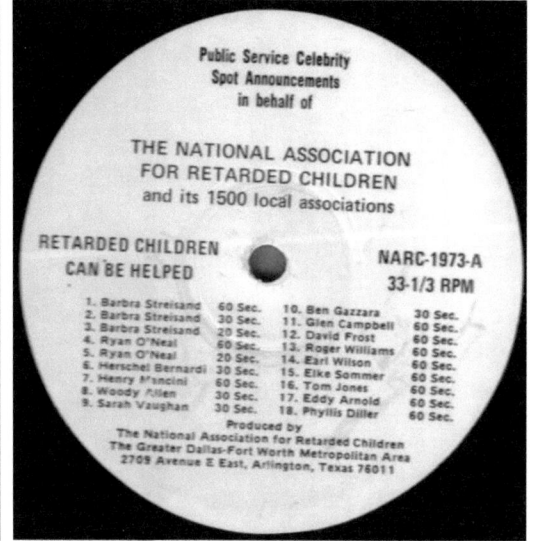

Radio Shows on LP

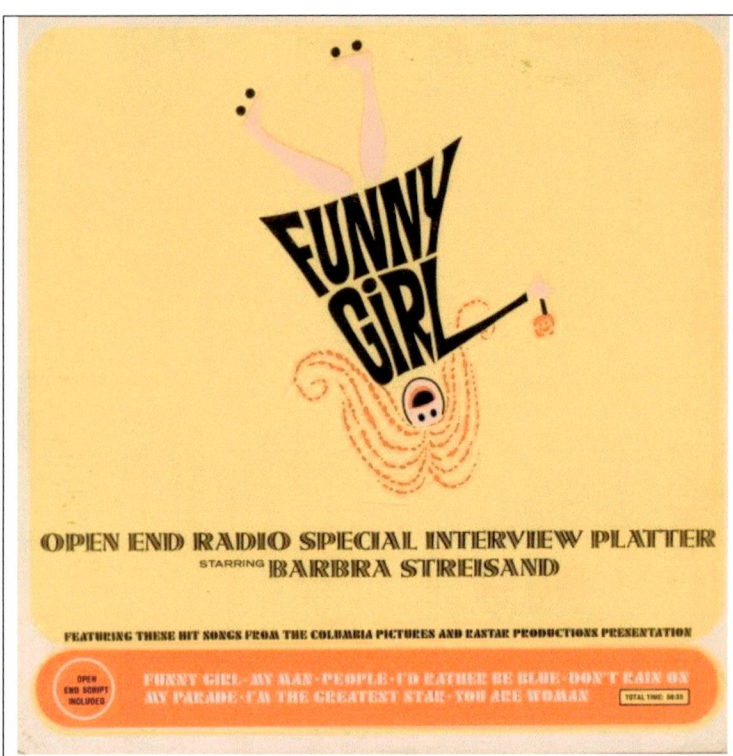

Funny Girl Open End Radio Special Interview Platter (1968)
#1168 2-LP Set with cue sheets. Promotional-only

1st LP contains 1-Hour program with Streisand interview and music. The 2nd LP (#968) has 10-minute interview program with Omar Sharif and 10-minute Featurette with Cast & Crew Interviews.

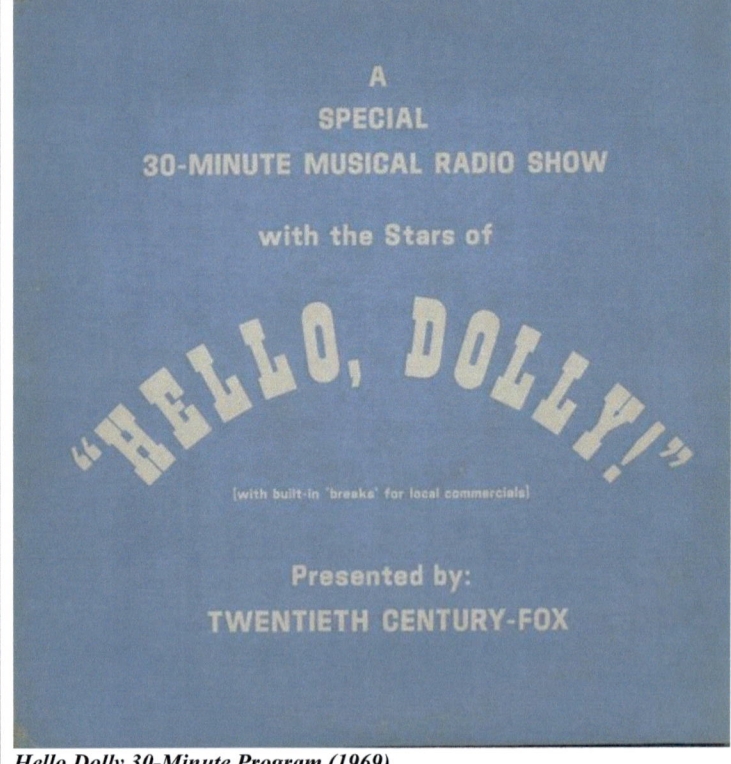

Hello Dolly 30-Minute Program (1969)
20th Century Fox #1069 Promotional-only release

Features interviews with Streisand, Ernest Lehman, Gene Kelly, Louis Armstrong & Walter Matthau.

Another version with interview (#1741) 20th Century Fox

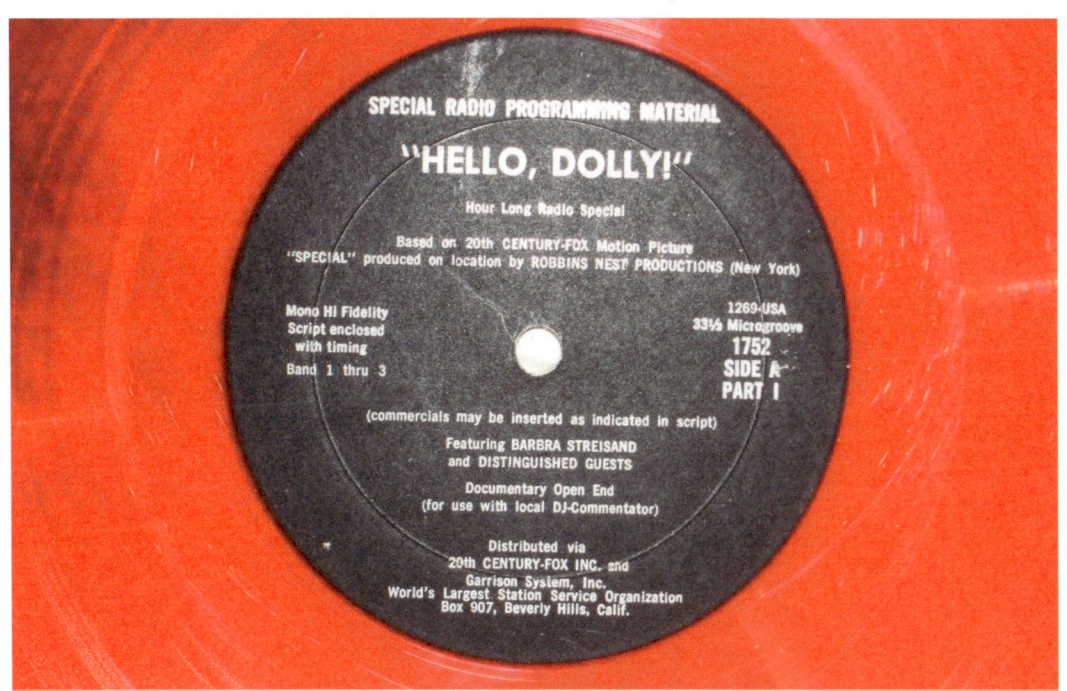

Hello Dolly 1-Hour Program Interview on Red Vinyl (1969) Promotional-only 20th Century Fox #1269 (also issued on black vinyl) with cue sheets

The Barbra Streisand Special (1979)
ABC Radio Network OCC 301-302 Promotional-only
2-LP set in custom box with four-page program card
1-Hour program with interview & music promoting The Main Event

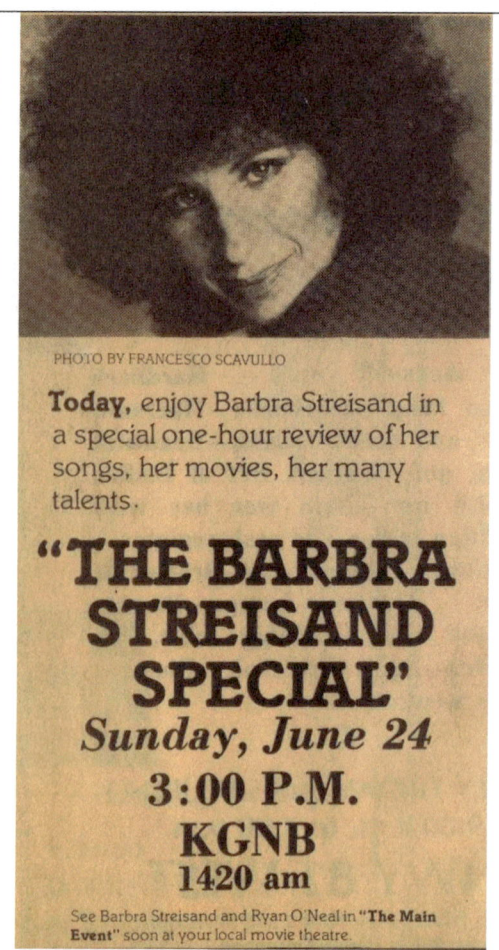

The Legend Of Barbra Streisand (1983)
Columbia #A2S 1779 Promotional-only
2-LP set features 1-Hour interview & music promoting Yentl

Portrait Of An Artist (1992)
Westwood One #S3-92-07 Promotional-only
4-LP set issued in plain white cover with cue sheets.
Features 2-Hour program with interview & music promoting Just For The Record

124

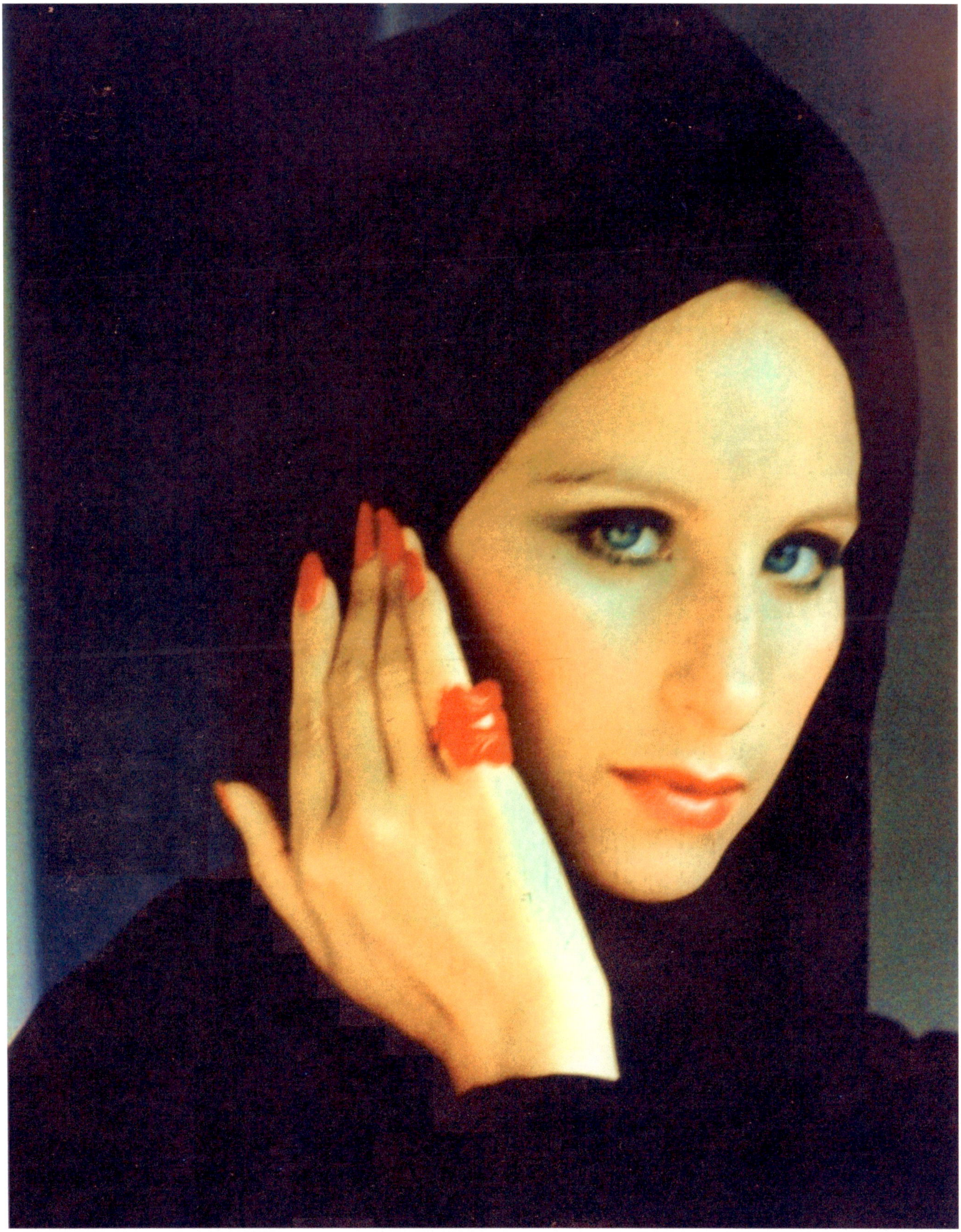

Autographed LP Box Sets

Early in Streisand's film career, she would often present autographed boxed album sets to fellow cast and crew members after filming was completed. What is unique about them is the custom box with Streisand's handwriting on the cover. Presented here are two rare finds.

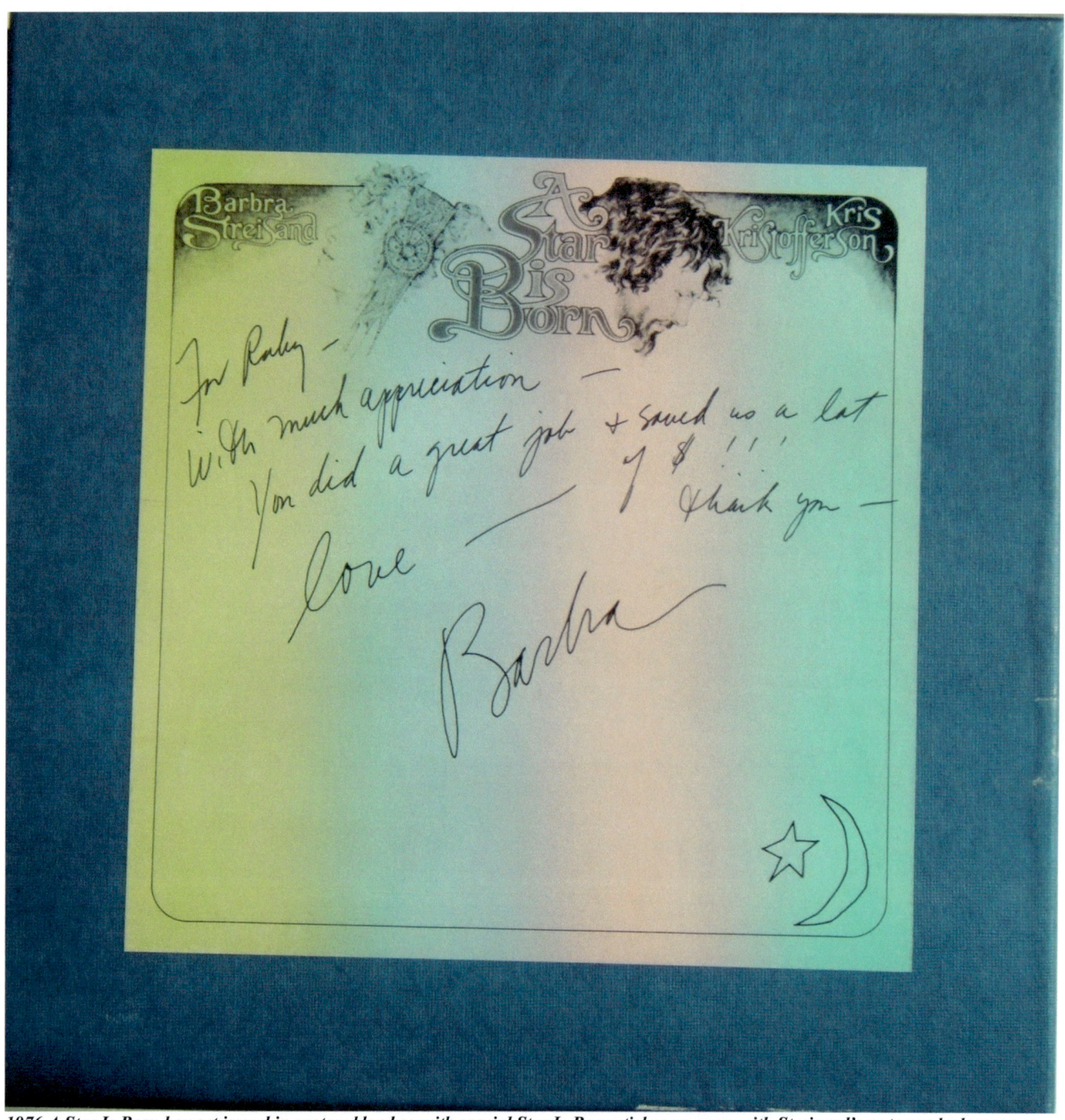

1976 A Star Is Born box set issued in custom blue box with special Star Is Born sticker on cover with Streisand's autographed message. The albums are Butterfly, Lazy Afternoon, & Classical Barbra.

126

1972 What's Up Doc boxed set with albums Stoney End and Barbra Joan Streisand. Issued in orange custom box with What's Up Doc sticker and has her signature gold embossed. Top right corner has Streisand's hand written message to Don Capel.

12" LP's International

The following are alternate releases of Streisand's albums. All CBS Records unless noted.

The Second Album (1963)
(England)# BPG 62216 with different back cover

The Second Album (1970's reissue)
Canadian edition without red strike on cover #8854

Funny Girl Broadway Cast (1964)
(France) Capitol #STTX 340855

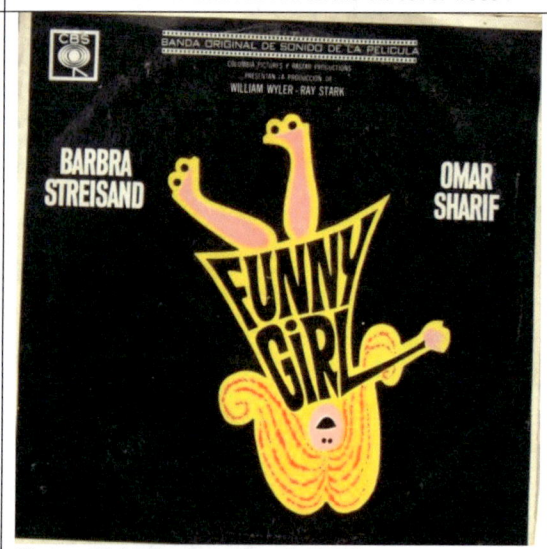

Funny Girl Film Soundtrack (1968)
(Uruguay) #8907

Funny Girl Sampler Album (1969)
(England) 1-sided promotional LP 11-tracks with commentary by Alan Freeman (#SC 26)(Issued in plain cover)

Hello Dolly (1974 reissue)
(France) 20th Century Fox #STEC 166

Color Me Barbra (1970's issue)
(Australia) Summit Records #MFP 5918

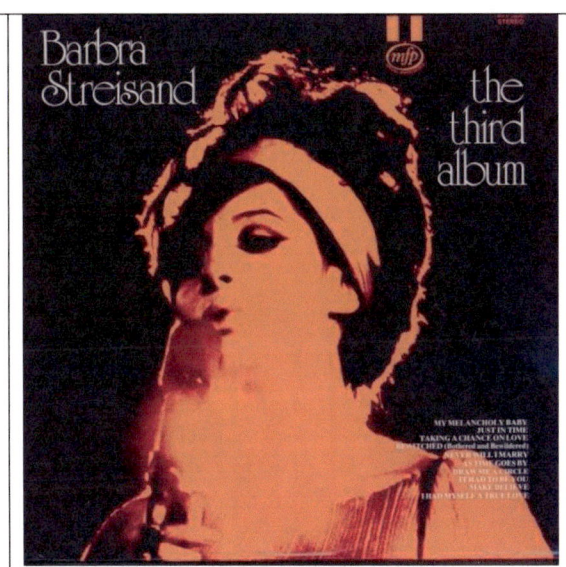

The Third Album (1970's reissue)
(Australia) Summit Records #MFP 5896

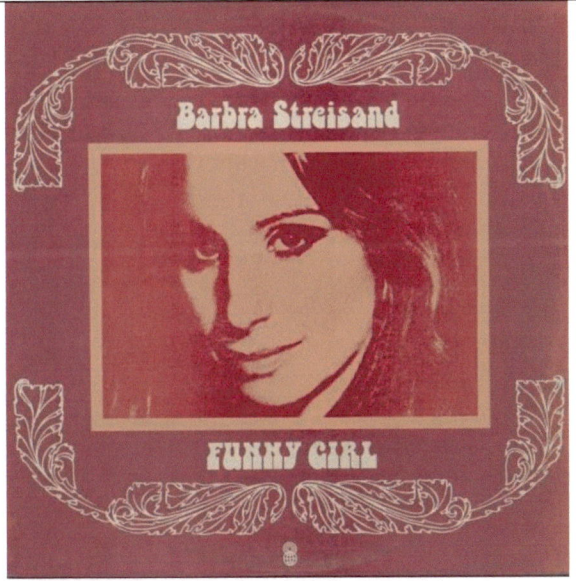

Funny Girl Broadway Cast (1970's reissue)
(Australia) Record Club issue Capital #S-5230

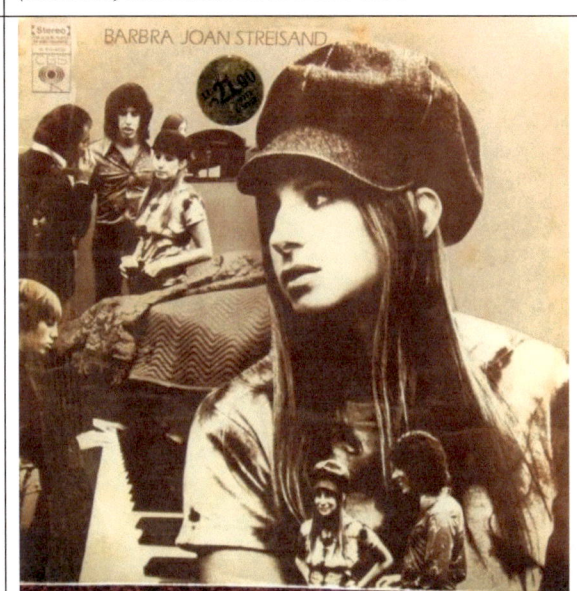

Barbra Joan Streisand (1971)
(Israel) #S 64459

Barbra Streisand And Other Musical Instruments (1973)
(England) Rare ATV Promotional issue with special gatefold cover #S 69052

My Name Is Barbra (1973 Reissue)
(England) #S 31481 (Reversed covers)

Butterfly (1974)
(England) #69079

Lazy Afternoon (1975)
(Russia) #33C60-10267-68

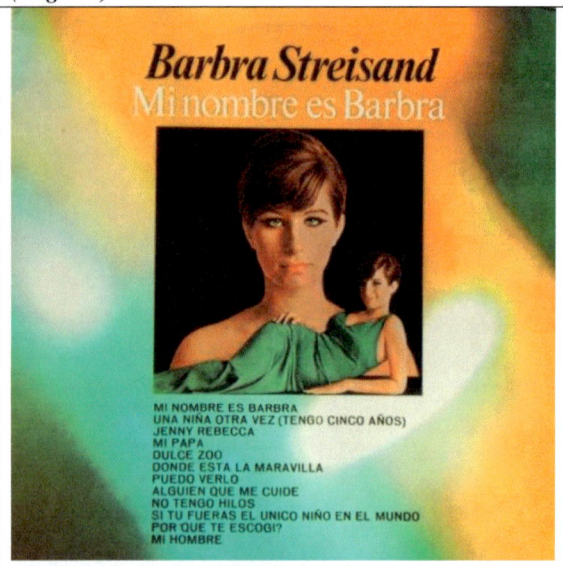

My Name Is Barbra (1975 Reissue)
(Spain) #32128

People (1975 Reissue)
(England) Hallmark Label #SHM 871

Greatest Hits (1976 Reissue)
(Holland) Different back cover #63921

My Name Is Barbra (1976 Reissue)
(Italy) #RB37

A Star Is Born (1977)
(Korea) #KJPL-0111

131

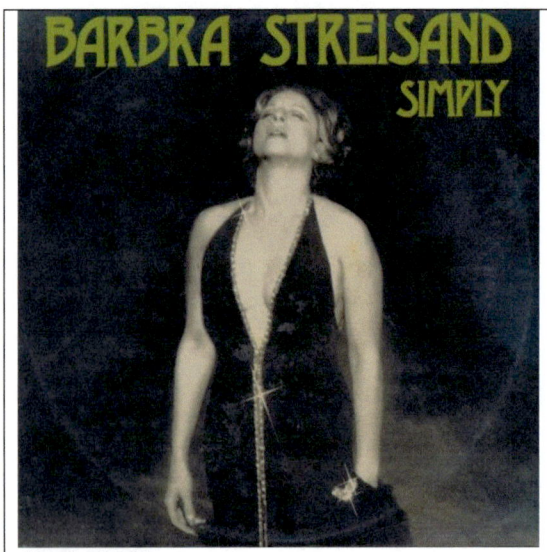

Simply (1976)
(Portugal) Record club issue of Simply Streisand #63151

A Star Is Born (1977)
(Taiwan) Holy Hawk #6304 (thin picture sleeve as cover)

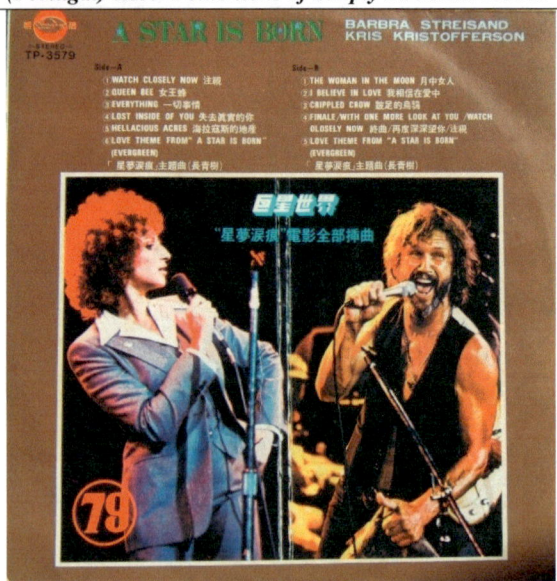

A Star Is Born (1977)
(Taiwan) #TP-3579

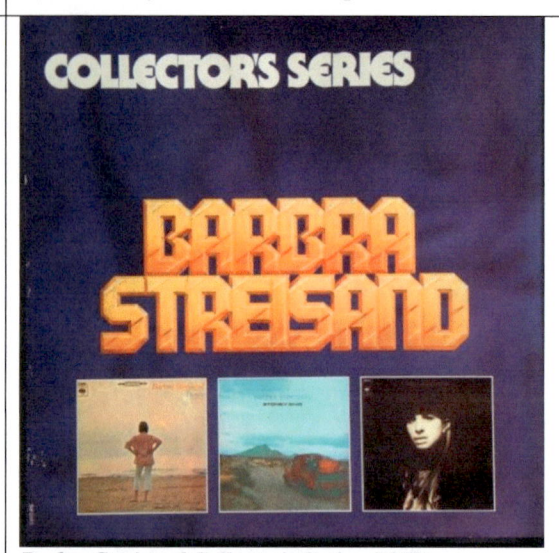

Barbra Streisand Collector's Series (1978)
(Holland) Box set of People, Stoney End, & Barbra Joan.
With four-page insert #66335

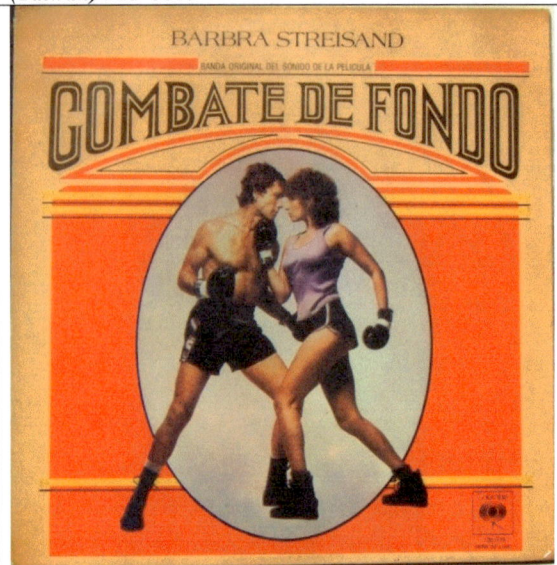

The Main Event (1979)
(Argentina) Gatefold cover #120019
(Argentina also issued gatefolds to Superman, Songbird & Wet)

Barbra Streisand Box Set (1980)
(England) Deluxe box set cover with LP's Greatest Hits
Volume 1 & 2 and Wet. No special catalog number on box, LP's
have regular UK CBS catalog numbers.

Barbra Streisand Box Set (1980)
(England) Deluxe cover box set of Greatest Hits, Stoney End, & Superman LP's. (No catalog number to box cover)

Guilty (1980)
(Italy) Reversed covers #86112

People (1981 Reissue)
(England) Pickwick #SHMV 871

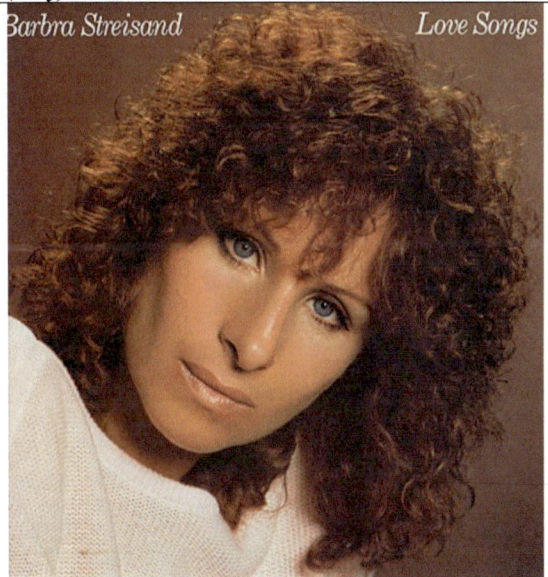

Love Songs (1981)
(England) #10031 Memories retiled with Wet, A Man I Loved, I Don't Break Easily, & Kiss Me In The Rain songs added.

Golden Highlights Volume 34 (1985)
(Holland) Reissue of A Christmas Album #54734

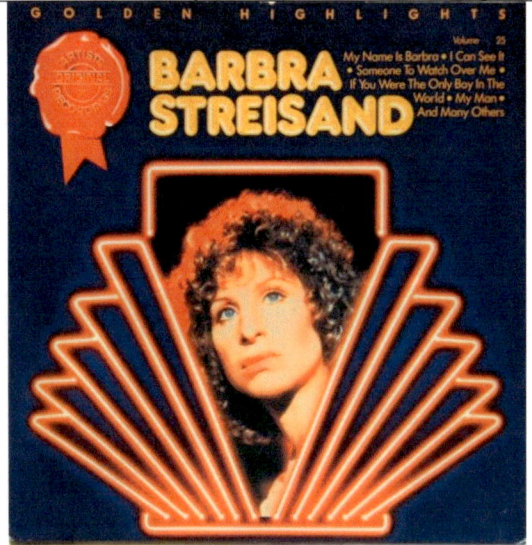

Golden Highlights Volume 25 (1985)
(Holland) Reissue of My Name Is Barbra #54715

The Broadway Album (1985)
(Mexico) Rare promotional copy on blue vinyl #141894
(Also pressed on blue vinyl in Colombia)

One Voice (1987)
(Colombia) Rare blue vinyl pressing #142054

Live At The Forum (1987 Reissue)
(Korea) Creato #2055

Nuts Soundtrack (1987)
(Holland) Issued as Maxi Single #6513796
(Also issued in France, Spain & UK #651379)

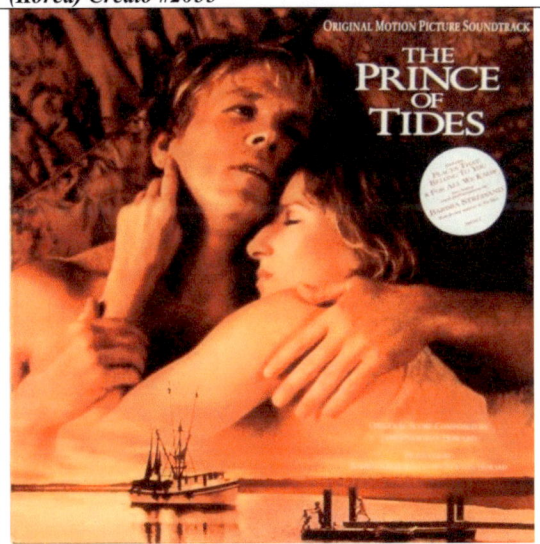

The Prince Of Tides Soundtrack (1991)
(England) #4687351 with insert sleeve
(Also issued in Holland)

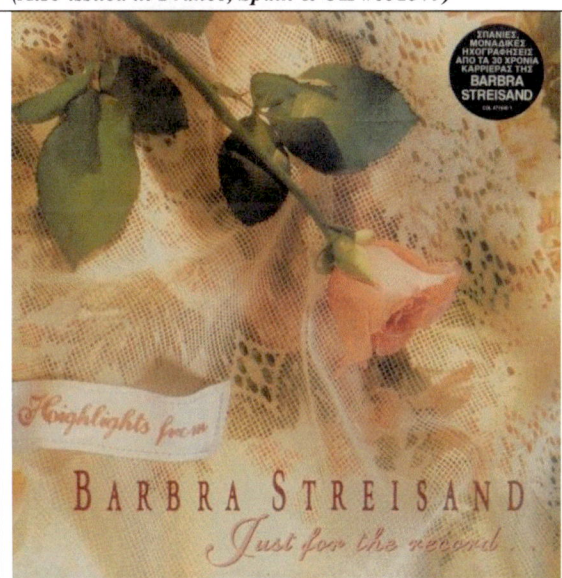

Highlights From Just For The Record (1992)
(Greece) #4716401 2-LP Set

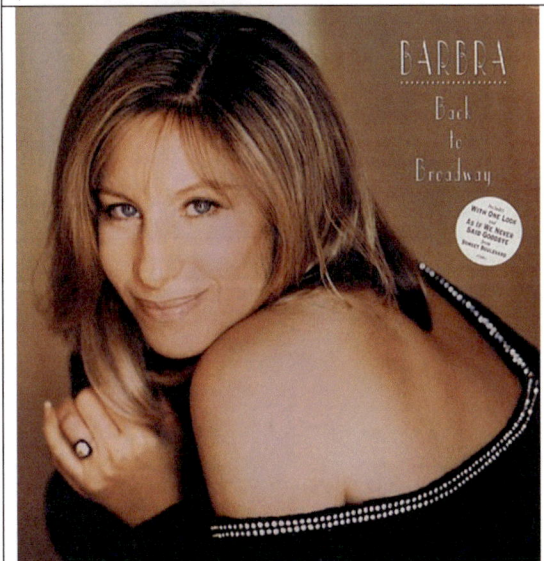

Back To Broadway (1993)   (England) #4738801 with insert
(Also issued in Holland & Brazil)

The Concert (1994)
(Spain) #4775991 Rare 2-LP set with insert sleeves

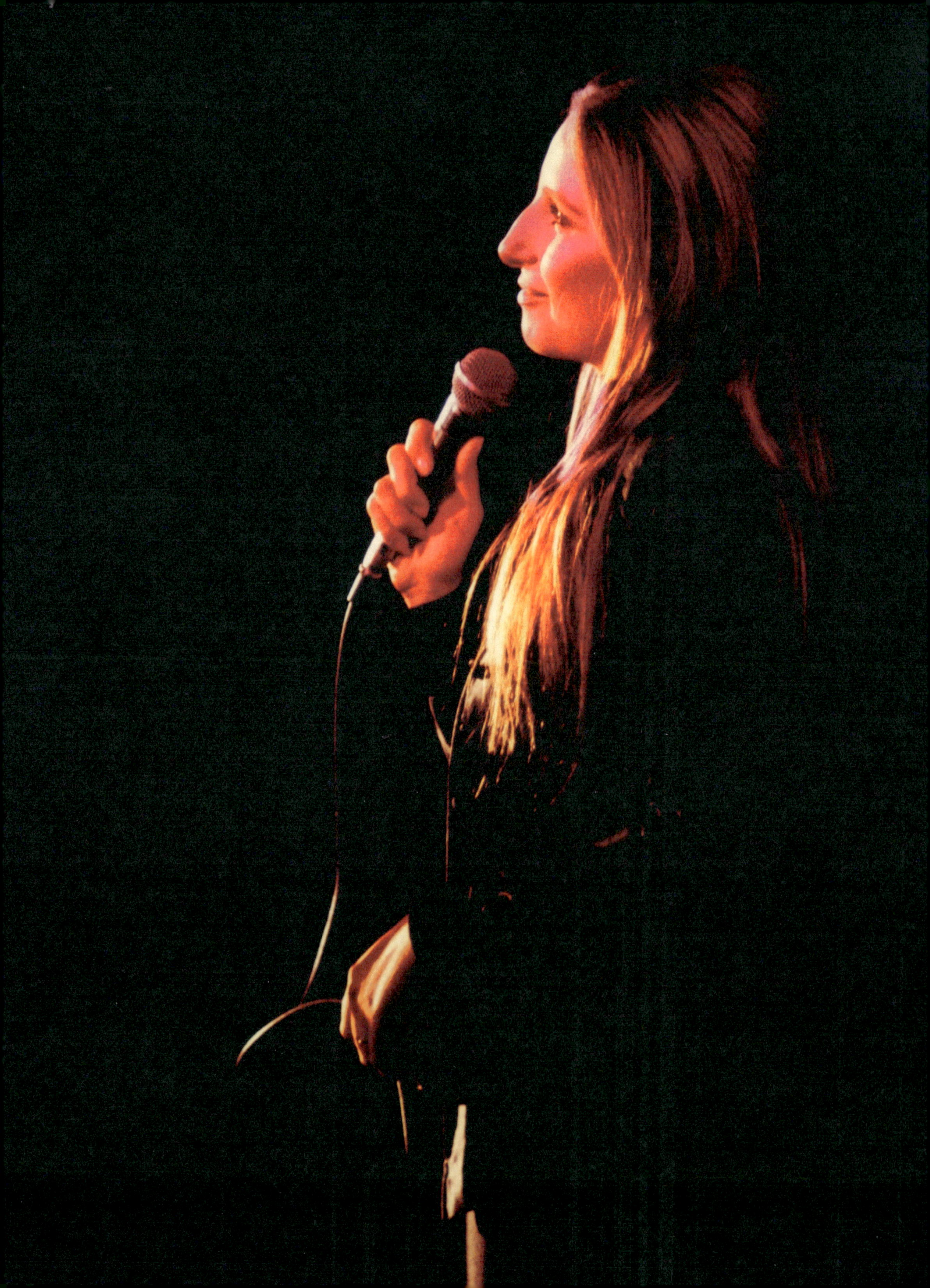

Taiwan LP's

The following were issued on colored vinyl with thin paper sleeves as covers on First Records label. Unsure if they are from the 1960's or 1970's reissues.

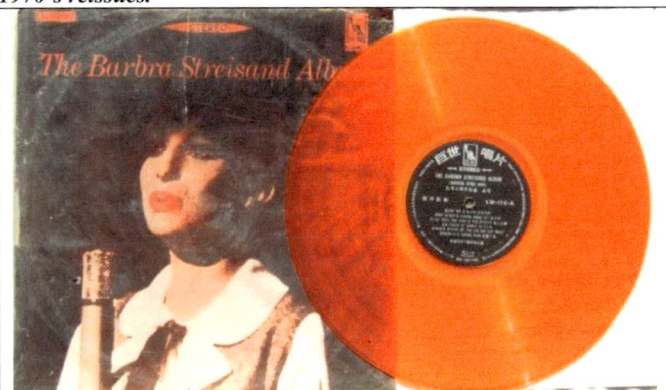

The Barbra Streisand Album (1963)
#LW-172 Orange vinyl
(Also issued on red vinyl)

People (1964)
#FL-S 1341 Red vinyl
(Also issued on orange vinyl)

Color Me Barbra (1966)
#FL-S 1348 Orange vinyl
(Also issued on red vinyl)

Je m'appelle Barbra (1966)
#HS 573 (Haishan Label) Orange vinyl

Simply Streisand (1967)
#FL-S 1587 Orange vinyl
(Also issued on red vinyl)

Funny Girl (1968)
#FL-1737 (not colored vinyl)

The following were released as hit compilation LP's

Barbra Streisand (1964)
(Argentina) #8491
(Lover Come Back To Me, My Melancholy Baby, As Time Goes By, Just In Time, Keepin' Out Of Mischief, Happy Days Are Here Again, Gotta Move, It Had To Be You, My Honey's Loving Arms, Any Place I Hang My Hat Is Home, Bewitched, My Coloring Book)

My Name Is Barbra-Barbra Streisand Sings For You (1965)
(Argentina) #8576
(My Name Is Barbra, A Kid Again-I'm Five, Sweet Zoo, People, Taking A Chance On Love, Who's Afraid Of The Big Bad Wolf?, Cry Me A River, I've Got No Strings, When In Rome, My Lord And Master, Funny Girl, Right As The Rain, My Man)

Las Grandes Creaciones De Barbra Streisand (1967)
(Argentina) #8878
(My Name Is Barbra, Second Hand Rose, Yesterdays, Cry Me A River, As Time Goes By, The Minute Waltz, Non C'est Rien, The Shadow Of Your Smile, People, Funny Girl, Lover Come Back To Me, My Melancholy Baby)

Second Hand Rose (1967)
(Germany) #H 048 (Record club issue)
(My Name Is Barbra, People, Cry Me A River, My Honey's Loving Arms, Sweet Zoo, Taking A Chance On Love, Love Is A Bore, When In Rome, Second Hand Rose, He Touched Me, The Minute Waltz, I've Got No Strings, My Man, Yesterdays, Non C'est Rien, Where Am I Going?)

138

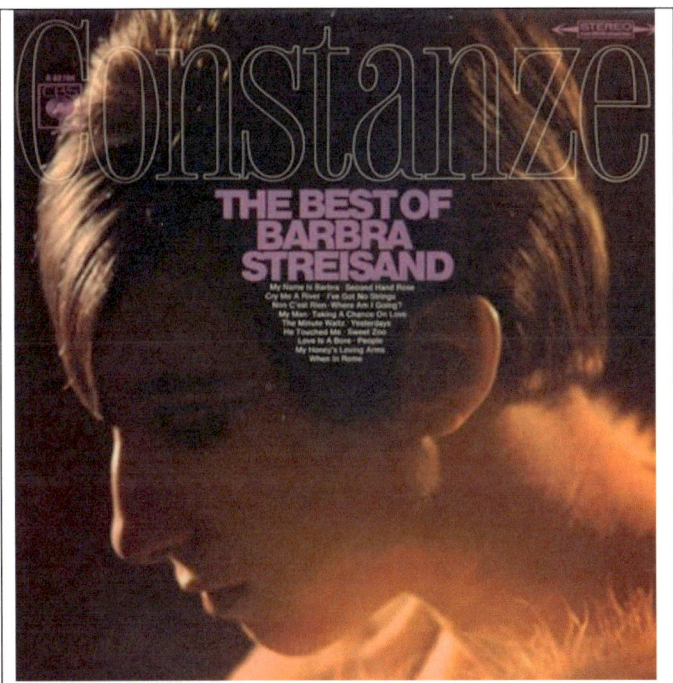

Constanze The Best Of Barbra Streisand (1968)
(Holland) #62788

(My Name Is Barbra, People, Cry Me A River, My Honey's Loving Arms, Sweet Zoo, Taking A Chance On Love, Love Is A Bore, When In Rome, Second Hand Rose, He Touched Me, The Minute Waltz, I've Got No Strings, My Man, Yesterdays, Non C'est Rien, Where Am I Going?)
(Also issued in Italy)

The Great Streisand (1970's issue)
(Australia) #MFP 2-398020 Summit Records (2-LP Set)
(Any Place I Hang My Hat Is Home, Right As The Rain, Down With Love, Who Will Buy?, When The Sun Comes Out, Gotta Move, My Coloring Book, I Don't Care Much, Lover Come Back To Me, I Stayed Too Long At The Fair, Like A Straw In The Wind, My Melancholy Baby, Just In Time, Taking A Chance On Love, Bewitched, Never Will I Marry, As Time Goes By, Draw Me A Circle, It Had To Be You, Make Believe, I Had Myself A True Love)

Barbra Streisand (1970)
(Czechoslovakia) #1130796

(Any Place I Hang My Hat Is Home, Just In Time, Bewitched, Never Will I Marry, A Taste Of Honey, When The Sun Comes Out, Gotta Move, Make The Man Love Me, Come To The Supermarket, My Funny Valentine, People, Like A Straw In The Wind)

Barbra Streisand (1970)
(Czechoslovakia) #1130796

(Same songs as other release, different cover)

Seguire Tu Camino (1971)
(Uruguay) #19147

(Where You Lead, Mother, Flim Flam Man, Love, Stoney End, If You Could Read My Mind, Beautiful, The Summer Knows, Space Captain, You've Got A Friend, Time And Love)
(Also released in Argentina)

Spectacular (1972)
(South Africa) #ASF 1695

(Mother, Where You Lead, I'll Be Home, If You Could Read Me Mind Love, You've Got A Friend, Stoney End, Time And Love, Flim Flam Man, Second Hand Rose, Don't Rain On My Parade, People, Honey Pie, With A Little Help From My Friends, Alfie, Silent Night, My Man, What Now My Love, On A Clear Day)

Greatest Hits (1975)
(New Zealand) #CSP-801

(Same tracks as 1968 Holland Best Of release)

Best Of Barbra Streisand (1977)
(Korea) Creato #1055

(The Way We Were, Evergreen, Stoney End, Cry Me A River, Don't Rain On My Parade, Sweet Inspiration, My Man, People, Didn't We, Sing-Happy Days Are Here Again, As Time Goes By, Starting Here Starting Now, On A Clear Day, Sing-Make Your Own Kind Of Music)

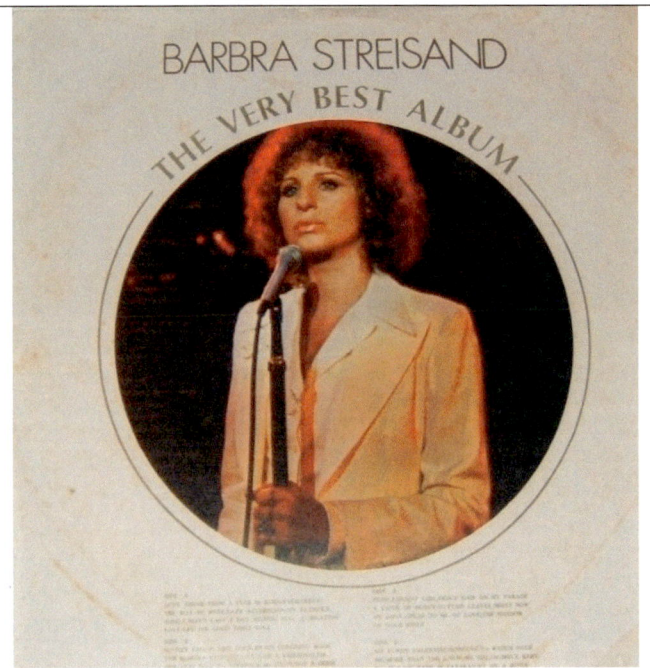

The Very Best Album Of Barbra Streisand (1977)
(Taiwan) Shan Shui Records #SB-20 (2-LP Set)
(Evergreen, The Way We Were, Lazy Afternoon, My Father's Song, I Won't Last A Day Without You, Jubilation, Love, Let The Good Times Roll, Stoney End, As Time Goes By, My Coloring Book, The Summer Knows, You've Got A Friend, Alfie, One Less Bell-House Is Not A Home, People, Funny Girl, Don't Rain On My Parade, Taste Of Honey, Autumn Leaves, What Now My Love, Speak To Me Of Love, Shadow Of Your Smile, My Funny Valentine, Someone To Watch Over Me, More Than You Know, My Melancholy Baby, My Man, My Name Is Barbra ,Cry Me A River)

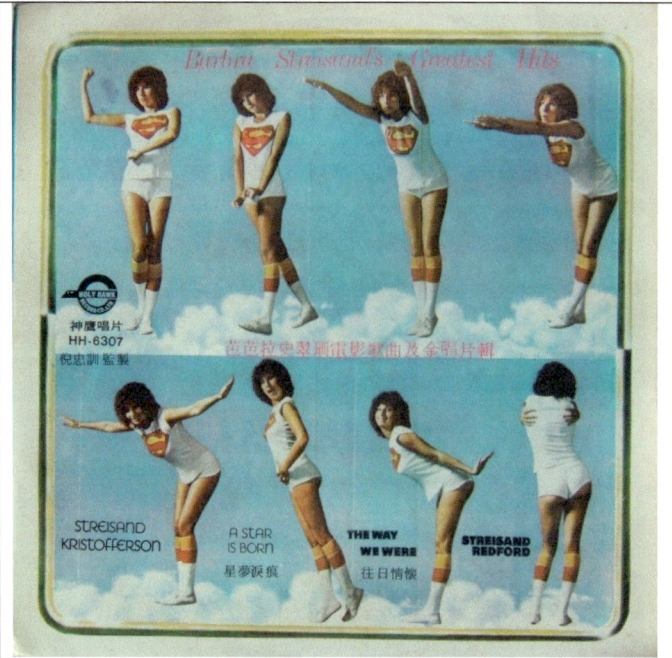

Barbra Streisand's Greatest Hits And Movie Songs (1977)
(Taiwan) 1977 Holy Hawk Records #6307

(Evergreen, My Heart Belongs To Me, Second Hand Rose, People, Sam You Made The Pants Too Long, Sweet Inspiration-Where You Lead, The Way We Were, Stoney End, My Man, Free Again, My Funny Valentine, Hello Dolly)

Spectacular (1980)
(South Africa) #10033

(Same tracks as 1972 release)

The Best Of Barbra Streisand (1981)
(China) #TP 3613

(Woman In Love, Guilty, What Kind Of Fool, Run Wild, You Don't Bring Me Flowers, My Heart Belongs To Me, Evergreen, Prisoner, The Way We Were, Main Event-Fight, The Love Inside, Superman)

141

Barbra Streisand (1981)
(Korea) Hanyang Records #CTAT-2028

(Woman In Love, Lost Inside Of You, You Don't Bring Me Flowers, Evergreen, The Love Inside, New York State Of Mind, Memory, Comin' In And Out Of Your Life, The Way We Were, No More Tears, My Heart Belongs To Me, Guilty)

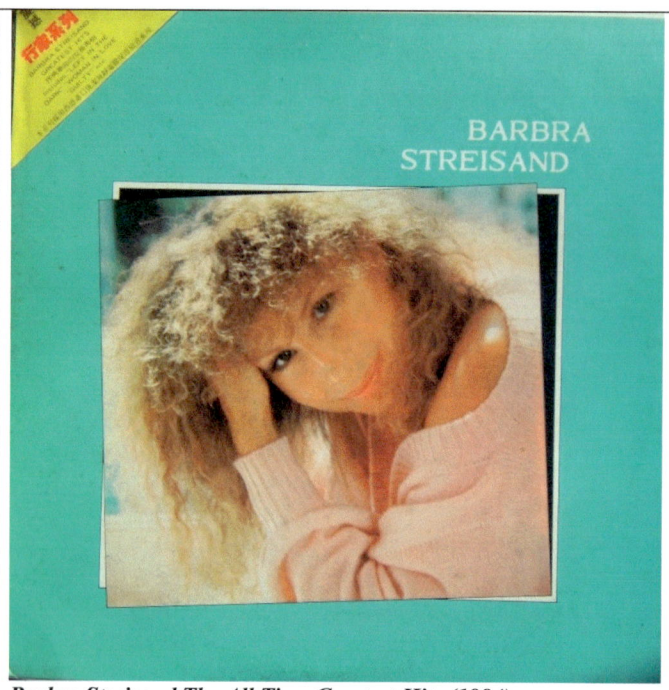

Barbra Streisand The All Time Greatest Hits (1984)
(Taiwan) #PRO-4027

(Left In The Dark, You Don't Bring Me Flowers, The Way We Were, Memory, Comin' In And Out Of Your Life, Evergreen, Woman In Love, Emotion, Guilty, The Way He Makes Me Feel, Make No Mistake, He's Mine, What Kind Of Fool)

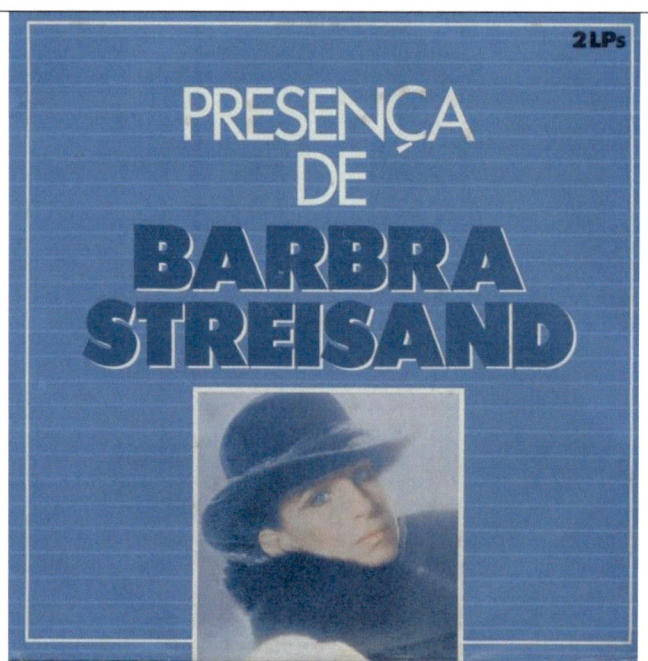

Presenca De Barbra Streisand (1985)
(Brazil) #138758 (2-LP Set)

(People, Fine And Dandy, Lazy Afternoon, No More Tears, Second Hand Rose, Stoney End, Free Again, Promises, New York State Of Mind, Guilty, A Taste Of Honey, You Don't Bring Me Flowers, Woman In Love, Yesterdays, Free The People, My Name Is Barbra, Cry Me A River, Happy Days, The Way We Were, Evergreen, A Child Is Born, Supper Time, The Shadow Of Your Smile, Me Melancholy Baby)

Stars: Barbra Streisand (1991)
(China) #SH0371-4 (issued with color insert with lyrics and picture label)

(Guilty, Woman In Love, Memory, You Don't Bring Me Flowers, My Heart Belongs To Me, Comin' In And Out Of Your Life, The Way We Were, Evergreen, Make No Mistake, He's Mine, When I Dream, Emotion, What Kind Of Fool, Promises)

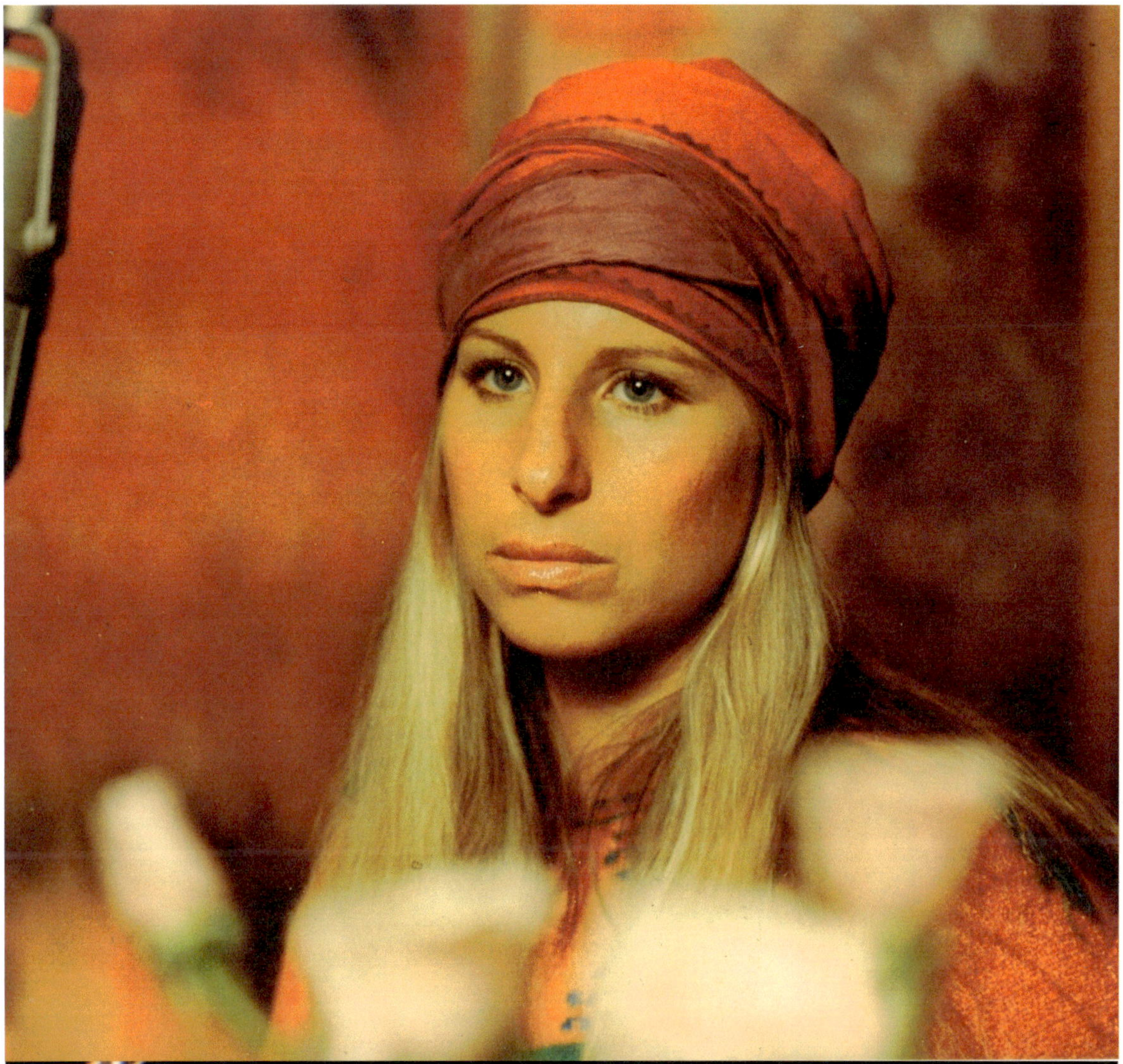

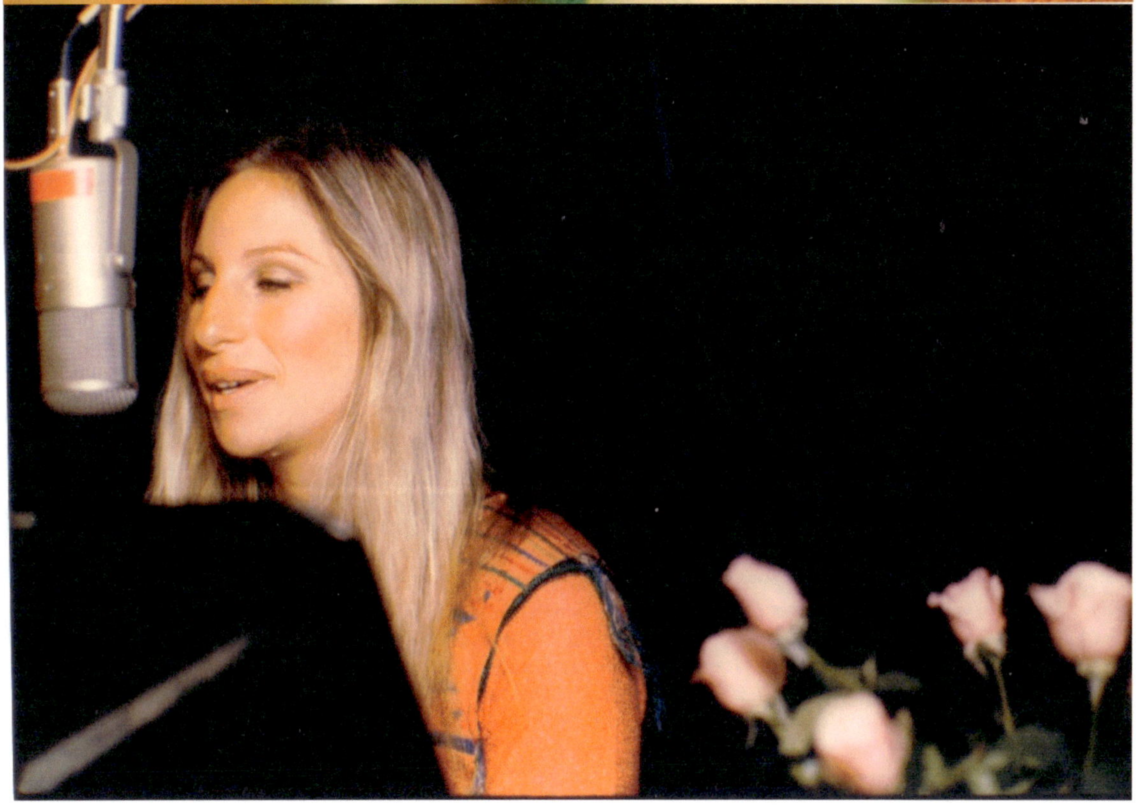

Japanese LP's

Japanese vinyl is a favorite among record collectors for its high quality pressings of vinyl. The covers are produced on a heavy stock paper; some LP's are beautifully packaged. All LP's include a Japanese/English lyric sheet/booklet, and most all Japanese LP's have what is called an 'OBI' strip around the LP cover, which is basically a fancy price tag. The older the record, the harder to find with the OBI. This section features all the Japanese-only compilation releases. Japan also released some various artists compilation LP's that featured Barbra as the full cover. One is pictured at the end of this section.

The Barbra Streisand Story (1967)
(#YS-842-3C) 2-LP set with beautiful gold embossed gatefold cover and four-page insert.

(Cry Me A River, A Taste Of Honey, Lover Come Back To Me, My Coloring Book, My Melancholy Baby, Just In Time, People, Taking A Chance On Love, Bewitched, As Time Goes By, It Had To Be You, Make Believe, The Shadow Of Your Smile, My Name Is Barbra, Someone To Watch Over Me, He Touched Me, Second Hand Rose, My Man, What Now My Love, The Minute Waltz, Autumn Leaves, C'est Si Bon, Yesterdays, Ma Premiere Chanson)

144

The Best Of Barbra Streisand (1967)
#YS-709-C Gatefold cover with four-page insert.

(The Shadow Of Your Smile, Yesterdays, My Melancholy Baby, Where Or When, Just In Time, As Time Goes By, People, A Taste Of Honey, C'est Si Bon, Bewitched, Cry Me A River, Lover Come Back To Me)

My Funny Valentine (1968)
#YS-925-C Beautiful gatefold cover with four-page insert
Simply Streisand was originally released in Japan as My Funny Valentine, until the 1975 reissue.

(My Funny Valentine, The Nearness Of You, When Sunny Gets Blue, Make The Man Love Me, Lover Man, More Than You Know, I'll Know, All The Things You Are, The Boy Next Door, Stout-Hearted Man)

Me, Funny Girl (1968)
#SONP 50002 With insert sheet

(People, Absent Minded Me, When In Rome, I'm All Smiles, How Does The Wine Taste, Fine And Dandy, The Shadow Of Your Smile, He Touched Me, Second Hand Rose, The Kind Of Woman A Man Needs, All That I Want, I Got Plenty Of Nothing)

All About Barbra Streisand (1971)
#SOPH 9-10 (2-LP Set) Silver embossed gatefold cover with insert

(Stoney End, One Less Bell To Answer-A House Is Not A Home, Alfie, Until It's Time For You To Go, What About Today?, Happy Days, Funny Girl, My Funny Valentine, What Now My Love, Autumn Leaves, C'est Si Bon, Yesterdays, Second Hand Rose, The Shadow Of Your Smile, He Touched Me, My Man, Someone To Watch Over Me, My Name Is Barbra, People, As Time Goes By, Lover Come Back To Me, My Coloring Book, A Taste Of Honey, Cry Me A River)

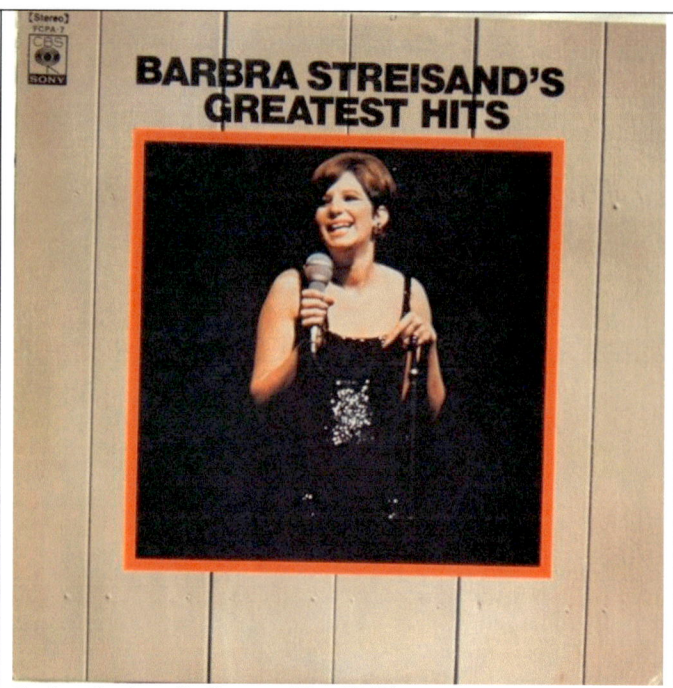

Barbra Streisand's Greatest Hits (1972)
#FCPA-7 Record Club issue with insert, no OBI

(People, Second Hand Rose, A Taste Of Honey, Alfie, My Coloring Book, One Less Bell-A House Is Not A Home, Stoney End, My Man, As Time Goes By, What Now My Love, Cry Me A River)

Gold Disc (1974)
#SOPN-97 Gorgeous gold foiled cover with four-page booklet and lyric insert sheet

(The Way We Were, All In Love Is Fair, You've Got A Friend, Stoney End, Love, One Less Bell-A House Is Not A Home, Until It's Time For You To Go, Free Again, My Funny Valentine, As Time Goes By, My Man, Autumn Leaves, Cry Me A River, People)

Cover of insert booklet. This was used on two different bootleg Asian LP's as a cover.

Golden Double Series (1974)
#SOPW 39-40 2-LP Set with beautiful gatefold cover with four-page insert

(The Way We Were, I Won't Last A Day Without You, Jubilation, You've Got A Friend, If You Could Read My Mind, One Less Bell-A House Is Not A Home, Stoney End, Love, The Summer Knows, Free Again, Alfie, Until It's Time For You To Go, People, As Time Goes By, The Shadow Of Your Smile, Autumn Leaves, What Now My Love, My Man, My Funny Valentine, A Taste Of Honey, My Name Is Barbra, Happy Days, My Coloring Book, Cry Me A River)

New Gold Disc (1975)
#SOPO 51 with four-page booklet

(The Way We Were, I Won't Last A Day Without You, You've Got A Friend, Love, Stoney End, One Less Bell-A House Is Not A Home, Until It's Time For You To Go, People, My Funny Valentine, Autumn Leaves, What Now My Love, A Taste Of Honey, Cry Me A River, My Man)
(This LP was also issued in the Philippines)

Grand Prix 20 (1976)
#29AP 44 with four-page booklet

(The Way We Were, My Father's Song, Jubilation, I Won't Last A Day Without You, Love, Stoney End, The Summer Knows, My Funny Valentine, What Now My Love, Alfie, People, You've Got A Friend, As Time Goes By, The Shadow Of Your Smile, A Taste Of Honey, My Man, More Than You Know, Speak To Me Of Love, Taking A Chance On Love, Cry Me A River)

Golden Grand Prix 30 (1977)
#40AP 475-6 (2-LP set) Beautiful gold embossed gatefold cover with four-page insert

(Evergreen, The Way We Were, Lazy Afternoon, My Father's Song, I Won't Last A Day Without You, Jubilation, Love, Let The Good Times Roll, Stoney End, As Time Goes By, My Coloring Book, The Summer Knows, You've Got A Friend, Alfie, One Less Bell-A House Is Not A Home, People, Funny Girl, Don't Rain On My Parade, A Taste Of Honey, Autumn Leaves, What Now My Love, Speak To Me Of Love, The Shadow Of Your Smile, My Funny Valentine, Someone To Watch Over Me, More Than You Know, My Melancholy Baby, My Man, My Name Is Barbra, Cry Me A River)

147

Japanese editions of Streisand's albums

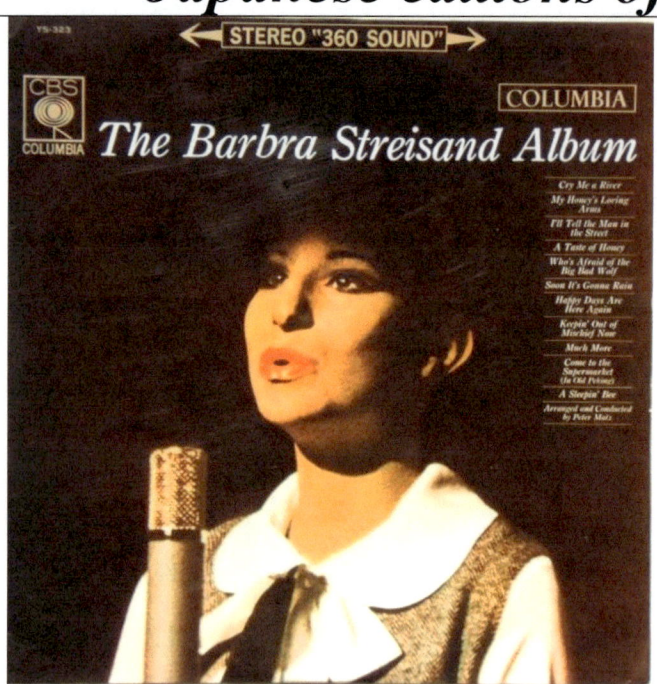

The Barbra Streisand Album (Released in Japan April 1964)
YS-323 with insert sheet

1975 Reissue SOPN-138 with insert sheet

The Second Album (Released in Japan August 1964)
(The Third Album originally was released in Japan as The Second Album, later reissued correctly)
YS-357-C with four-page insert

The Third Album (1975 Reissue)
SOPN-139 with insert sheet

The Third Album (Released in Japan Oct. 1964)
YS-399-C with insert sheet (The Second Album retiled as The Third Album)

Funny Girl Broadway Cast Recording (1969 Great Musical Series on Red vinyl)
Capitol Records CP-8477 gatefold with four-page insert

Promotional Red vinyl test pressing of above release comes in plain white sample sleeve
CP-8477 (1969) Capital

1977 Reissue ECS-80821 Capital Records with insert

149

People (1964)
YS-465-C with insert sheet

My Name Is Barbra (1965)
YS-534-C Unique gatefold cover with four-page insert

My Name Is Barbra, Two (1965)
YS-632-C Unique gatefold cover with six-page insert

Color Me Barbra (1966)
SONX 600400 Gatefold cover with four-page Chemstrand insert

Je m'appelle Barbra (1966)
YS-744-C with six-page insert booklet

Simply Streisand (1975 Pressing)
SOPN-142 with insert sheet
(The original 60's pressing was retitled My Funny Valentine)

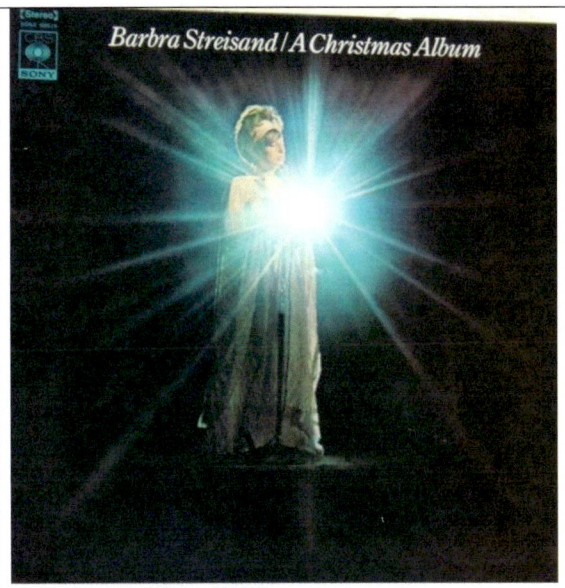

A Christmas Album (1967)
SONX 60019 Unique gatefold cover with insert

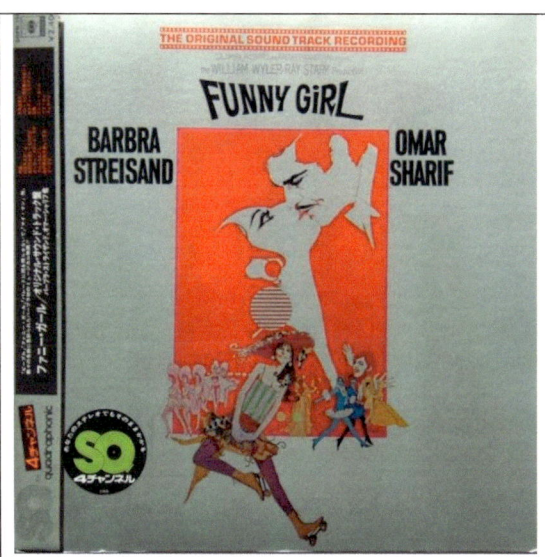

Funny Girl (1971 Quad Pressing)
SOPN 134 Beautiful silver finish gatefold cover with insert sheet
Original 1968 release SONX 60011 Gatefold with insert sheet

A Happening In Central Park (1968)
SONP 50035 with four-page insert

What About Today? (1969)
SONX 60090 Beautiful gatefold cover with insert sheet

Hello Dolly (1969)
20th Century Fox Records SWG-7170 Gatefold with 16-page color insert booklet

Greatest Hits (1970)
SONX 60129 Unique gatefold cover with four-page insert sheet

On A Clear Day You Can See Forever (1970)
SONX 60190 Unique gatefold cover with insert sheet

Stoney End (1971 Quad Pressing)
SOPN 44008 Unique silver finish cover with insert sheet (Original Stereo release SOPC 57128)

Barbra Joan Streisand (1971 Quad Pressing)
SOPN-19 Unique silver finish gatefold cover with insert & poster (Original Stereo release SOPC-57151)

Live At The Forum (1972)
SOPM-35 Gatefold cover with insert sheet

Barbra Streisand …And Other Musical Instruments (1973)
SOPM-117 Not gatefold cover, with insert sheet

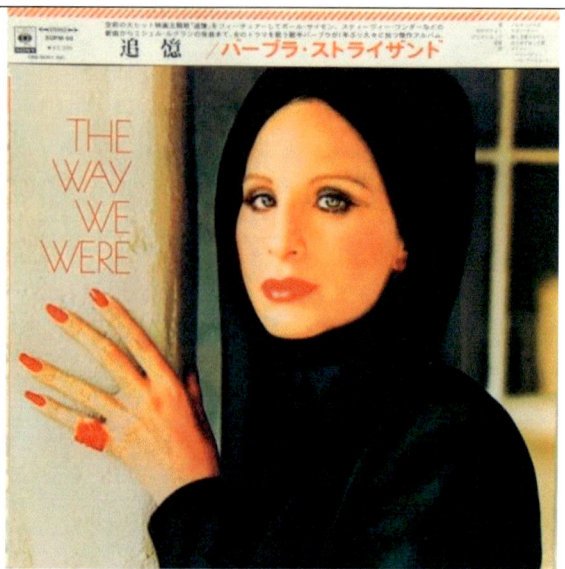

The Way We Were (1974)
SOPM-98 with insert sheet

The Way We Were (1974)
SOPM-89 Gatefold cover with no insert
1977 Reissue (Non-gatefold with insert) #25AP-519

Butterfly (1974)
SOPO-19 Gatefold cover with four-page booklet and insert sheet

Funny Lady (1975)
Arista BLPO-10-AR Gatefold cover with four-page insert

Lazy Afternoon (1975)
SOPO-110 Gatefold cover with insert sheet

Classical Barbra (1976)
#25AP-7 with four-page booklet

A Star Is Born (1976)
#25AP325 Gatefold cover with unique four-page booklet

Superman (1977)
#25AP 590 Includes four-page color booklet (same as US) & unique four-page insert booklet

Songbird (1978)
#25AP-1065 with four-page insert

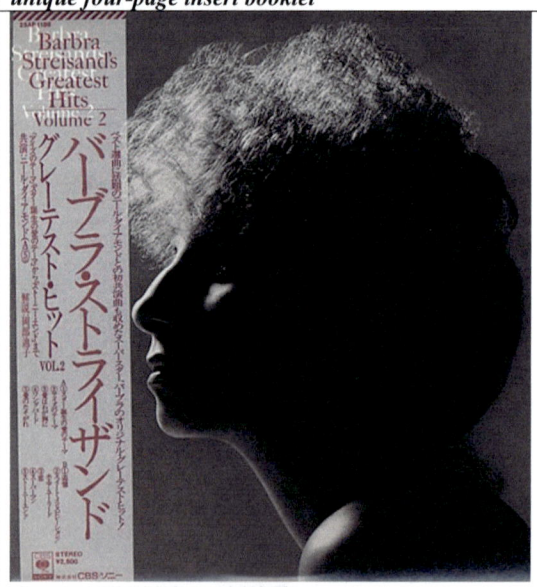

Greatest Hits Volume 2(1978)
#25AP 1188 with insert sheet

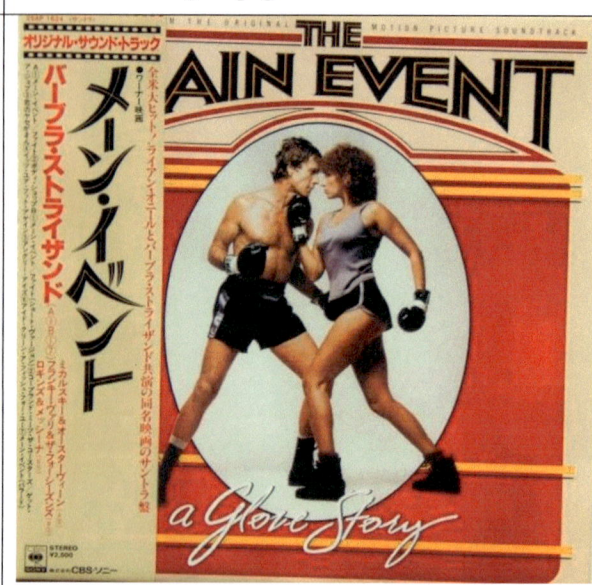

The Main Event (1979)
#25AP 1624 with insert sheet

Wet (1979)
#25AP 1724 with four-page booklet

Guilty (1980)
#25AP 1930 Gatefold cover with four-page booklet

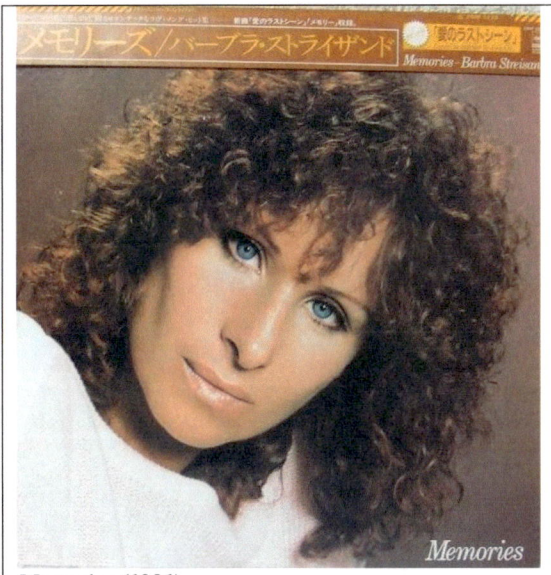

Memories (1981)
#25AP 2229 with unique four-page insert

Yentl (1983)
#25AP 2734 Gatefold cover with six-page insert

Emotion (1984)
#28AP 2940 with four-page insert (Also issued as MasterSound)

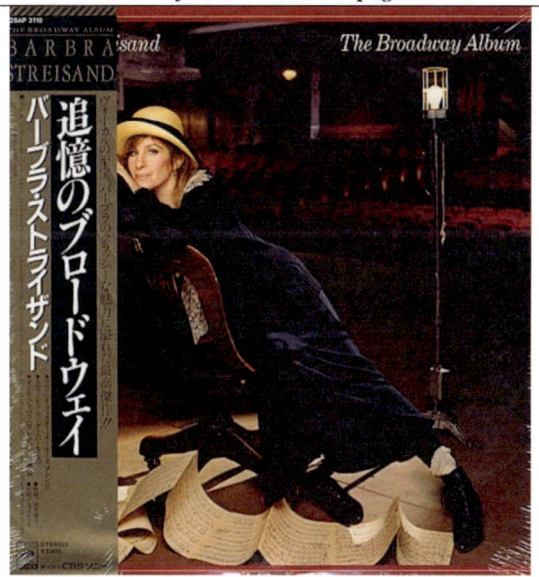

The Broadway Album (1985)
#28AP 3118 with four-page insert

One Voice (1987)
#28AP 3333 with six-page insert
(Last of the Japanese LP's)

Screen Music (1975)
Music Rainbow #MRS-8009 issued with oversized 26-page book
with 3 tracks: Hello Dolly, People & The Way We Were

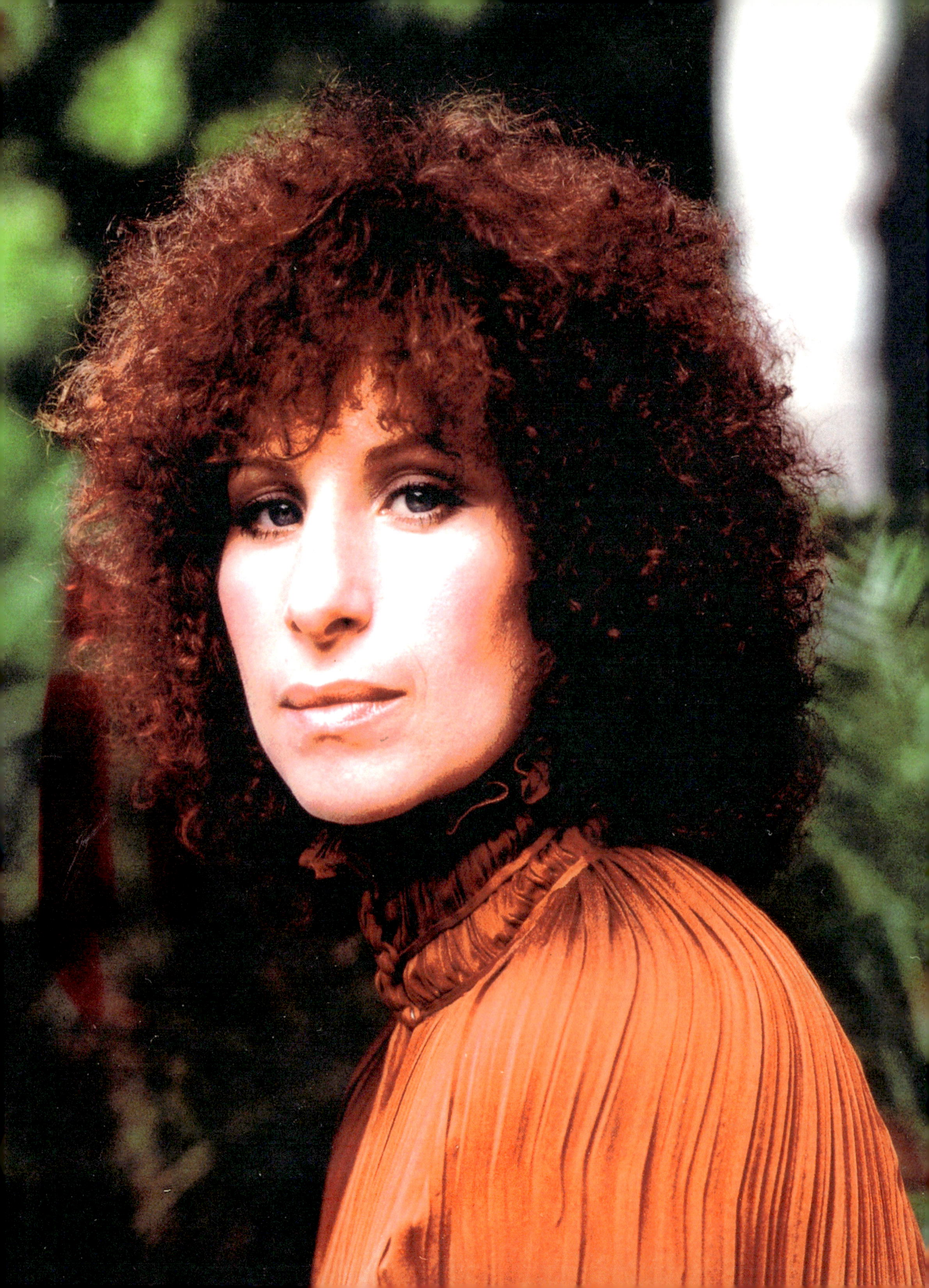

CD's US Release
Streisand's entire album catalog is issued on CD, all on Columbia/SONY label unless noted.

I Can Get It For You Wholesale CK 53020 (out of print)

Pins And Needles CK 57380 (out of print)

The Barbra Streisand Album CK 57374 (1st pressing #8807)

The Second Album CK 57378 (1st pressing #8854)

The Third Album CK 57379 (1st pressing #8954)

People CK 86103 (1st pressing #9015)
2002 UK Bonus CD with I Am Woman #506357-2

My Name Is Barbra CK 9136

My Name Is Barbra, Two CK 9209

Color Me Barbra CK 9278

Harold Sings Arlen CK 52722 (out of print)

Je m'appelle Barbra CK 9347

Simply Streisand CK 9482

Funny Girl Film Soundtrack CK 85151 (1st pressing #3220)
2002 UK Bonus CD with I'd Rather Be Blue (single version) #5063582

A Happening In Central Park CK 9710

What About Today? CK 47014

Hello Dolly Philips #810368-2

On A Clear Day CK 57377 (1st pressing #A20716)

Stoney End CK 725022

Barbra Joan Streisand CK 30792

Live At The Forum CK 31760

Barbra Streisand And Other Musical Instruments CK 32655

The Way We Were CK 85153 (1st pressing #32801)
2002 UK Bonus CD with Soundtrack version #5063592

The Way We Were Soundtrack CK 57381

Butterfly CK 33005

Lazy Afternoon CK 33452

Classical Barbra CK 33452

A Star Is Born CK 86119 (1st pressing #57375)
2002 UK Bonus CD with Spanish Evergreen #5063602

Superman CK 34830

Songbird CK 35375

Greatest Hits Volume 2 CK 35679

The Main Event CK 57376 (out of print)

Wet CK 36258

Guilty CK 36750

Memories CK 37678

Yentl CK 3915

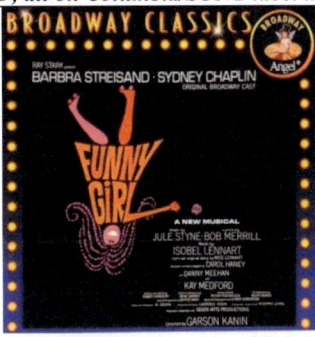

Funny Girl Broadway (Angel Label) #64661 (1st pressing 7466342 Capital)

A Christmas Album 2004 reissue CK 92708
Original release CK9557

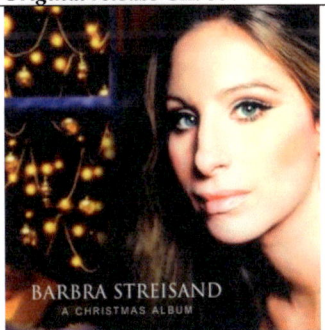

A Christmas Album 2008 reissue #A712043

Greatest Hits 2005 Release with slipcase CK 9968

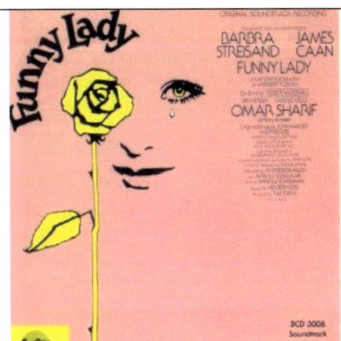

Funny Lady 1st edition Bay Cities Label BCD 3006 (out of print)

157

Emotion CK 39480

The Broadway Album CK 85159 (1st pressing #40092)
2002 UK Bonus CD with I Know Him So Well (#5063612)

One Voice CK 40788

Till I Loved You CK 40880

A Collection Greatest Hits & More CK 45369

The Prince Of Tides Soundtrack CK 48627

Highlights Just For The Record CK 52849

Back To Broadway CK 44189

The Concert 2-CD Set C2K 66109

The Concert Highlights CK 67100

The Mirror Has Two Faces Soundtrack CK 67887

Higher Ground CK 66181

A Love Like Ours CK 69601

Timeless 2-CD Set #63778

Christmas Memories CK 86203

The Essential 2-CD Set C2K 86123

Funny Lady 1998 Reissue
Arista #19006
Contains alternate Let's Hear It For Me (extra line), different version of Great Day, and bonus track How Lucky Can You Get (Single version)

Classical Barbra (2013 Remastered Special Edition)
Contains two unreleased bonus tracks An Sylvia & Auf dern Wasser zu singen
Sony Masterworks #88691922552

Also UK Promotional CD issued with picture sleeve in plastic wallet #LC 12723

Nuts Soundtrack 1987 CXK 40876 (out of print)
(Long box shown)
(Note: CD's were first packaged in a large cardboard designed box, referred to as 'Long box')

Just For The Record

1998 Edition in thick jewel box with 56-page booklet (4-CD set) CXK 68614

1991 Original Deluxe 4-CD set. Issued in 6x12 pink linen box with 92-page booklet C4K 44111

2003 Edition 6x10 glossy finish box with foldout cover (inside shown) C4K 89077

159

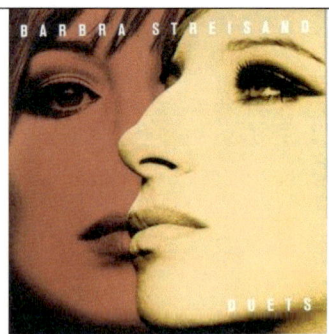

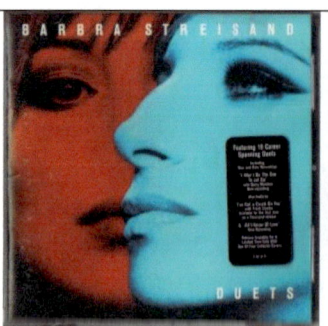

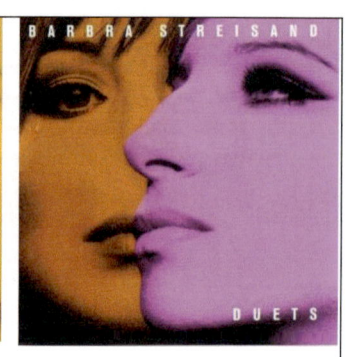

Duets CK 86126
Limited Edition of Four Covers

The Movie Album
Deluxe Edition with DVD in digipak
CK 90742
Regular Edition CK 89018
SACD (Super Audio) Edition
CH-90748

The Movie Album Interview CD
CSK 56602 (6:38 interview)
Promotional-only release
Comes in black card sleeve

Guilty 25th Anniversary Edition (2005) DualDisc CN96524
Contains DVD with videos & interview segments

Guilty Pleasures
DualDisc CN 94997
Contains DVD with videos & Interview
Regular Edition CK 93559

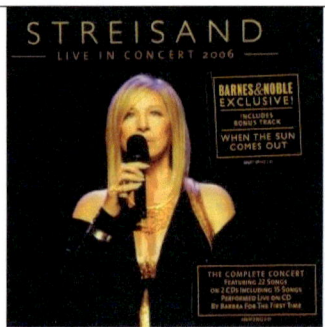

Live In Concert 2006
2-CD Set in Digipak #88697019222
Barnes & Noble Edition with bonus track When The Sun Comes Out
#88697094402-BC (2007 release)

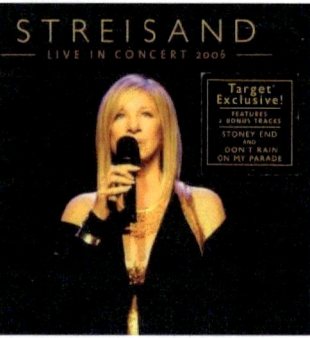

Live In Concert 2006 (2-CD Set)
Target Edition with 2 Bonus Tracks Stoney End & Don't Rain On My Parade #88697084492-BG (2007)

Love Is The Answer
Promotional acetate copy
Issued in Columbia card sleeve, no catalog number

Love Is The Answer
Deluxe Edition 2-CD Set
Bonus Disc Quartet Arrangements (digipak)
#88697482832-7
Regular Edition #88697433542-9

Love Is The Answer
Starbucks Edition in gatefold card sleeve
#88697571502-2

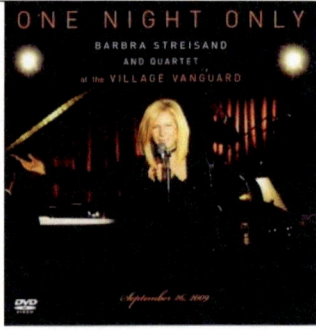

One Night Only Live At The Village Vanguard 2009
DVD/CD Digipak
#88697684119 (2010 Release)

One Night Only CD Program

Intro, Here's To Life, In The Wee Small Hours Of The Morning, Gentle Rain, Spring Can Really Hang You The Most, If You Go Away, Where Do You Start?, Nobody's Heart Belongs To Me, Make Someone Happy, My Funny Valentine, Bewitched Bothered & Bewildered, Thankyou's & Intros, Evergreen, Exit Music, Some Other Time, The Way We Were

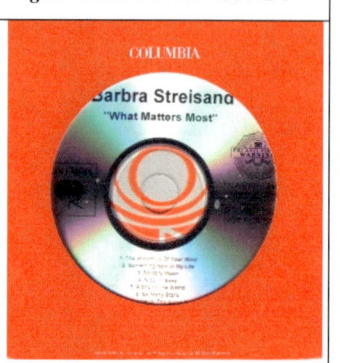

What Matters Most
Promotional Acetate CD issued in Columbia red card sleeve, no catalog number.

What Matters Most- Deluxe Edition
2-CD Set Digipak #8869786257-2
(Previously released Bergman Hits on other disc)

Regular Edition #8869794057-2

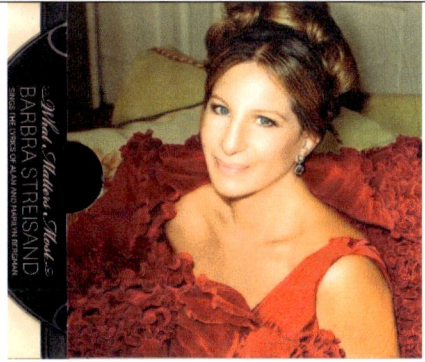

What Matters Most-Starbucks Edition
Beautiful gatefold cardsleeve with bonus tracks The Way We Were, You Don't Bring Me Flowers, & What Are You Doing The Rest of Your Life?
#8869794194-2

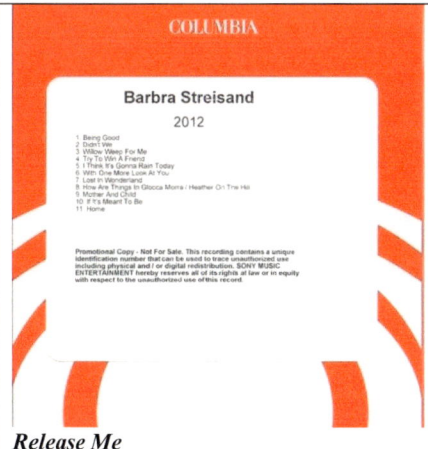

Release Me
Promotional Acetate issued in Columbia red card sleeve, no catalog number.

Release Me
#88725458552
Issued in digipak. Back cover shown.

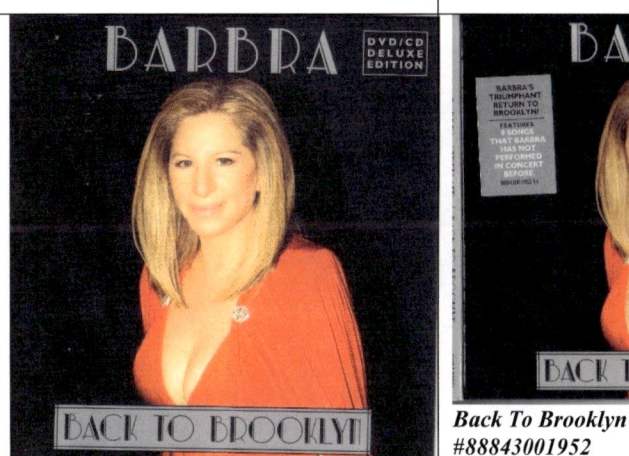

Back To Brooklyn
DVD/CD Deluxe Edition
#88843007589 issued in jewel case

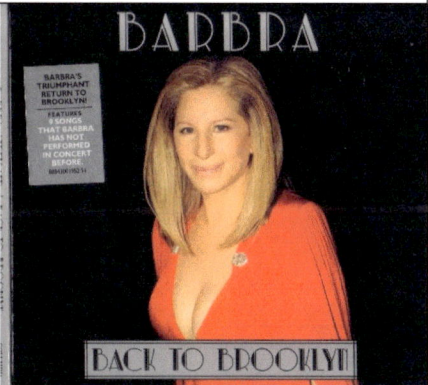

Back To Brooklyn
#88843001952
Issued in digipak.

Promotional Acetate CD also issued.

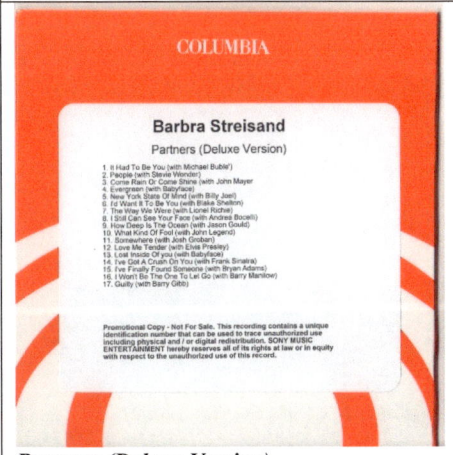

Partners (Deluxe Version)
Promotional acetate pressing
Issued in Columbia Records card sleeve, no catalog number

Partners
#88843091142
Issued in jewel case

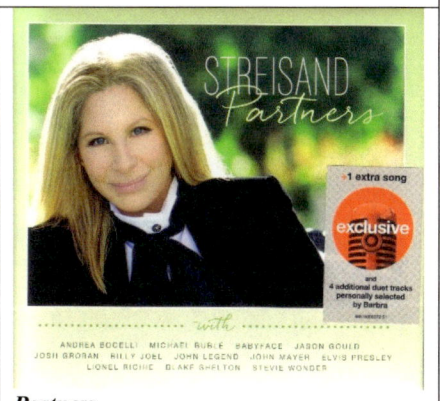

Partners
Target Deluxe (2-CD Set)
#8887500807251 Issued in digipak
Bonus Disc: Lost Inside Of You (with Babyface) plus 4 previously released tracks

161

Collectible CD's

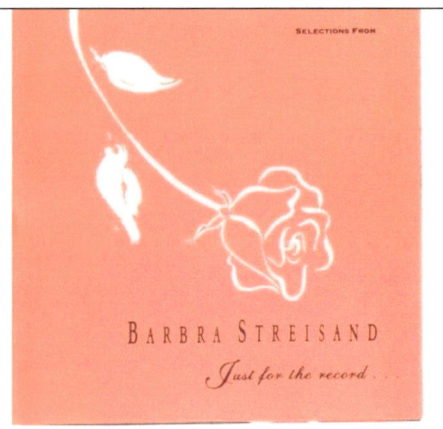

Selections From Just For The Record (1991)
CSK 4200 12-track promo-only release

Second promotional disc with 12 different tracks
CSK 4196 (1991)

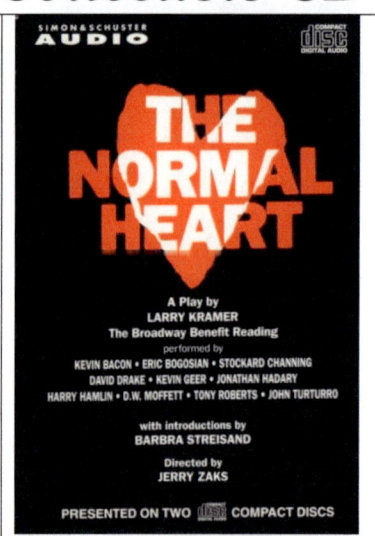

The Normal Heart Broadway Benefit Reading (1993) Simon & Schuster ISBN 0-671-88285-6
Contains introduction by Streisand

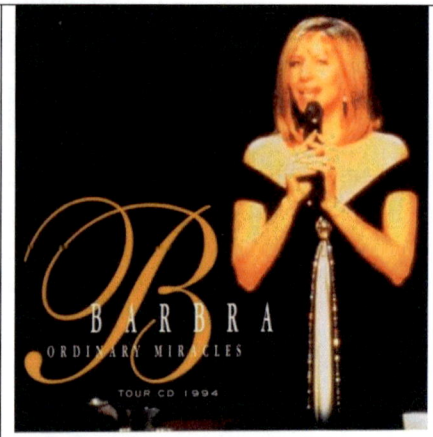

Ordinary Miracles Tour CD 1994
CSK 6120 Promotional-only
Contains 19-track compilation of hits plus Ordinary Miracles live & studio versions, both non-LP cuts.

The Mirror Has Two Faces-Advanced Promotional CD (1996)
ACK 67887 S1

Comes in clear jewel case with sticker on back

Selections From Timeless (2000)
CSK 16154 Promotional-only
(Cry Me A River, Lover Come Back To Me, Alfie, Something Wonderful-Being Alive, Send In The Clowns, The Main Event, I've Dreamed Of You, Happy Days)

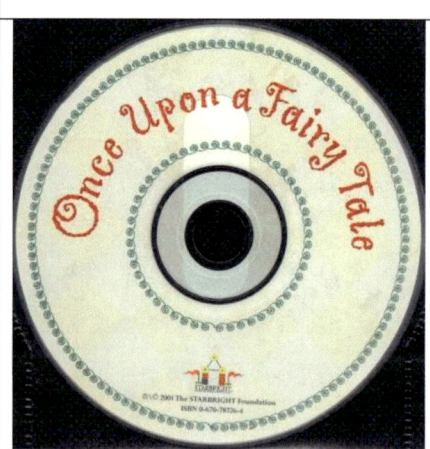

Once Upon A Fairy Tale-Starlight Foundation
Book with Celebrity Narrative CD (2001)
ISBN-10:0670035009
Streisand appears on The Frog Prince

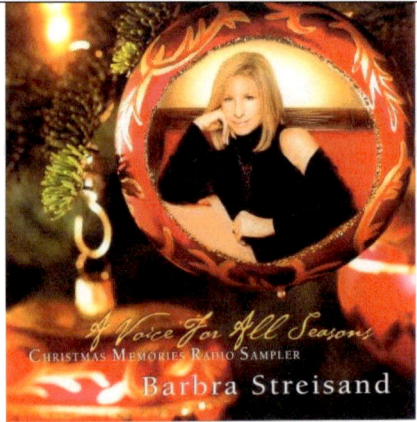

A Voice For All Seasons Christmas Memories Radio Sampler (2001)
CSK 54903 Promotional-only release
(Grown-Up Christmas List, It Must Have Been The Mistletoe, I'll Be Home For Christmas, Closer, One God)

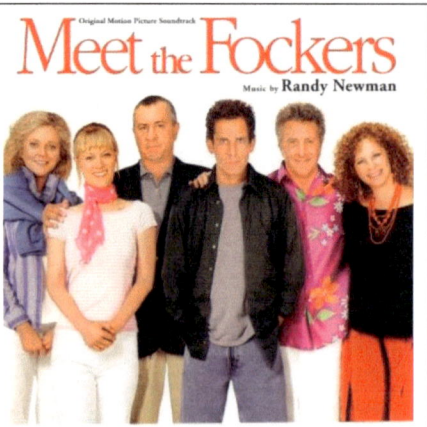

Meet The Fockers Soundtrack (2004)
Varese Sarabande Label #3020666302

(Contains no Streisand vocals)

Baby, It's Cold Outside (2005)
Starbucks Exclusive CD EMI #LMM-644
Contains rare unreleased English version of Gounod's Ave Maria

The Lyrics Of Alan & Marilyn Bergman (1996)(4-CD Set)
Threesome Music DIDX 403206-9 Rare Promotional-only release Issued in custom 12x6 black box with 16-page booklet.
Songs included are: A Child Is Born, A Piece Of Sky, After The Rain, Ask Yourself Why?, Between Yesterday And Tomorrow, Can You Tell The Moment?, I Believe In Love, If I Close My Eyes, No Matter What Happens, One Day, Ordinary Miracles (studio version), Papa, Can You Hear Me?, The Summer Knows, Summer Me Winter Me, The Way He Makes Me Feel, The Way We Were, What Are You Doing The Rest Of Your Life?, Will Someone Ever Look At Me That Way?, You Don't Bring Me Flowers.

What is unique about this box set is that One Day is included. This has never been released on CD. The track is the same as what appears on the 1990 Earth Day TV Special, except the ending has newly recorded verses of Somewhere. Streisand recorded three versions of One Day in the late 60's for the What About Today album, but remained unreleased. The TV Special is one of the 60's versions produced by Jack Gold and music by Michel Legrand.

The Collection (2004) C3K 24639
3-CD set issued in beautiful custom 6x10 box with Funny Girl, The Way We Were, & A Star Is Born albums.

The Collection 2004 Slipcase version C3K 94970

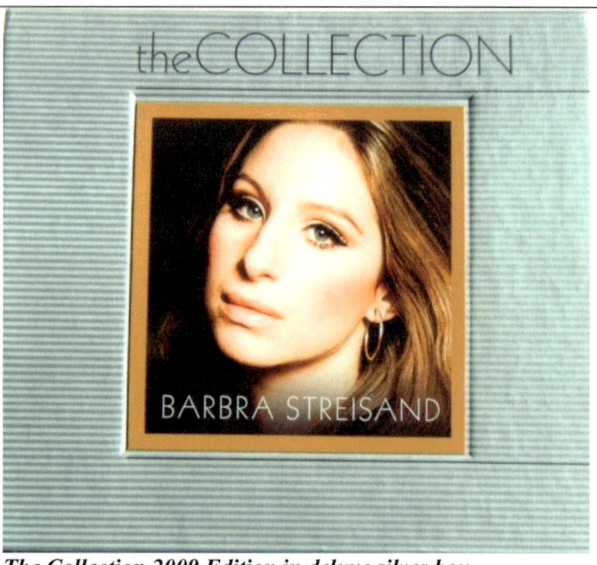

The Collection 2009 Edition in deluxe silver box #88697559612

The Essential 3.0 Limited Edition (2008) #88687345702 3-CD Set issued in unique digipak with bonus disc (Letting Go, A Love Like Ours, At The Same Time, By The Way, Unusual Way, Evergreen-Live, Wild Is The Wind, On My Way To You, After The Rain)

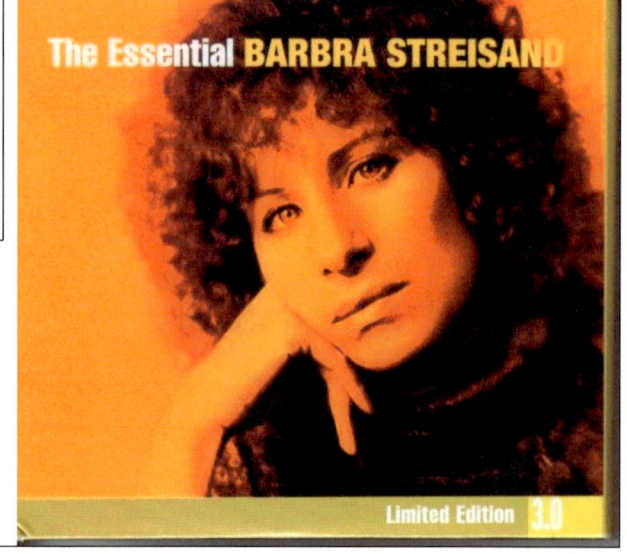

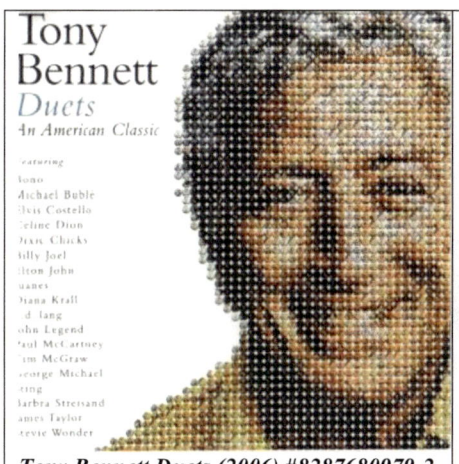

Tony Bennett Duets (2006) #8287680979-2
Contains duet with Streisand (Smile)

Live In Concert 2006 Sampler (2007 release) #88697103222 Promo-only (1-CD) Act 1 Program

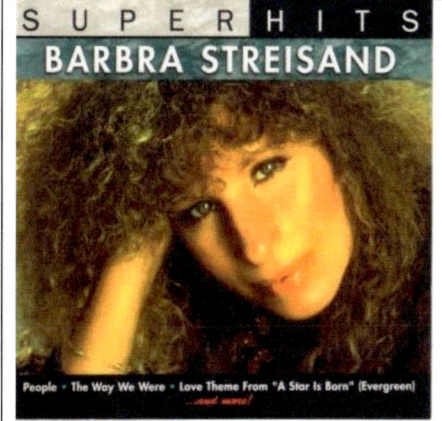

Super Hits (2007) #A 721560
Miss Marmelstein, People, Funny Girl, The Way We Were, Evergreen, Main Event, Woman In Love, Somewhere, If I Could, I Dreamed Of You

Little Fockers Soundtrack (2010) Varese Sarabande #3020670582
Contains no Streisand vocals

This Christmas John Travolta & Olivia Newton John (2012)
Universal Music #B0017624-02
Streisand recorded a special vocal for the duo on I'll Be Home For Christmas

Super Hits (2007) Misprint with Look & Our Corner Of The Night listed on back CD cover, disc has correct tracks

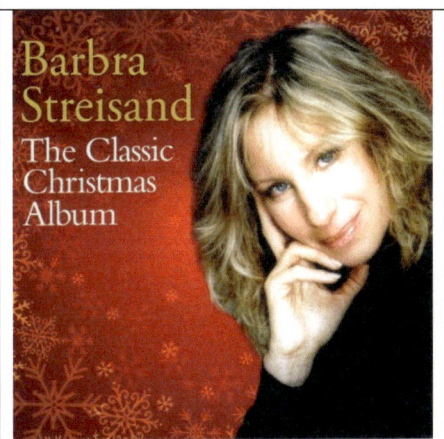

The Classic Christmas Album (2013) #88883769332 Sony Legacy
Have Yourself A Merry Little Christmas, The Christmas Song, I'll Be Home For Christmas, A Christmas Love Song, The Best Gift, It Must Have Been The Mistletoe, I Remember, I Wonder As I Wander, Silent Night, Snowbound, Jingle Bells?, My Favorite Things, Christmas Lullaby, O Little Town Of Bethlehem, Christmas Mem'ries, White Christmas

There's also a Sony promo copy issued with picture sleeve in plastic wallet, no catalog number

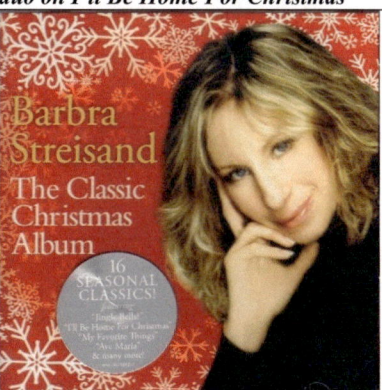

2014 Edition with revised cover and different back cover and change in selection of songs #888430130821

Mary J Blige-A Mary Christmas (2013) #B0018910-02 Verve Music
Duet with Streisand on When You Wish Upon A Star (featuring Chris Botti)

Funny Girl Broadway Cast Recording Deluxe 50th Anniversary Edition (2014)
#B0019958-02 Capital Records Digitally Remastered issued in custom box with LP, CD and 48-page book.

Radio Shows on CD

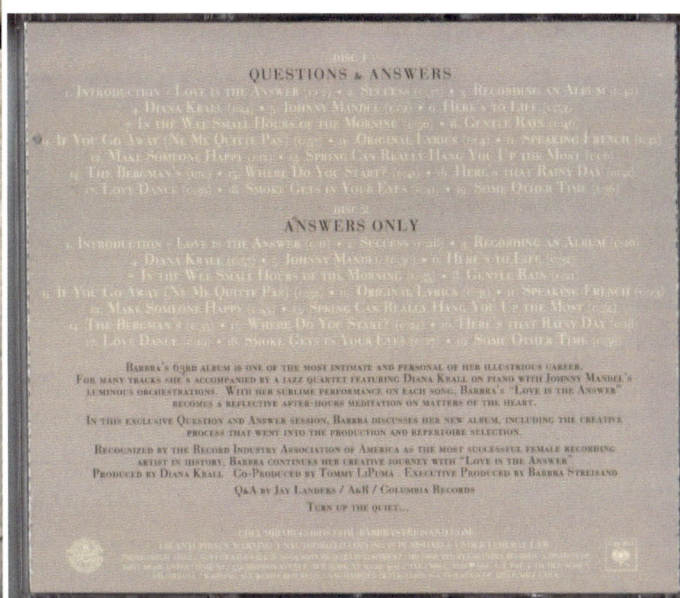

Love Is The Answer Interview Q & A (2009)
Rare promotional-only 2-CD set with disc 1 featuring the questions and answers, and disc 2 with only the answers.
Includes eight-page booklet issued in jewel case. Q&A 20-minutes.
#886975973-1-2

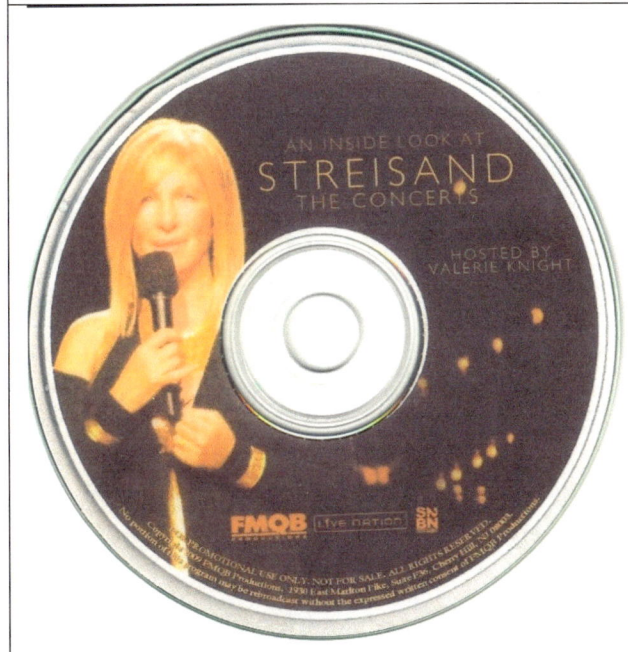

An Inside Look At Streisand: The Concerts (2009) Hosted by Valerie Knight. Promotional-only release with highlights from the 2006 Concert TV special (which aired in 2009).
Features song selections with commentary by host.
FMQB Productions (no catalog #).

From The Way We Were To The Way We Are (2011) (England) BBC Radio 2 Promotional-only (no catalog #) plain sleeve. 90-minute program of music and interview with Don Black to promote What Matters Most.

CD's International

The following are alternate releases to Streisand's albums. All CBS/Sony Label unless noted.

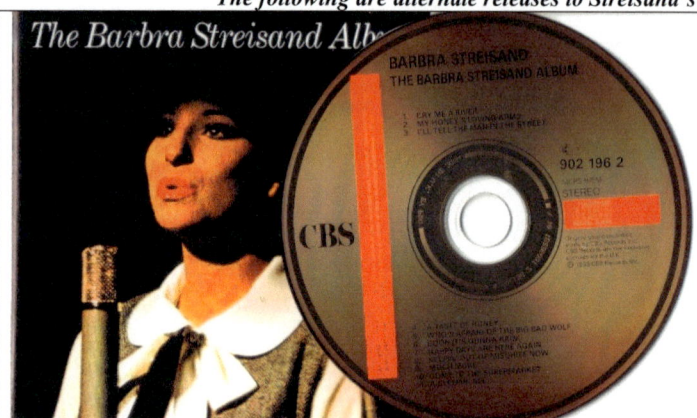

The Barbra Streisand Album (1990's Reissue with Gold top CD)
(England) #9021962

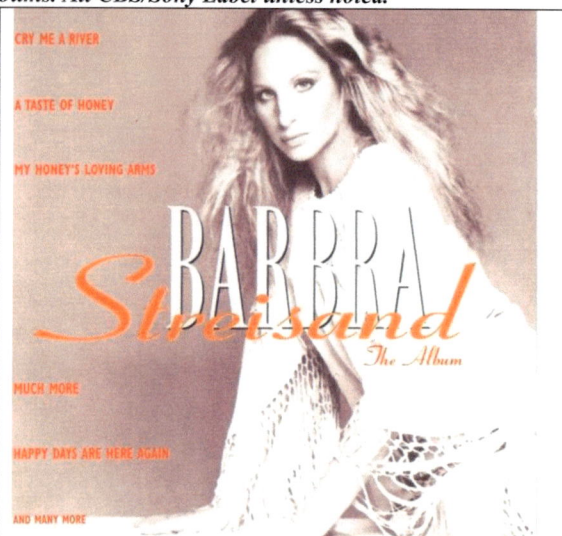

The Album (1995 Reissue of The Barbra Streisand Album)
(Germany) #4510862

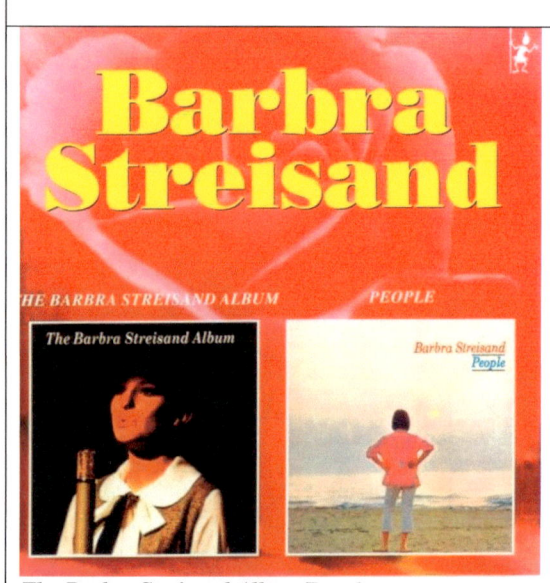

The Barbra Streisand Album/People
(Russia) 2001 Landy Star (no catalog number) (both on one disc)

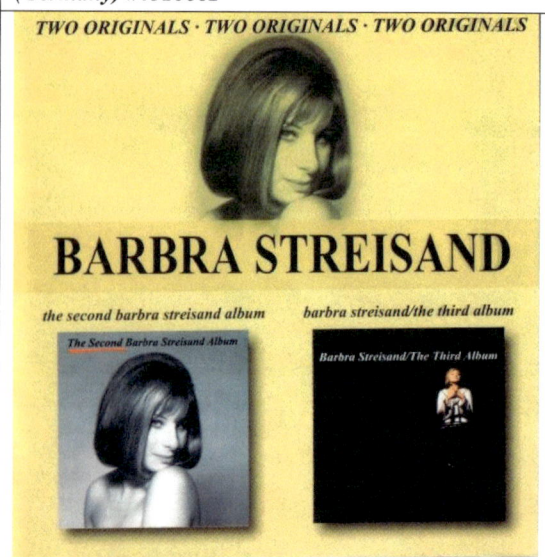

Two Originals-The Second Album & The Third Album
(Russia) 2001 #M311 (Picture Disc) (both on one disc)

People (2003 Reissue)
(England) #4604982

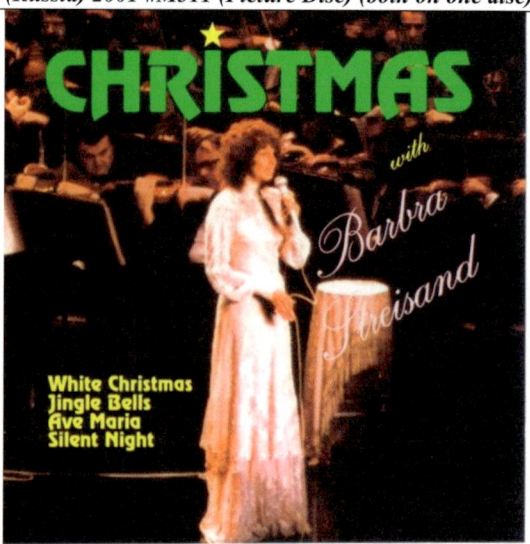

Christmas With Barbra (1990 Reissue of The Christmas Album)
(Germany) Duchesse Label #352093

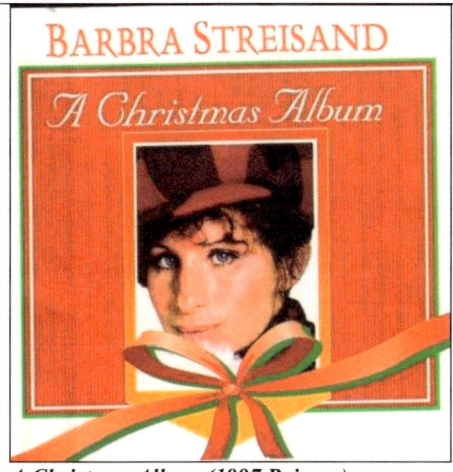

A Christmas Album (1997 Reissue)
(Australia) Rainbow Label #699007

The Way We Were (1990's)
(Taiwan) #4749112 Gorgeous Deluxe 24K Gold CD issued in gold jewel case

Butterfly (1994 Reissue)
(England)#9828322

A Star Is Born (1990's)
(Taiwan) #4749052 Gorgeous Deluxe 24K Gold CD issued in gold jewel case

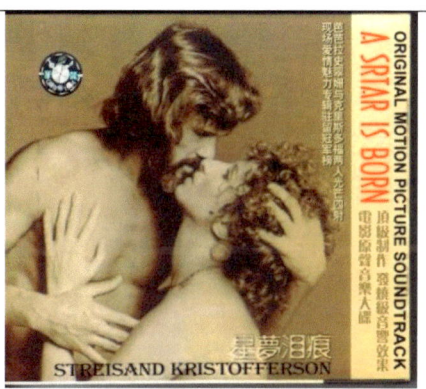

A Star Is Born (2002 Reissue)
(China) #B0108 issue in slip case with picture disc (misprint in title)

The Way We Were/A Star Is Born (2002)
(France) #CB872 2-CD set in custom box

UK version in plain slip cover
#5175562

Superman (1993 Reissue)
(England) #CDCBS 86030
Special edition with extended booklet includes the 1977 original insert pages & photos

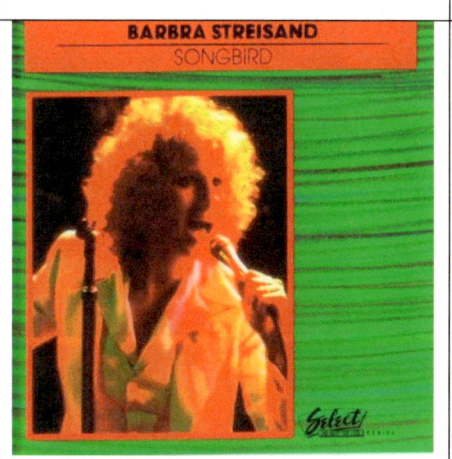

Songbird (1988 Reissue)
(Australia) #4627282

Guilty (2011 Reissue)
(Germany) #88697995652
Issued in book-style cover

169

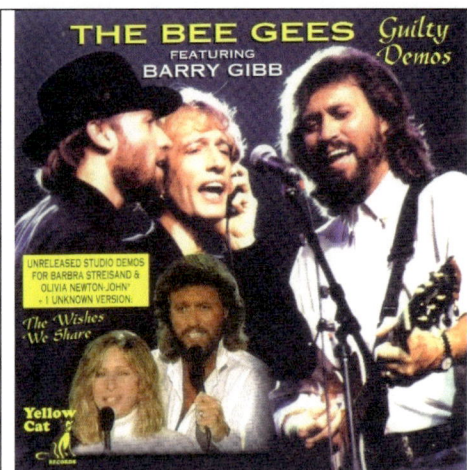

Guilty Demos (1993 pressing)
(Italy) Yellow Cat #005
Features Barry Gibb rehearsal vocals on songs for the Guilty album. Contains no Streisand vocals.

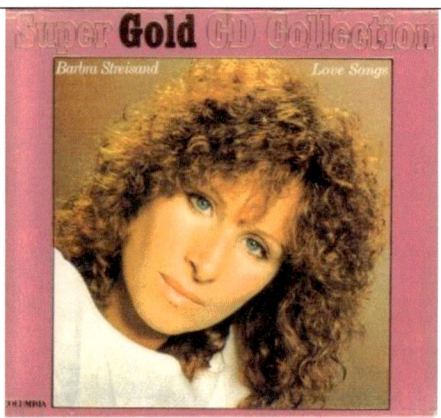

Love Songs (Memories)(1990's issue)
(China) (Disc says made in Australia)
SMPT 3038-9 Beautiful Gold CD with slip cover

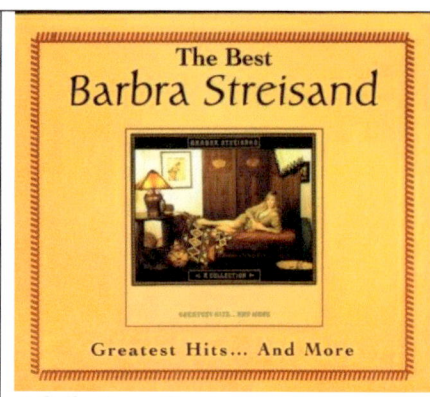

A Collection…Greatest Hits & More (1989)
(France) (Made in Austria for French Market) #4658459
Issued in custom slip cover

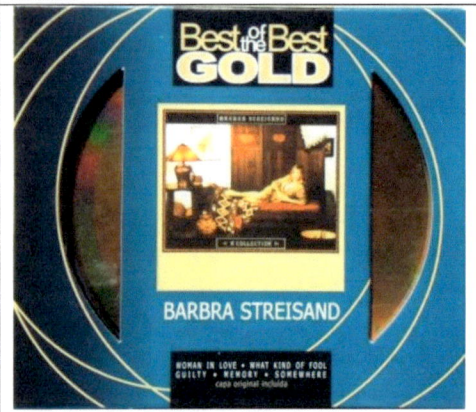

A Collection…Greatest Hits & More
(Brazil) #700439/2-465845
Gold CD pressing

A Collection…Greatest Hits And More (1999 Bootleg reissue)
(Germany) Storm label #KJF-31-876

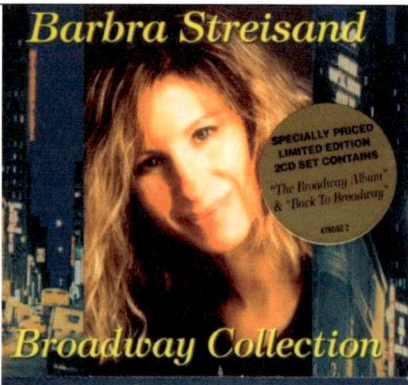

Broadway Collection (The Broadway Album & Back To Broadway) (1993)
(Australia) #476592-2 (2-CD Set)
Custom slip cover

The Broadway Album/Back To Broadway (2007 Reissue) #88697127822
(England) slip cover

(UK also released these other sets with designed slip covers: Yentl/Emotion #7842; The Barbra Streisand Album/People #7792; Guilty/Guilty Too #7782)

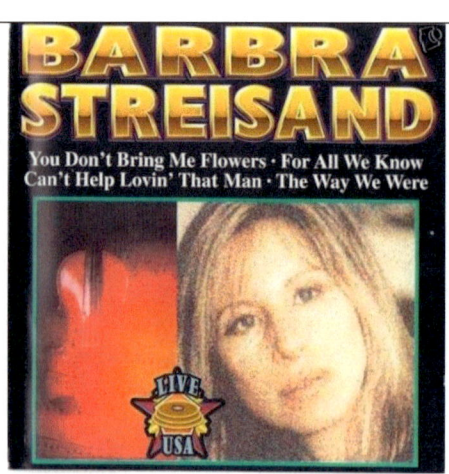

Barbra Streisand Live (1994 Bootleg of Anaheim Concert)
(Germany) LSD#15224

I'm Still Here (1994 Bootleg of Anaheim Concert)
(Germany) #P910118

170

Barbra Streisand Live (1994 Bootleg of Anaheim Concert) (Germany) Imprat Records #409346	**Higher Ground (2007 Reissue)** (China) #1193 (Different back cover)	**Studio Selections From Timeless (2000)** XPCD-1308 Promotional-only (England) Issued in card sleeve (The Way We Were, Evergreen, Tell Him, People, Guilty, & You Don't Bring Me Flowers)
Timeless DVD with Bonus CD My Name Is Barbra (2001) (Brazil) #746056/2-468784	**The Christmas Collection (2002)** (England) #518970-2 (2-CD Set) Beautiful Box set with A Christmas Album & Christmas Memories (Same release issued exclusive at Boarders)	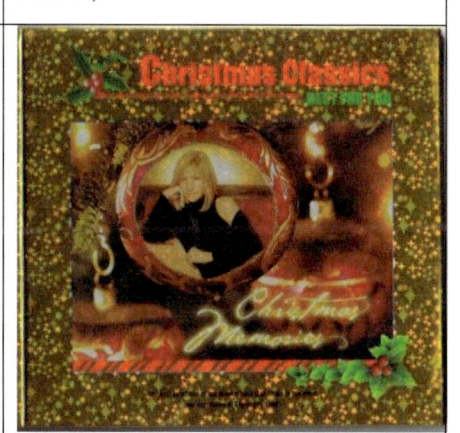 **Christmas Memories (2009 Issue)** (China)# SD0027 Issued in beautiful book-style gatefold cover
The Essential (2002) (Taiwan) C2K86123 (2-CD Set) Issued in slipcover with lyric sheet & foldout insert with photos	**The Essential (2002)** (Taiwan) C2K86123 (2-CD Set) Beautiful Gold CD Limited Edition with slipcover (with lyric sheet & foldout insert	**Duets (2002)** (China) #D2CD-236 (2-CD Set) Slip cover with bonus disc of A Love Like Ours with tracks Woman In Love & Memory

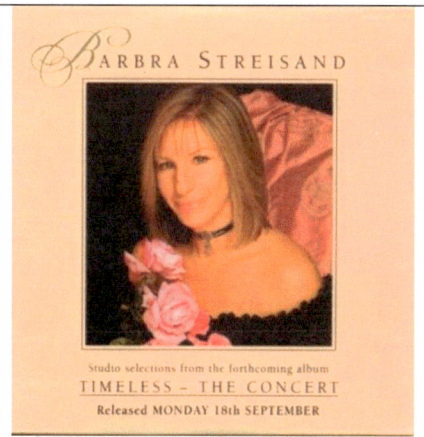

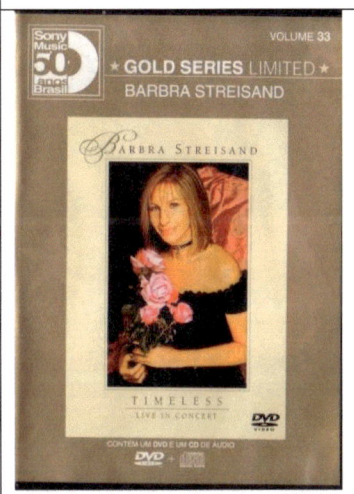

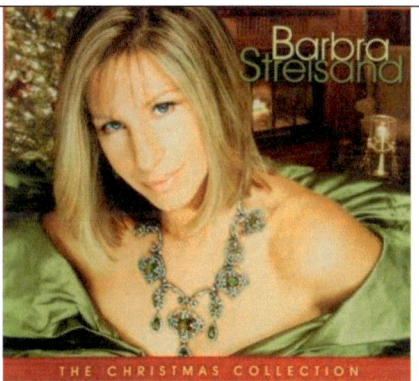

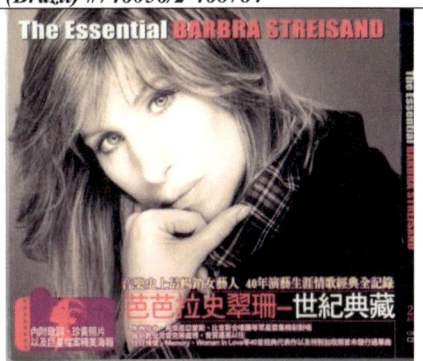

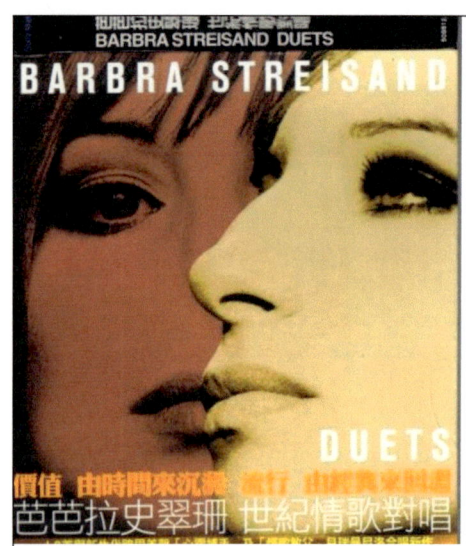

Duets (2002)
(Taiwan) #5098129
Slip cover with special insert booklet

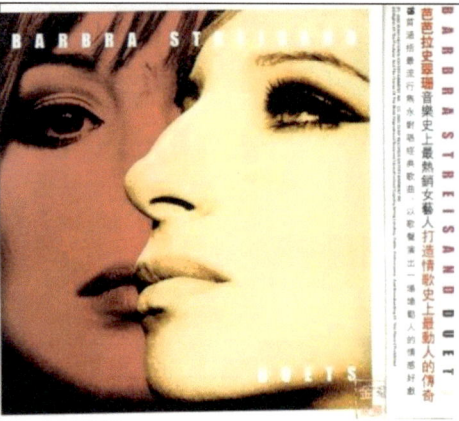

Duets (2002)
(China) #HL-1299
Gold CD in custom slip cover

Duets (2002)
(China) #509812-9
Issued in slip cover with lyric sheet

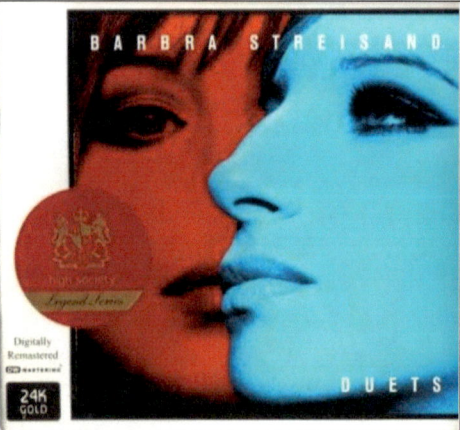

Duets (2007 Reissue)
(Made in Japan for Asian Market)
#88697051022
24K Gold CD issued in gatefold book-style cover

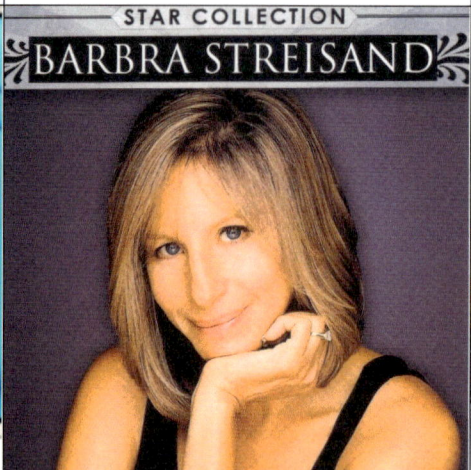

Star Collection (2013)
(Venezuela) Sony re-release of Duets
#5099750981290

The Movie Album (2003)
(China) Universal #H790
Gold 2-CD Set with Duets CD as bonus in custom box

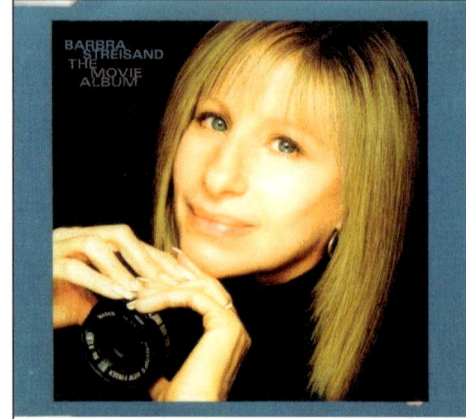

The Movie Album (2003)
(Austria) Promotional CD
#SAMPCD 13487-2
Issued with picture sleeve in slim jewel case

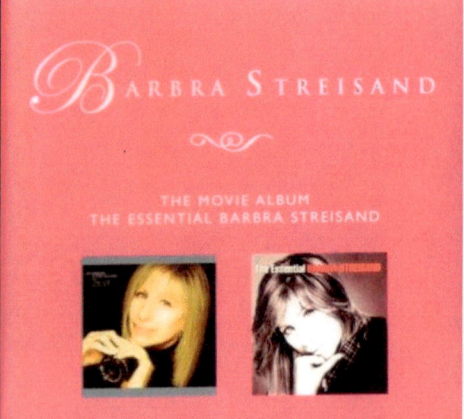

The Movie Album/The Essential (2003)
(England) #514840-2
2-CD set in custom slipcase

The Movie Album (2003)
(Taiwan) #513421-2
Slip cover with fold-out poster insert

The Movie Album/Duets/Guilty (2007) (India) 3-CD Box set Sony/BMG (catalog number of each CD listed on back cover)	**Best Of The Best (2011 release)** (Canada) 3-CD box set with Higher Ground, The Movie Album, & Guilty Pleasures) (Unknown catalog number)	**Guilty Too/Guilty (2005)** (England) Sony Promotional-only 2-CD set issued in black glossy box (no catalog number; CD's have regular CBS UK catalog numbers) (Guilty Pleasures was renamed Guilty Too in the UK)
Guilty Pleasures (2005) (Taiwan) #82876726632 CD/DVD set with unique OBI & insert sheet	**Guilty Pleasures (2005)** (China) Universal #DSD-1931 (2-CD set) Gold CD's with bonus CD Duets in custom box	**Guilty Too/Guilty (2006 Reissue)** (England) #828767788029 2-CD set in custom box
Live In Concert 2006 (2007) (Taiwan) #88697019222 (2-CD set) With OBI & lyric insert sheet (in jewel case) Also China Gold pressed 2-CD set Polydor #725684796246	**Love Is The Answer (2009)** (Taiwan) Deluxe 2-CD set #88697482832 With OBI & lyric insert sheet (in jewel case	**Love Is The Answer (2009)** (Poland-EEC) #8897593682 Eco-Style designed box where CD slides out, no insert booklet.

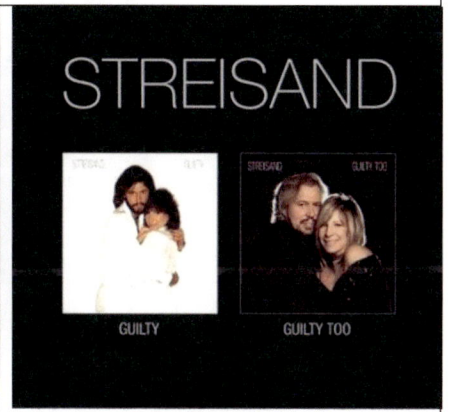

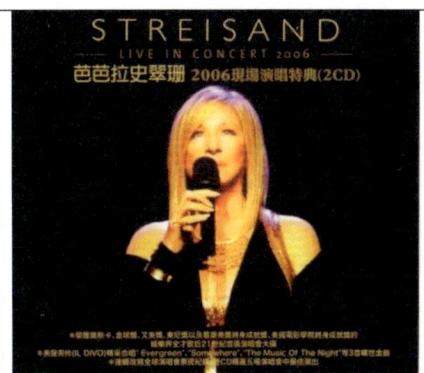

One Night Only (2010)
(China) #CY0220 DVD/CD set (Duets CD)
Unique metallic-style designed box with poster

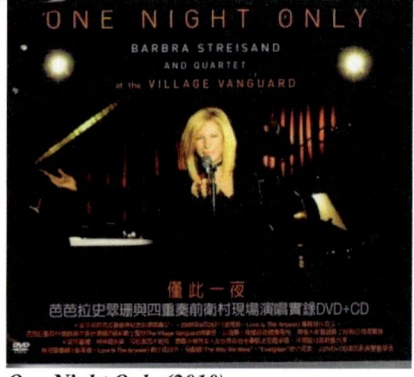

One Night Only (2010)
(Taiwan) #8869788798-9 (DVD/CD)
With slip cover in jewel case

What Matters Most (2011)
(Taiwan) #88697940572 (Deluxe 2-CD set)
With OBI & lyric insert sheet in glossy digipak

What Matters Most (2011)
(Poland) #88697954402
Eco-Style designed box where CD slides out, no booklet.

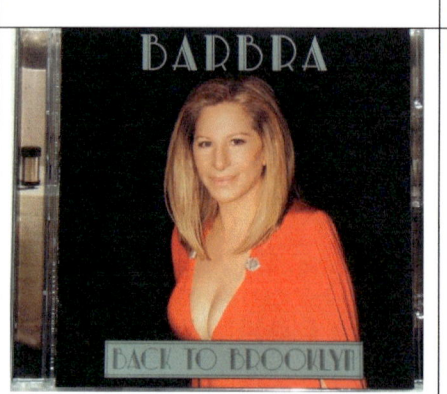

Back To Brooklyn (2013)
(Russia) #88843021642
Issued in jewel case with four-page insert sleeve

Partners (2011) Deluxe Edition 2-CD set
(Taiwan) #888750141620
Issued in custom slipcover with lyric insert sheet. In glossy finish digipak.
(UK Deluxe edition on one disc, issued in jewel case #888750-1640-25)

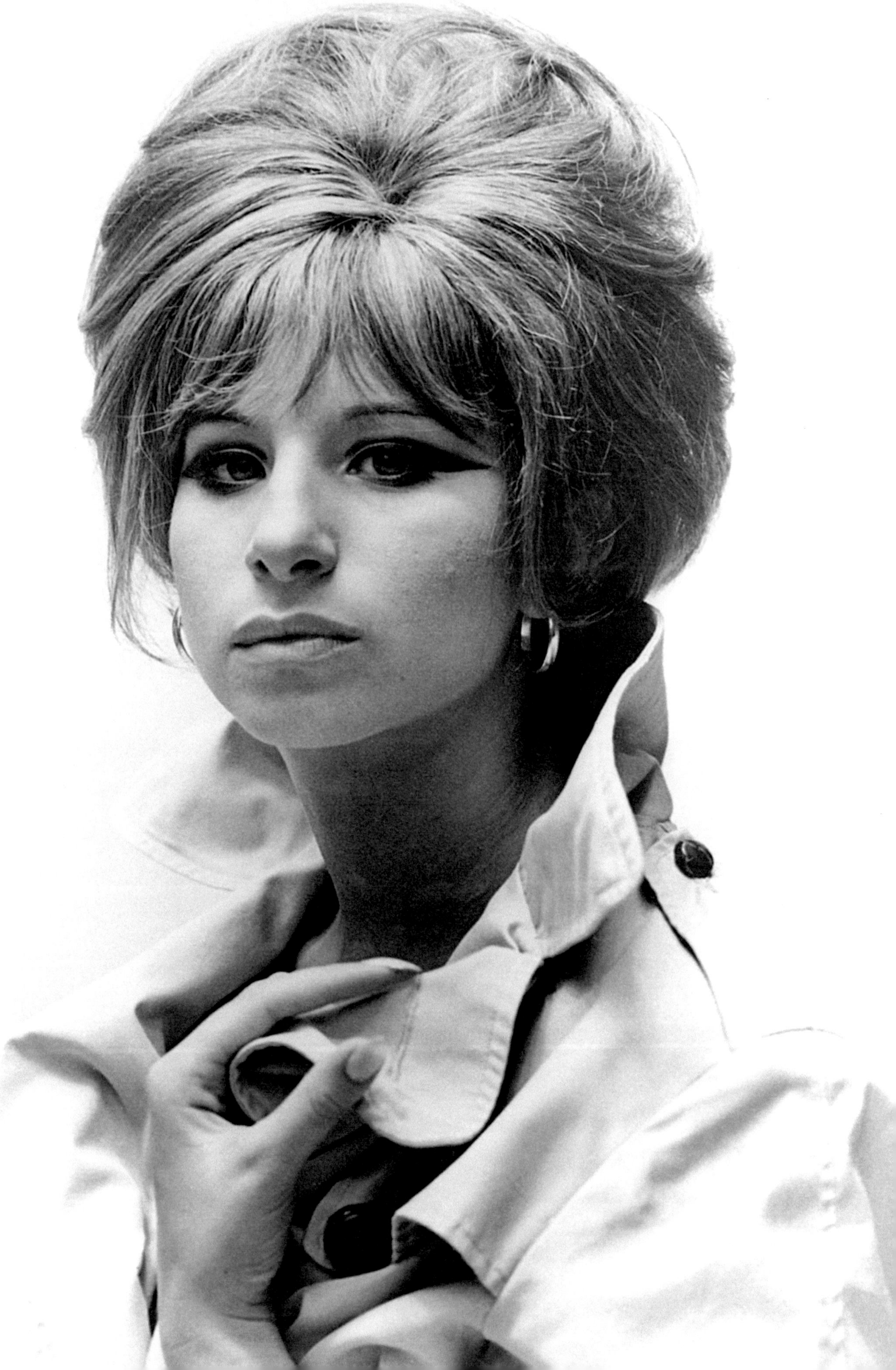

Japanese CD's

Like the Japanese vinyl, Music Collector's are interested in the Japanese CD's for the premium quality pressings. In the same tradition as the LP's, the Japanese CD's are issued with a decorative OBI strip and include a Japanese/English lyric sheet or booklet. Presented here are some of the Japanese editions of Streisand's albums. It's interesting to note that the first few CD's released in the US in the 1980's had Japanese pressed CD's.

(Front cover) *(Back cover)*

One of the rarest CD's is this Promotional-only release limited to 100 pressings, issued with no OBI. Gorgeous double foldout digipak.

Special Selection (1992) XDDP-93080-1 (2-CD Set)
Disc 1: Places That Belong To You, For All We Know, Evergreen, Prisoner, My Heart Belongs To Me, You Don't Bring Me Flowers, The Way We Were, All In Love Is Fair, Stoney End, We're Not Makin' Love Anymore, Woman In Love, All I Ask Of You, Guilty, Memory, Somewhere. Disc 2: (from Just For The Record) Moon River, Family-Recording 1965 Second Hand Rose (Barbra's Mother), Act II Medley from My Name Is Barbra, 1965 Emmy Awards, Hello Dolly, Friars Club Tribute, Since I Fell For You, Cryin' Time, You Don't Bring Me Flowers, You'll Never Know, A Piece Of Sky (Demo/Soundtrack)

(Inside foldout digipak)

Color Me Barbra (1992 pressing)
SRCS 5955 with lyric booklet and the original 1966 four-page color insert is included

A Christmas Album (1990 Edition)
#28DP 5291 Picture Disc with box-style OBI and lyric booklet

Hello Dolly (1995 pressing)
Philips #PHCP 1437
With lyric booklet

Greatest Hits (1992 pressing)
SRCS 5851 with lyric booklet

Live At The Forum (1992 pressing)
SRCS 5853 with lyric insert

The Way We Were (1992 pressing)
SRCS 5854 with lyric booklet

Butterfly (1992 pressing)
SRC 55885 with lyric booklet

Lazy Afternoon (1992 pressing)
SRCS 5886 with lyric booklet

Classical Barbra (1987 pressing)
35DP 163 Box-OBI with lyric booklet
Reissued 1992 with full back cover
SRCS 5855

Greatest Hits Volume 2 (1980's pressing)
35DP 161 Box-OBI with lyric booklet

Guilty (1983 pressing)
35DP7 Box-OBI with lyric booklet
Also issued 3DP7-1 1A1 with Gold top-pressed CD (Rare)
Reissued 1992 SRCS 5857

Memories (1992 pressing)
SRCS 5889 with lyric booklet

Emotion (1984)
#32DP 188 Box-style OBI with lyric book and rare back cover
Also reissued 1992

The Broadway Album (1985)
#32DP 293 Box-OBI with lyric booklet
Also reissued 1992

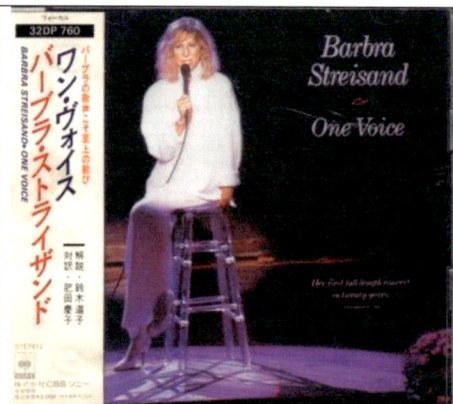

One Voice (1987)
#32DP 760 with lyric booklet

Till I Loved You (1988)
#25DP 5293 with lyric insert sheet

A Collection…Greatest Hits And More (1989)
CSCS 5062 with lyric insert sheet

The Prince Of Tides Soundtrack (1991)
SRCS 5778 with lyric booklet

Highlights Just For The Record (1992)
SRCS 5980 with lyric booklet

Just For The Record Box Set SRCS 5811-4 (1991) with lyric booklet

Back To Broadway (1993)
SRCS 6778 with lyric insert sheet

The Concert (1994)
SRCS 7546-7 (2-CD set) with lyric booklet

Highlights-The Concert (1995)
SRCS 7846 with lyric sheet

The Mirror Has Two Faces Soundtrack (1996)
SRCS 8247 with insert lyric sheet

Higher Ground (1997)
SRCS 8513 with lyric insert sheet

A Love Like Ours (1999)
SRCS 2142 with lyric insert sheet

Timeless (2000)
SRCS 2373-4 with lyric booklet (2-CD Set)

Christmas Memories (2001)
SICP 26 with lyric booklet

The Essential (2002) SICP 131-2 with lyric booklet (2-CD set)	*The Essential Blu-Spec CD* (2009 Release) SICP 20190/1 with lyric booklet (2-CD set) (Super Audio Disc)	*Duets* (2002) SICP-325 with lyric booklet
The Movie Album (2003) SICP 504 with lyric booklet	*Guilty 25th Anniversary Edition* (2005) SICP 984 with lyric booklet	*Guilty Pleasures* (2005) SICP 905 with lyric booklet
Live In Concert 2006 (2007 Release) SICP 1478-9 (2-CD set) with lyric booklet (Digipak)	*Love Is The Answer* (2009) Deluxe Edition SICP 2442-3 with lyric booklet (2-CD Set) (Digipak)	*What Matters Most* (2011) Deluxe Edition SICP 3280-1 with lyric booklet (2-CD set) (Digipak)
Release Me (2012) SICP 3563 with lyric booklet Issued in jewel case	*Back To Brooklyn* (2013) BSCD2 (Blu-Spec) SICP 30429 With lyric booklet (Digipak)	*Partners* (2014) BSCD2 (Blue-Spec) SICP 30729 Deluxe edition on one disc issued in jewel case. With lyric booklet

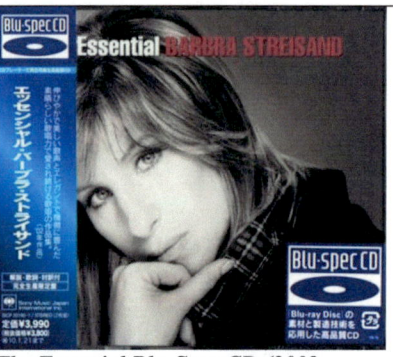

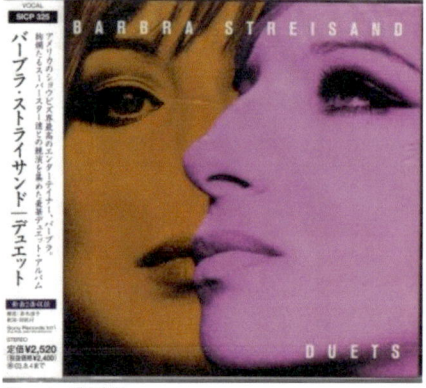

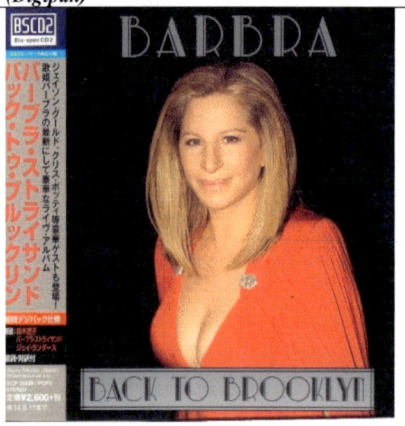

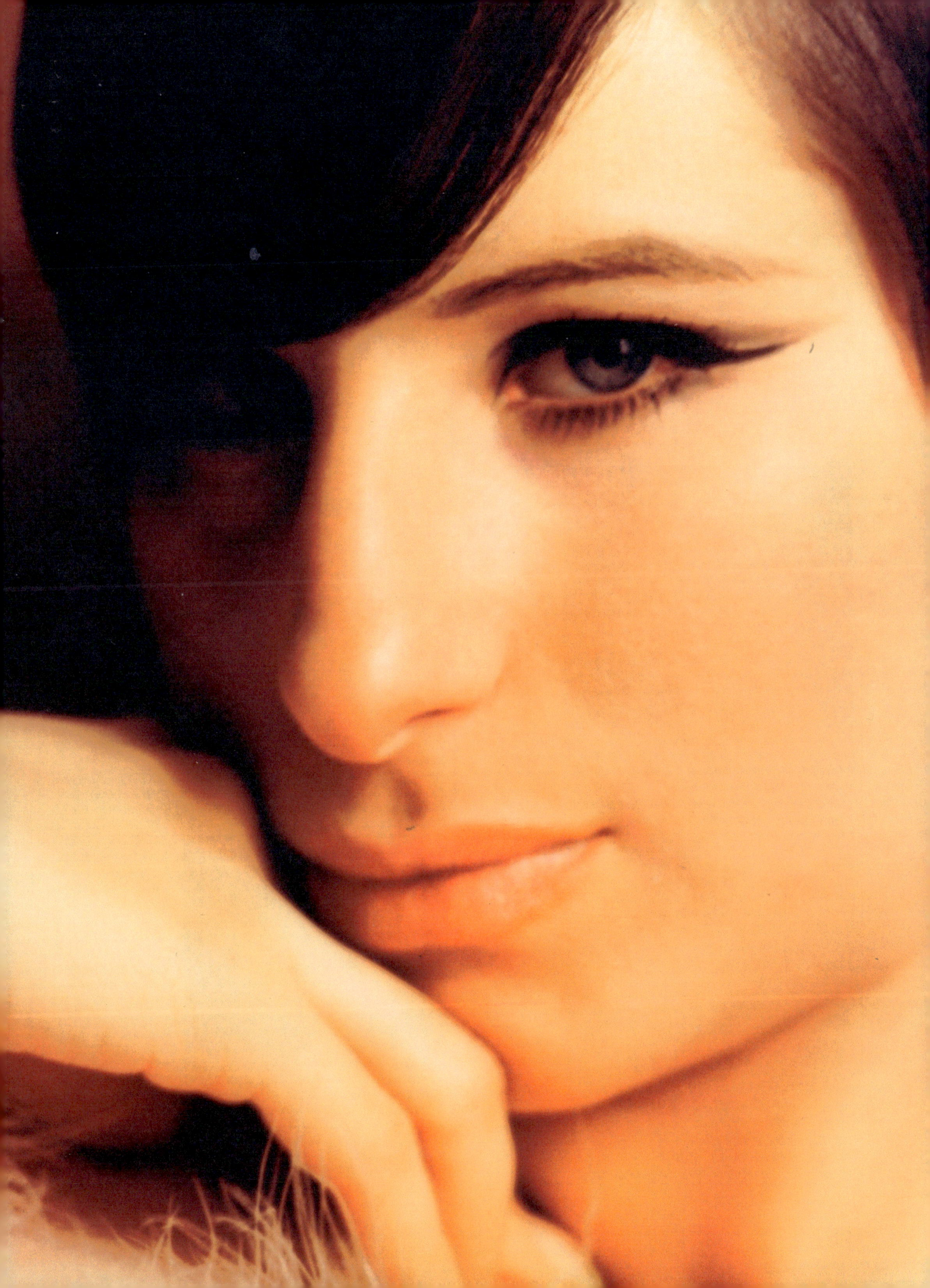

The following International CD's are compilation releases.

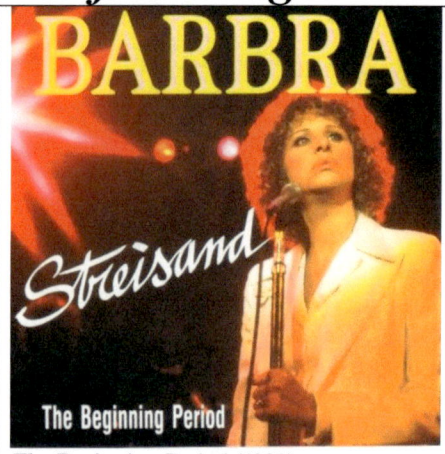

The Beginning Period (1988)
(Germany) Duchesse Label #352040
(People, Second Hand Rose, The Shadow Of Your Smile, I Got Plenty Of Nothing, All That I Want, Where's That Rainbow?, Absent Minded Me, Fine And Dandy, How Does The Wine Taste?, He Touched Me, No More Songs For Me, Quiet Night, When In Rome, Supper Time, Love Is A Bore, Autumn) (Also issued on LP (1990) #152040)

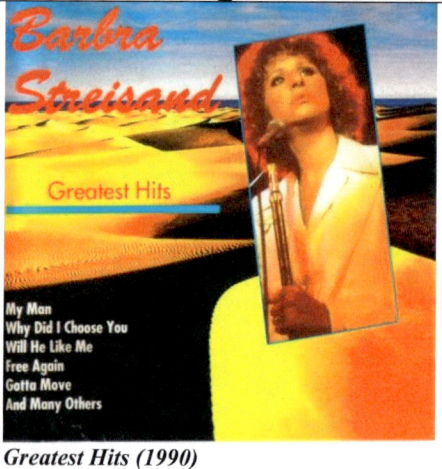

Greatest Hits (1990)
(Germany) Universe #UN3041
(My Man, How Much Of The Dream Comes True, Kind Of Man A Woman Needs, Why Did I Choose You, Will He Like Me, I'm All Smiles, My Lord And Master, Don't Like Goodbyes, Free Again, Don't Rain On My Parade, Happy Days, My Coloring Book, Gotta Move, Sam You Made The Pants Too Long, My Name Is Barbra Medley)

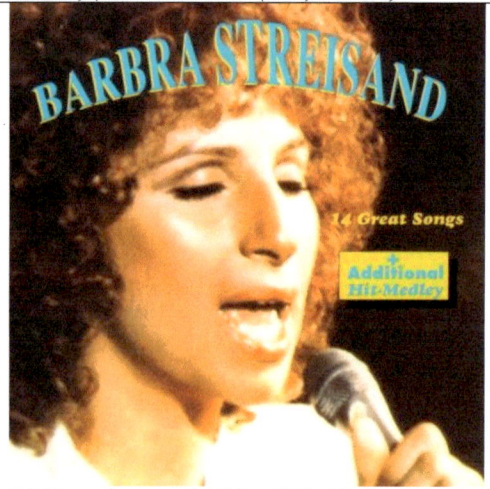

14 Great Songs + Additional Hit Medley (1990)
(Germany) Duchesse #352088
(Same tracks as 1990 Germany Greatest Hits release)
Also issued on LP #152088

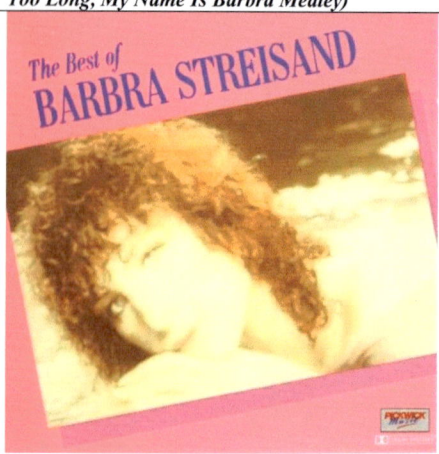

The Best Of Barbra Streisand (1990)
(Australia) Pickwick Music #PKD 3086
(My Name Is Barbra, A Kid Again, I'm Five Jenny Rebecca, My Pa, Sweet Zoo, Where Is The Wonder, I Can't See It, Someone To Watch Over Me, I've Got No Strings, If You Were The Only Boy In The World, Why Did I Choose You, My Man)

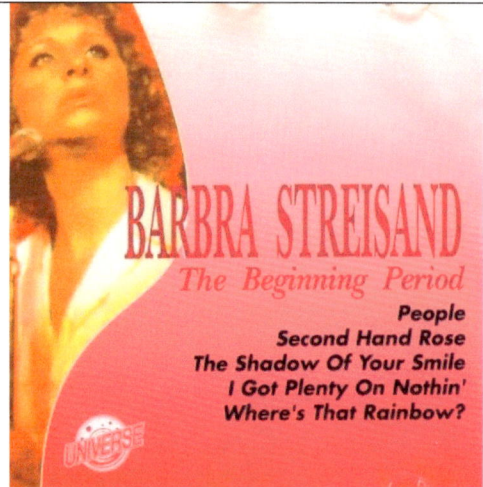

The Beginning Period (1991)
(Germany) Universe #UN 3039
(Same tracks as original 1988 German release)

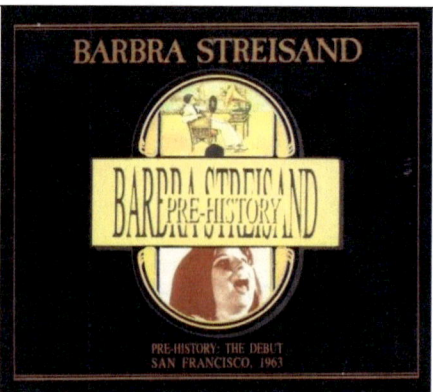

Pre-History: The Debut San Francisco 1963 (1991)
(Italy) Dejavu Label #DVRECD65 (Hungry i nightclub show)
(Any Place I Hang My Hat Is Home, Keepin Out Of Mischief, Cry Me A River, Lover Come Back To Me, I Stayed Too Long At The Fair, My Honey's Loving Arms, Soon It's Gonna Rain, When The Sun Comes Out, Much More, Like A Straw In The Wind, Right As The Rain, Down With Love, Bewitched, Happy Days)

Original Tracks (1991)
(Spain) Eltoro #T8904
(People, Second Hand Rose, Shadow Of Your Smile, I Got Plenty Of Nothing, All That I Want, Where's That Rainbow?, Absent Minded Me, Fine And Dandy, How Does The Wine Taste?, He Touched Me, No More Songs For Me, Quiet Night, When In Rome, Supper Time, Love Is A Bore, Autumn)

Barbra Streisand (1991)
(Singapore) CTAT-2028
(Woman In Love, Lost Inside Of You, You Don't Bring Me Flowers, Evergreen, The Love Inside, New York State Of Mind, Memory, Comin' In And Out Of Your Life, The Way We Were, No More Tears, My Heart Belongs To Me, Guilty)

The Very Best Of Barbra Streisand (1992)
(Korea) Aridna Label #DRC-378
(Woman In Love, Memory, Evergreen, You Don't Bring Me Flowers, Guilty, People, What Kind Of Fool, The Way We Were, The Main Event, Way He Makes Me Feel, Somewhere, No More Tears, Comin' In And Out Of Your Life)

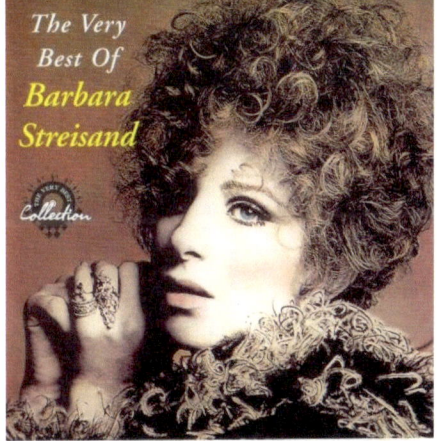

The Very Best Of Barbra Streisand (1993)
(Germany) Bootleg-no catalog number
(Free The People, Let Me Go, People, Who's Afraid Of The Big Bad Wolf? Sam You Made The Pants Too Long, Guilty, Woman In Love, Run Wild, Promises, The Love Inside, Life Story, Lover Man, My Funny Valentine, Honey Pie, That's A Fine Kind Of Freedom, Memory, Second Hand Rose, My Heat Belongs To Me, New York State Of Mind, Way We Were, I'm All Smiles, Comin' In And Out Of Your Life)

Barbra Streisand (1993)
(Germany) Universe DCD 22026 (2-CD Set)

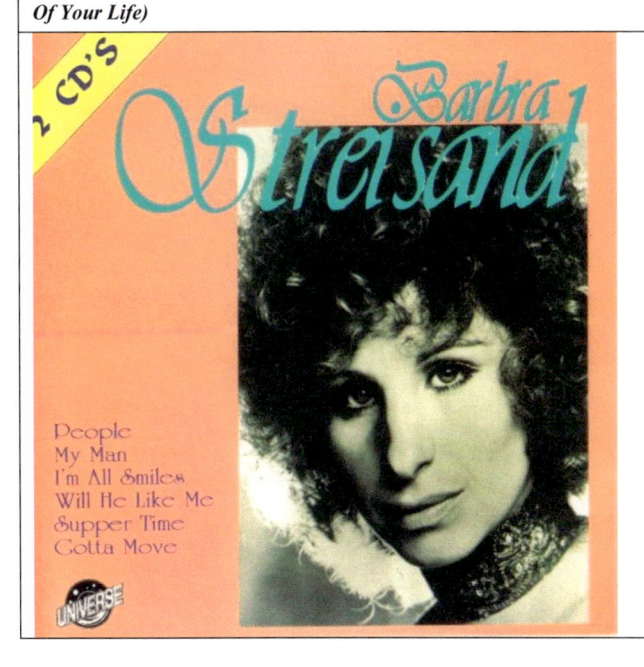

Disc 1
My Man, How Much Of The Dream Comes True, Kind Of Man A Woman Needs, Why Did I Choose You, Will He Like Me, I'm All Smiles, My Lord And Master, Don't Like Goodbyes, Free Again, Don't Rain On My Parade, Happy Days Are Here Again, My Coloring Book, Gotta Move, Sam You Made The Pants Too Long, Medley (My Name Is Barbra)

Disc 2
People, Second Hand Rose, The Shadow Of Your Smile, I Got Plenty Of Nothing, All That I Want, Where's That Rainbow?, Absent Minded Me, Fine And Dandy, How Does The Wine Taste?, He Touched Me, No More Songs For Me, Quiet Night, When In Rome, Supper Time, Love Is A Bore, Autumn)

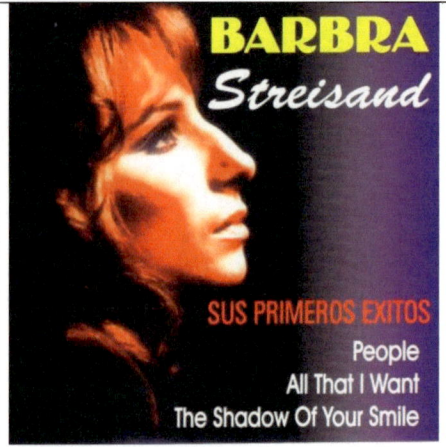

Sus Primeros Exitos (1994)
(Spain) Lamejor Label #50508
(People, Second Hand Rose, Shadow Of Your Smile, I Got Plenty Of Nothing, All That I Want, Where's That Rainbow?, Absent Minded Me, Fine And Dandy, How Does The Wine Taste?, He Touched Me, No More Songs For Me, Quiet Night, When In Rome, Supper Time, Love Is A Bore, Autumn)

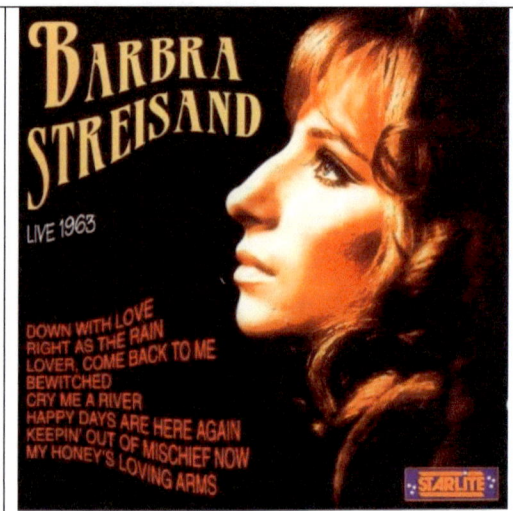

Live 1963 (1994)
(Germany-EEC) Starlite #CDS 51226
(Same tracks as the 1991 Italian CD release)

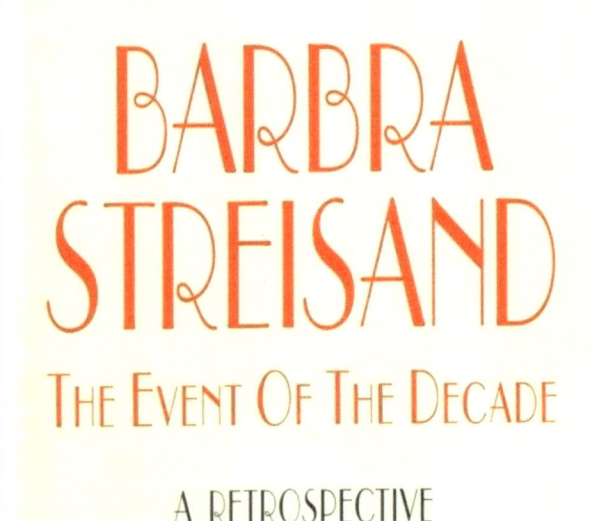

The Event Of The Decade A Retrospective (1994)
(England) #XPCD417 (2-CD Set) Rare Promotional-only release

Disc 1
You'll Never Know, People, Second Hand Rose, He Touched Me, Don't Rain On My Parade, My Man, Happy Days Are Here Again, The Way We Were, You Don't Bring Me Flowers, Evergreen, Memory, Stoney End, No More Tears, Guilty, Way He Makes Me Feel, Somewhere, All I Ask Of You, We're Not Makin Love Anymore, The Places That Belong To You, With One Look

Disc 2
Cry Me A River, Any Place I Hang My Hat Is Home, It Had To Be You, Will He Like Me, Lover Man (Oh Where Can He Be?), Starting Here Starting Now, Can't Help Lovin' That Man Of Mine, I'll Know, Ask Yourself Why, One Less Bell-A House Is Not A Home, By The Way, Speak Low, Papa Can You Hear Me?, Not While I'm Around, Answer Me, Everybody Says Don't, On A Clear Day, Places You Find Love, Here We Are At Last, Two People, As If We Never Said Goodbye, For All We Know

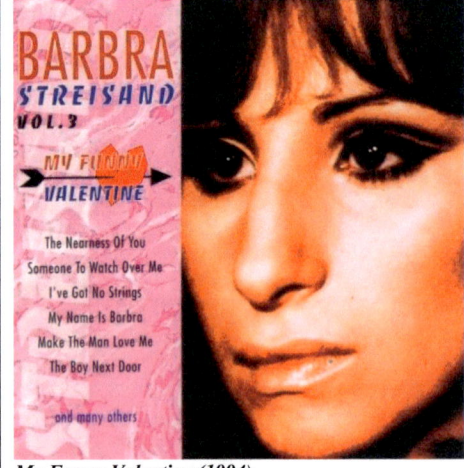

My Funny Valentine (1994)
(Germany) Duchesse #352147 Vol. 3
(My Funny Valentine, Someone To Watch Over Me, I've Got No Strings, If You Were The Only Boy In The World, My Pa, Nearness Of You, When Sunny Gets Blue, I'll Know, My Name Is Barbra, Make The Man Love Me, Lover Man, Jenny Rebecca, Sweet Zoo, Where Is The Wonder, I Can See It, The Boy Next Door)

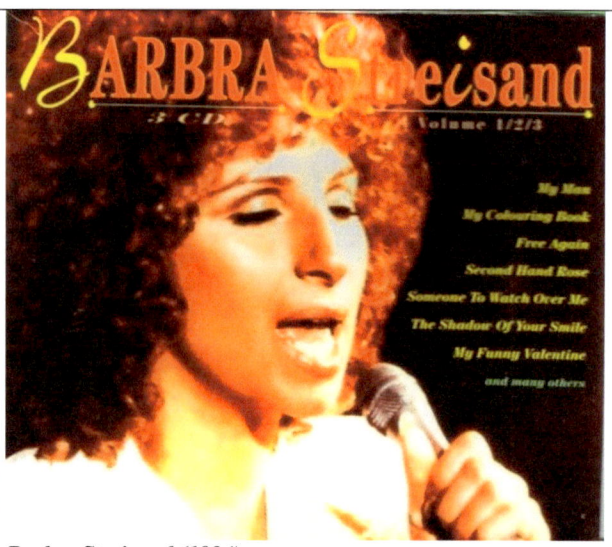

Barbra Streisand (1994)
(Germany) Duchesse #333512 (3-CD Box Set)
Contains The Beginning Period, 14 Great Songs + Additional Medley & My Funny Valentine

184

I'm All Smiles (1994)
(Germany) Cedar Label #CRB 528
(People, Why Did I Choose You, My Man, My Coloring Book, Gotta Move, Don't Rain On My Parade, My Melancholy Baby, Just In Time, As Time Goes By, He Touched Me, Absent Minded Me, Supper Time, How Does The Wine Taste?, I'm All Smiles, Second Hand Rose, Free Again)

Book Of Memories (1995)
(Germany) A Prori #791313
(My Man, How Much Of The Dream Comes True, Kind Of Man A Woman Needs, Why Did I Choose You, Will He Like Me, I'm All Smiles, My Lord And Master, Don't Like Goodbyes, Free Again, Don't Rain On My Parade, Happy Days, My Coloring Book, Sam You Made The Pants Too Long, Medley My Name Is Barbra)

The Sound Of Barbra Streisand (1995)
(Germany) Back Bitter BB 61056
(I'm All Smiles, Don't Like Goodbyes, Free Again, Happy Days, Gotta Move, Sam You Made The Pants Too Long, When In Rome, I Got Plenty Of Nothing, Don't Rain On My Parade, My Man, Will He Like Me, People, Second Hand Rose, Why Did I Choose You, Fine And Dandy, He Touched Me, Supper Time, Autumn)

As Grandes Interpretacoes de Barbra Streisand (1990's issue)
(Brazil) #746145/2-464491
(Free Again, Yesterdays, My Melancholy Baby, As Time Goes By, Shadow Of Your Smile, Second Hand Rose, People, Cry Me A River, A Taste Of Honey, My Coloring Book, My Name Is Barbra, Gotta Move)
(Originally issued on LP in 1969 #137543)

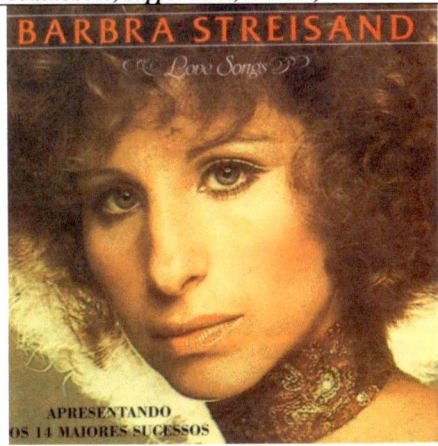

Love Songs (1996)
(Brazil) #419088
(Woman In Love, Memory, You Don't Bring Me Flowers, Guilty, All In Love Is Fair, I'd Rather Be Blue, No More Tears, Promises, Evergreen, Comin' In And Out Of Your Life, The Way We Were, Cry Me A River, Lost Inside Of You, People)
(Originally issued on LP 1983 #412042)

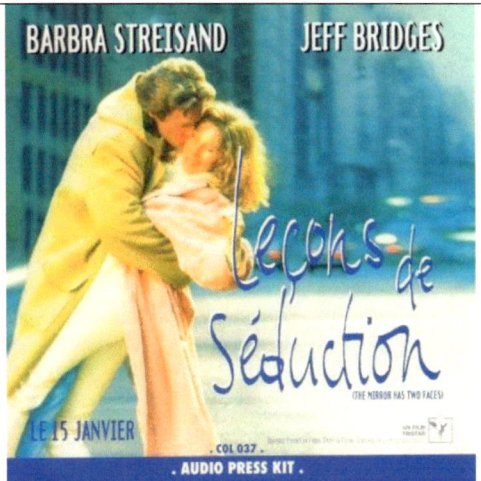

The Mirror Has Two Faces Audio Press Kit (1997)
(France) #037
Rare Promotional-only issued CD contains Radio Spots, Press Interview segments, and the single I Finally Found Someone.

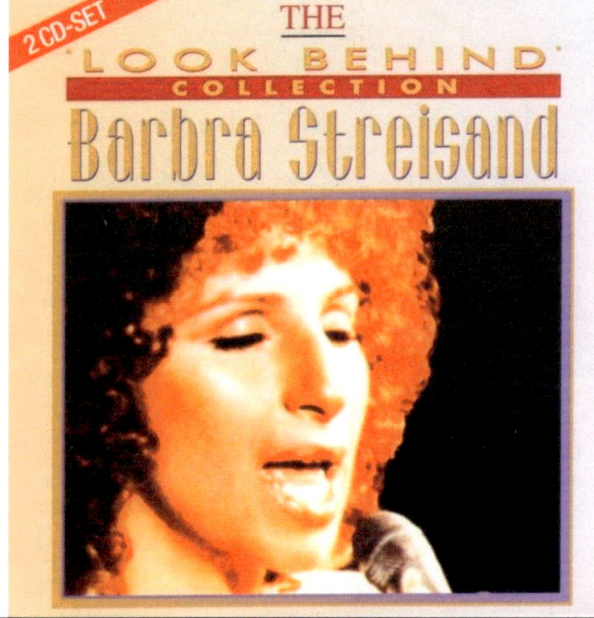

The Look Behind Collection (1997)
(Germany) Duchesse #LB 018 (2-CD Set)

Disc 1
People, Second Hand Rose, Shadow Of Your Smile, I Got Plenty Of Nothing, All That I Want, Where's That Rainbow?, Absent Minded Me, Fine And Dandy, How Does The Wine Taste?, He Touched Me, No More Songs For Me, Quiet Night, When In Rome, Supper Time, Love Is A Bore, Autumn

Disc 2
My Funny Valentine, Someone To Watch Over Me, I've Got Plenty Of Strings, If You Were The Only Boy In The World, My Pa, The Nearness Of You, When Sunny Gets Blue, I'll Know, My Name Is Barbra, Make The Man Love Me, Lover Man Oh Where Can You Be, Jenny Rebecca, Sweet Zoo, Where Is The Wonder, I Can See It, The Boy Next Door

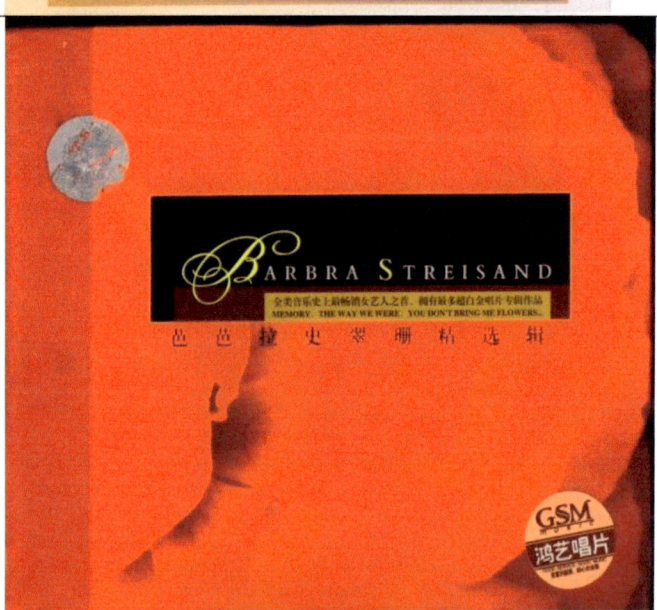

Barbra Streisand (1998)
(China) Cool Label #FA-03082 Gold Disc 2-CD Set in slip case

Disc 1
Memory, The Way We Were, Evergreen, You Don't Bring Me Flowers, Cry Me A River, Tell Him, I Finally Found Someone, Woman In Love, Guilty, Somewhere, People, Papa Can You Hear Me?, The Way He Makes Me Feel, My Heart Belongs To Me, Comin' In And Out Of Your Life, Wet

Disc 2
I Believe In Love, If I Loved You, Love Inside, Being Alive

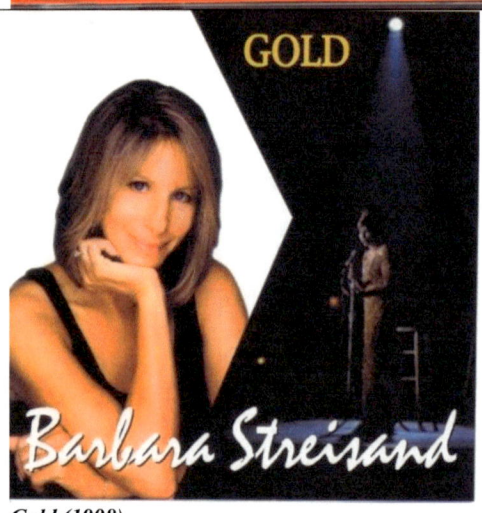

Gold (1998)
(Israel) Typhoon Records (Bootleg-no catalog number)
(I Finally Found Someone, Comin' In And Out Of Your Life, Memory, Papa Can You Hear Me?, With One Look, Woman In Love, Evergreen, Guilty, I Believe In Love, The Way We Were, Way He Makes Me Feel, Wet, Some Good Things Never Last, Somewhere, Sweet Inspiration-Where You Lead, Tell Him, As If We Never Said Goodbye, Kiss Me In The Rain)

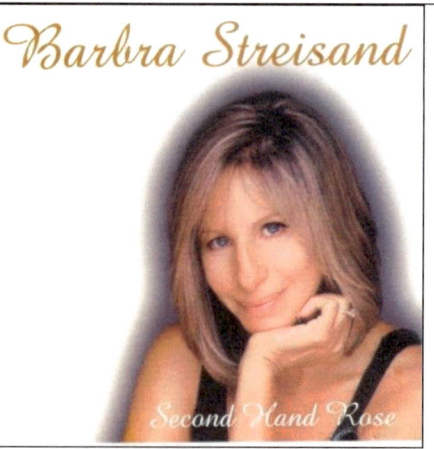

Second Hand Rose (1998)
(Hungry) Westline Coop #WL-103
(Shadow Of Your Smile, Second Hand Rose, The Minute Waltz, Gotta Move, Yesterday, I Got Plenty Of Nothing, Color Me Barbra Medley, Non C'est Bien, C'est Si Bon, Where Or When, Starting Here Starting Now, One Kiss, He Touched Me, Quiet Night, He Touched Me, How Much Of The Dream Comes True?, Kind Of Man A Woman Needs, No More Songs For Me, All That I Want, Where's That Rainbow?, My Name Is Barbra Medley)

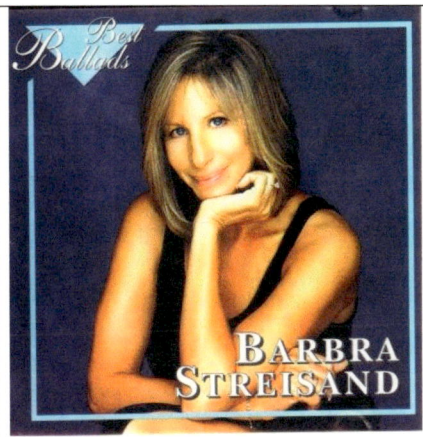

Best Ballads (1998)
(Austria) #488532-2
(Woman In Love, Tell Him, Memory, Guilty, Evergreen, You Don't Bring Me Flowers, Shadow Of Your Smile, I've Got A Crush On You, I Believe-You'll Never Walk Alone, Comin' In And Out Of Your Life, We're Not Makin' Love Anymore, The Way We Were, New York State Of Mind, A Man I Loved, Higher Ground, Superman, What Kind Of Fool, Kiss Me In The Rain)

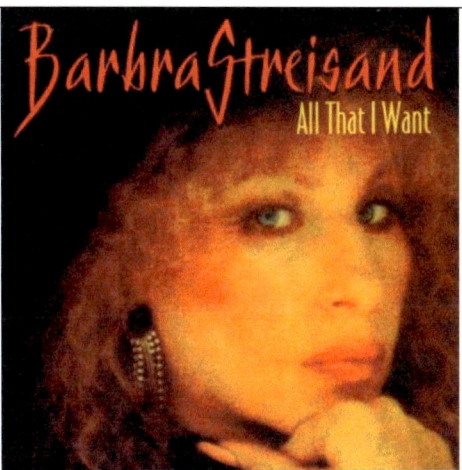

All That I Want (2000)
(Germany) Universe #3592
(Happy Days, Second Hand Rose, I Got Plenty Of Nothing, My Man, Kind Of Man A Woman Needs, People, My Lord And Master, Free Again, He Touched Me, Fine And Dandy, Why Did I Choose You, Don't Like Goodbyes, How Much Of The Dream Comes True, Love Is A Bore)

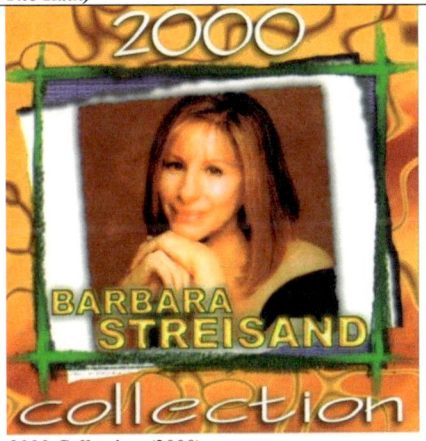

2000 Collection (2000)
(Germany-EEC) Ploy star (Bootleg-no catalog number)
(Woman In Love, I Finally Found Someone, Memory, Evergreen, If I Didn't Love You, What Kind Of Fool, Shadow Of Your Smile, If You Ever Leave Me, We Must Be Loving Right, Way He Makes Me Feel, We're Not Makin' Love Anymore, Superman, A Love Like Ours, I Won't Last A Day Without You, I've Got A Crush On You, New York State Of Mind, Somewhere, By The Way, Tell Him)

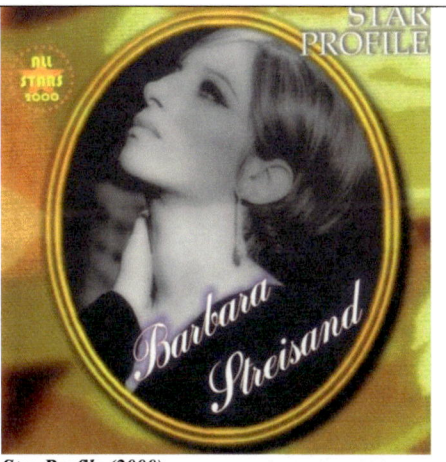

Star Profile (2000)
(Russia) All Stars Music (Bootleg-no catalog number)
(Guilty, Run Wild, Promises, I Finally Found Someone, What Kind Of Fool, Life Story, Make It Like A Memory, If I Didn't Love You, We Must Be Loving Right, Shadow Of Your Smile, I Won't Last A Day Without You, I've Got A Crush On You, If You Ever Leave Me, Superman, New York State Of Mind, Tell Him)

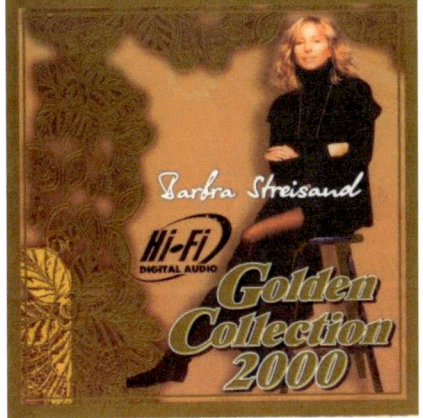

Golden Collection (2000)
(England) EMI #8-289932
(Woman In Love, Somewhere, Life Story, Tell Him, Promises, I've Got A Crush On You, New York State Of Mind, Guilty, We're Not Makin' Love Anymore, Comin' In And Out Of Your Life, You're The Top, If You Ever Leave Me, Run Wild, If I Didn't Love You, I Finally Found Someone, What Kind Of Fool, I Won't Last A Day Without You, Someone That I Used To Love, I Know Him So Well)

MTV History (2000)
(Germany) #HAL-357
(Woman In Love, Life Story, Memory, Run Wild, Who's Afraid Of The Big Bad Wolf?, By The Way, The Island, What Kind Of Fool, Simple Man, Someone That I Used To Love, A Love Like Ours, Way He Makes Me Feel, Isn't It A Pity, Crying Time, A Taste Of Honey, Male It Like A Memory, Tell Him, If You Ever Leave Me)

Grand Collection (2001)
(Russia) #GCR-034
(Woman In Love, Cry Me A River, Happy Days, My Man, People, Supper Time, My Lord And Master, On A Clear Day, I've Got No Strings, Go To Sleep, Gotta Move, Yesterdays, Love With All The Trimmings, When In Rome, Fine And Dandy, I'm All Smiles, Don't Like Goodbyes, Love Is A Bore)

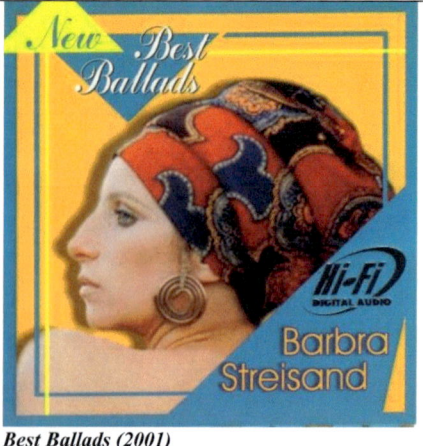

Best Ballads (2001)
(England) EMI #8-290138
(Woman In Love, I Finally Found Someone, We're Not Makin' Love Anymore, I've Dreamed Of You, The Island, If You Ever Leave Me, Run Wild, What Kind Of Fool, Tell Him, Someone That I Used To Love, All I Ask Of You, Way He Makes Me Feel, If I Didn't Love You, Comin' In And Out Of Your Life, I've Got A Crush On You, Just One Lifetime, I Won't Last A Day Without You, I Know Him So Well)

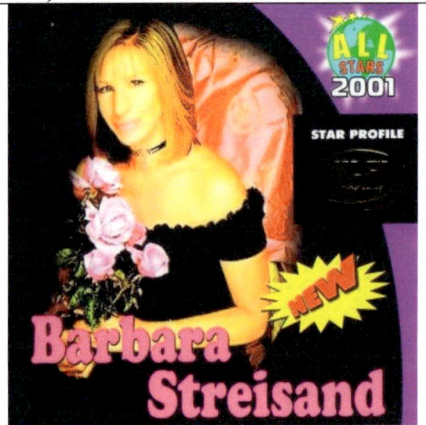

Star Profile (2001)
(Germany-EEC) All Stars Music (Bootleg-no catalog number)
(Guilty, Run Wild, Woman In Love, Promises, I Finally Found Someone, What Kind Of Fool, Life Story, Make It Like A Memory, If I Didn't Love You, We Must Be Loving Right, Shadow Of Your Smile, I Won't Last A Day Without You, I've Got A Crush On You, If You Ever Leave Me, Superman, New York State Of Mind, Tell Him)

The Very Best Of Barbra Streisand (2002)
(Germany) Universe #4092
(Shadow Of Your Smile, Where's That Rainbow?, Absent Minded Me, How Does The Wine Taste?, No More Songs For Me, Quiet Night, When In Rome, Super Time, Autumn, Will He Like Me, I'm All Smiles, Don't Rain On My Parade, My Coloring Book, Gotta Move, Sam You Made The Pants Too Long, My Name Is Barbra Medley)

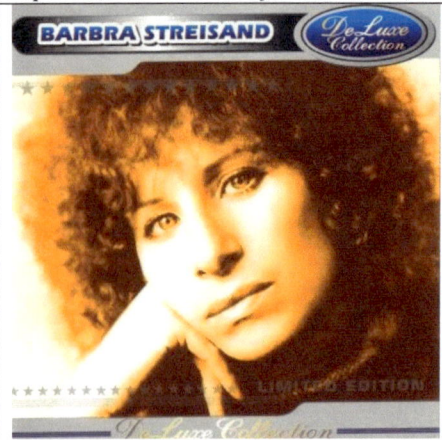

De Luxe Collection (2002)
(Russia) Dream Sound (Bootleg-no catalog number)
(Guilty, Woman In Love, Memory, The Way We Were, The Main Event, All In Love Is Fair, Comin' In And Out Of Your Life, Someone That I Used To Love, Somewhere, Evergreen, No More Tears, My Heart Belongs To Me, What Kind Of Fool, All I Ask Of You, We're Not Makin' Love Anymore, Tell Him, I've Dreamed Of You, Someday My Prince Will Come, People)

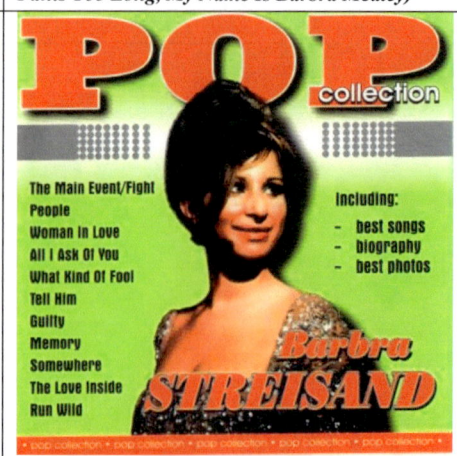

Pop Collection (2002)
(Russia) Celstion label #W8326220CD
(People, We're Not Makin' Love Anymore, Woman In Love, You Don't Bring Me Flowers, All I Ask Of You, Comin' In And Out Of Your Life, New York State Of Mind, What Kind Of Fool, Tell Him, The Main Event, Someone That I Used To Love, Who's Afraid Of The Big Bad Wolf?, Guilty, Memory, Way He Makes Me Feel, Somewhere, Love Inside, Sam You Made The Pants Too Long, Run Wild)

Hits (2002)
(China) Universal #D2CD-005 (2-CD Set with slip cover)

Disc 1
I've Dreamed Of You, Isn't It A Pity, The Island, A Love Like Ours, If You Ever Leave Me, We Must Be Loving Right, If I Never Met You, It Must Be You, Just One Lifetime, If I Didn't Love You, Wait, The Music That Makes Me Dance, Woman In Love, Tell Him, What Kind Of Fool, Guilty, Memory

Disc 2
Evergreen, People, You'll Never Know, You Don't Bring Me Flowers, Between Yesterday And Tomorrow, Second Hand Rose, A Sleepin' Bee, Cry Me A River, What Are You Doing The Rest Of Your Life?, I Finally Found Someone, All I Ask Of You, You'll Never Walk Alone, My Heart Belongs To Me, No More Tears, Somewhere, Lover Come Back To Me, As If We Never Said Goodbye, Comin' In And Out Of Your Life

Barbra Streisand (2002)
(Taiwan) #02ED494 with slip cover 2-CD Set

Disc 1
We're Not Makin' Love Anymore, All I Ask Of You, What Kind Of Fool, Someone That I Used To Love, Memory, A Love Like Ours, If You Ever Leave Me, Woman In Love, Comin' In And Out Of Your Life, The Main Event, By The Way, Guilty, The Way He Makes Me Feel, I've Dreamed Of You, Isn't It A Pity, If I Never Met You, It Must Be You

Disc 2
Cry Me A River, My Honey's Loving Arms, I'll Tell The Man In The Street, A Taste Of Honey, Who's Afraid Of The Big Bad Wolf?, Soon It's Gonna Rain, Happy Days Are Here Again, Keepin' Out Of Mischief, Much More, Come To The Supermarket, A Sleepin' Bee, Just One Lifetime, Memory, Wait, If I Didn't Love You, The Island, Tell Him, We Must Be Loving Right

Pop Collection (2002)
(Russia) #881632-185 (bootleg)
People, We're Not Makin' Love Anymore, Woman In Love, You Don't Bring Me Flowers, All I Ask Of You, Comin' In & Out Of Your Life, New York State Of Mind, What Kind Of Fool, Tell Him, Main Event, Someone That I Used To Love, Who's Afraid Of The Big Bad Wolf?, Guilty, Memory, Way He Makes Me Feel, Somewhere, The Love Inside, Sam You Made The Pants Too Long, Run Wild

Gold Greatest Hits (2005)
(Taiwan) DSD-07111 (2-CD Set) Gold CD's in unique foldout cover

Disc 1
Smile, Moon River, I'm In The Mood For Love, Wild Is The Wind, How Do You Keep The Music Playing, Calling You, Woman In Love, Memory, If I Didn't Love You, A Love Like Ours, Between Yesterday And Tomorrow, A Man I Loved, Kiss Me In The Rain, Evergreen, Shadow Of Your Smile, Lullaby For Myself, Free Again, I Won't Last A Day Without You, Superman

Disc 2
I Won't Be The One To Let Go, Guilty, You Don't Bring Me Flowers, I Finally Found Someone, Tell Him, No More Tears, What Kind Of Fool, Lost Inside Of You, Till I Loved You, Make No Mistake He's Mine, Ding Dong The Witch Is Dead, If You Ever Leave Me, The Music Of The Night, Get Happy-Happy Days Are Here Again, All I Know Of Love, Make It Like A Memory, New York State Of Mind

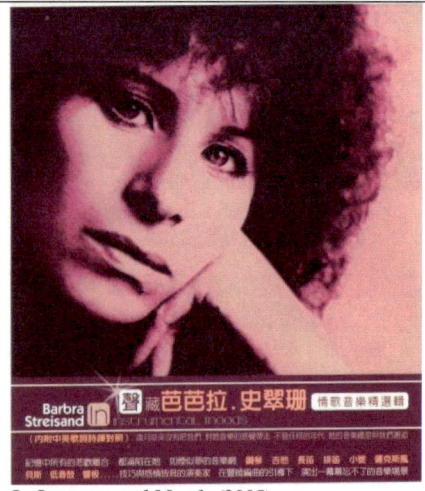

In Instrumental Moods (2005)
(Taiwan) Two Camlet Music #SDC-1027 Instrument only-no vocals
(Woman In Love, Guilty, Tell Him, I Finally Found Someone, Papa Can You Hear Me?, I've Dreamed Of You, No More Tears, The Way We Were, Evergreen, Memory, With One Look, Music Of The Night, As If We Never Said Goodbye, People, Second Hand Rose, You Don't Bring Me Flowers)

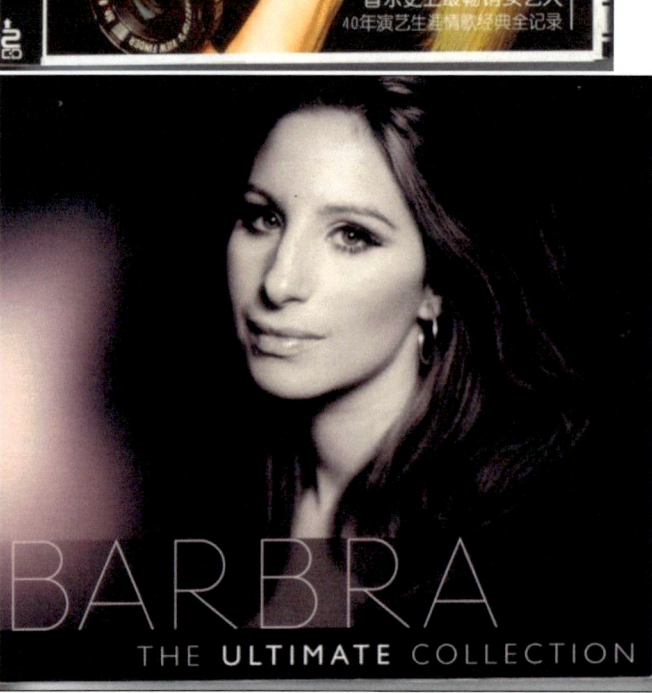

Nur Das Beste (2006)
(Germany) #82876 88272-2
(Memory, You Don't Bring Me Flowers, My Heart Belongs To Me, Wet, New York State Of Mind, A Man I Loved, No More Tears, Comin' In And Out Of Your Life, Evergreen, I Don't Break Easily, Kiss Me In The Rain, Lost Inside Of You, The Love Inside, The Way We Were)

Barbra Streisand (2006)
(China) Universal #XR-0826 LG-0344 (2-CD Set in digipak)

Disc 1
Come Tomorrow, Stranger In A Strange Land, Hideaway, It's Up To You, Night Of My Life, Above The Law, Without Your Love, All The Children, Golden Dawn, Don't Throw It All Away, Letting Go, I Won't Be The One To Let Go, Guilty, You Don't Bring Me Flowers, I Finally Found Someone, Tell Him, What Kind Of Fool, The Way We Were

Disc 2
Smile, Moon River, I'm In The Mood For Love, Wild Is The Wind, Emily, More In Love With You, How Do You Keep The Music Playing, But Beautiful, Calling You, The Second Time Around, Goodbye For Now, You're Gonna Hear From Me

The Ultimate Collection (2010)
(England) #88697793542 Deluxe Edition with 5 postcards in custom box
(Woman In Love, Evergreen, The Way We Were, You Don't Bring Me Flowers, Guilty, No More Tears, Don't Rain On My Parade, Memory, Papa Can You Hear Me?, As If We Never Said Goodbye, Tell Him, Stranger In A Strange Land, I've Dreamed Of You, Send In The Clowns, People, Smile, In The Wee Small Hours Of The Morning, Somewhere)
UK Promotional copy #88697806252 (Issued in gatefold cardsleeve)

Taiwan Edition #88697790432 with slip case and lyric insert sheet, same tracks as UK

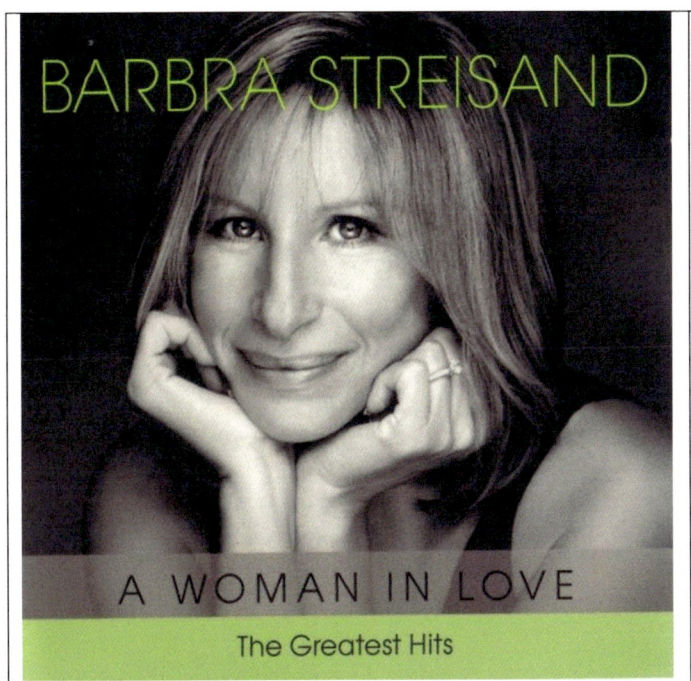

A Woman In Love-The Greatest Hits (2012)
(Germany) #88691992562
(Same tracks as Ultimate Collection 2010 release)

Streisand (2013)
(England) Sony/BMG promotional-only (no catalog number)
Issued with title sleeve in plastic wallet
(Guilty, People, The Way We Were, Tell Him, Evergreen, Woman In Love, No More Tears, On A Clear Day, I Finally Found Someone, A Piece Of Sky)

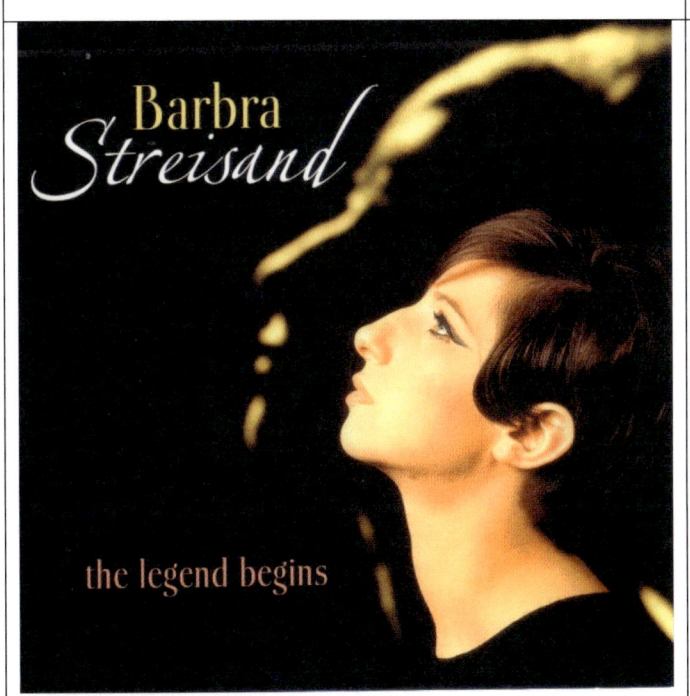

There is also the following International CD's issued:
Funny Girl Broadway Cast (Spain) Lamejor Musica 1995 #50578 (Cover has Clear Day photo)
Classical Barbra (Austria) 1993 Edition in custom slip case with calendar #MK 33452
Compilations CD's:
Barbra Streisand (Australia) 1999 Hins Records #4713836005724
World Ballad Collection (Germany-EEC) 2000 Breeze #47779039
Grand Collection (Russia) 2001 Cdap#008922
Barbra Streisand (Russia) 2002 boktokvk #251-01
It Must Be You 2002 (Germany-EEC) 2002 Tornado Records

The Legend Begins (2013)
(Holland) Remember Records #RMB75189

(Happy Days/My Coloring Book/Love Come Back To Me/Pins And Needles Tracks: Doing The Reactionary/Nobody Makes A Pass At Me/Not Cricket To Picket/Status Quo/What Good Is Love?/From Wholesale: I'm Not A Well Man/Miss Marmelstein/Jack Paar Show: A Sleepin' Bee/PM East: Moon River/Gary Moor Show When The Sun Comes Out/Happy Days/Backstage with Lee Jordan 1962 Wholesale interview/1962 Tonight Show with G Marx/Ed Sullivan 1962 My Coloring Book & Lover Come Back To Me)

The first three tracks are the Remastered single versions

191

Sheet Music

Popular with music collectors is sheet music. This section features all of the Streisand releases except unable to obtain He Could Show Me (1968). Songbooks for several Streisand albums were also issued.

Minute Waltz (1966)

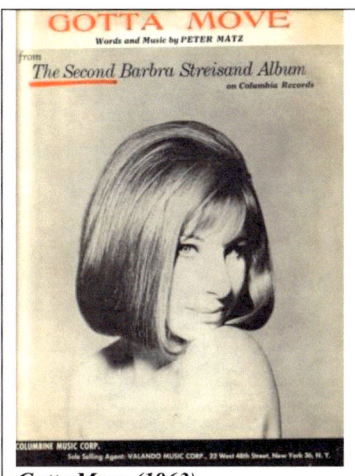

Gotta Move (1963)	*People (England) (1964)*	*You Are Woman, I Am Man (England) 1964*
The Music That Makes Me Dance (1964) (People & other titles issued with same cover	*Funny Girl (1964)* Absent-Minded Me issue as same cover	*I'm All Smiles (1964)*
Autumn (1965)	*A Kid Again (1965)*	*Where Is The Wonder? (1965)*
Why Did I Choose You? (1965)	*My Love (1965)*	*My Love (UK) (1965)*

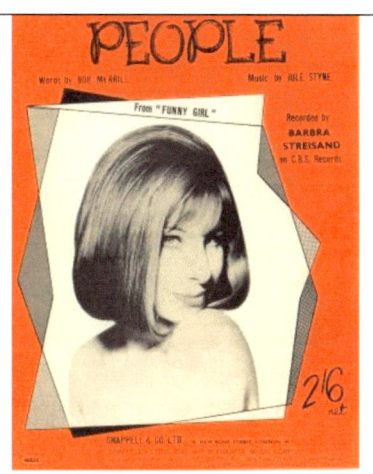

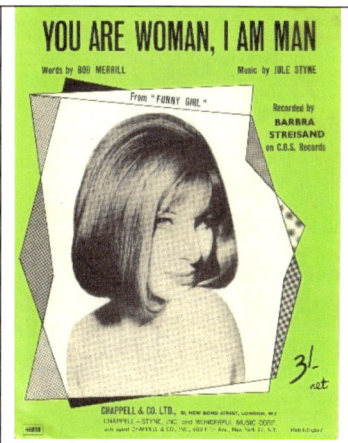

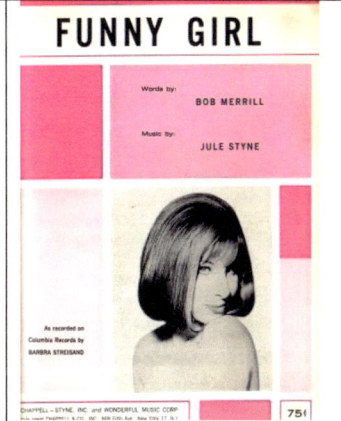

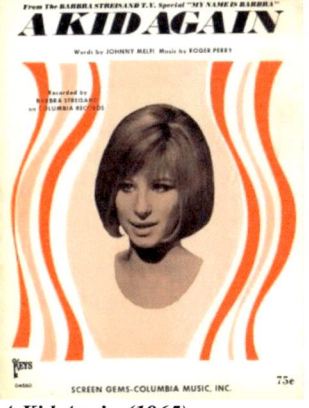

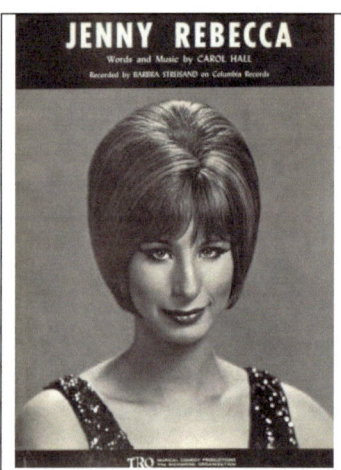

Jenny Rebecca (1965)  | *Second Hand Rose (1965)*  | *Second Hand Rose (1965)*

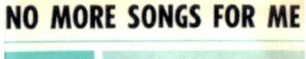

No More Songs For Me (1965) 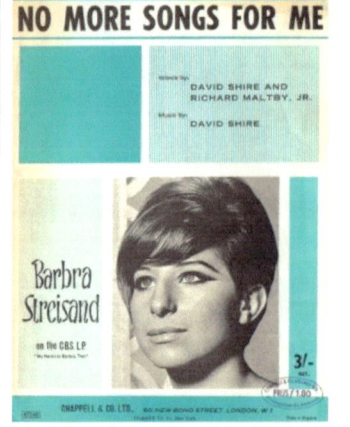 | *No More Songs For Me (UK) (1965)*  | *Free Again (1966)*

Free Again (1966)  | *I've Been Here! (1966)* 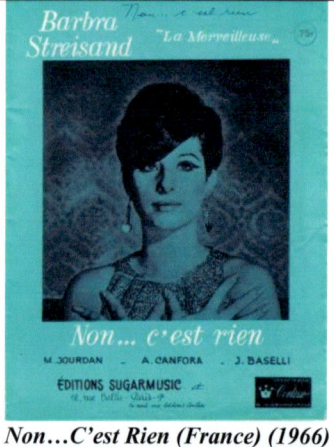 | *Non…C'est Rien (France) (1966)*

Sam You Made The Pants Too Long (1966)  | *Starting Here, Starting Now (1966)* 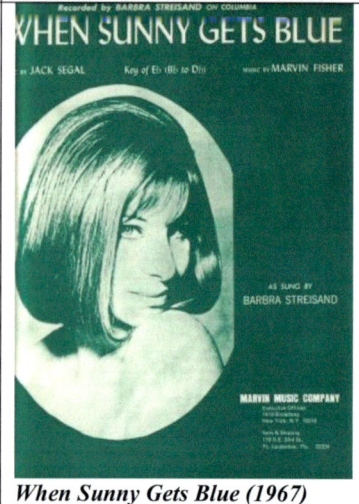 | *When Sunny Gets Blue (1967)*

Our Corner Of The Night (1968)	*Love Is Like A Newborn Child (1968)*	*I'd Rather Be Blue (1968)*
I'd Rather Be Blue (UK)(1968)	*I'd Rather Be Blue (1968)* *Second Hand Rose issued as same cover*	*My Man (1968)*
Second Hand Rose (1968)	*The Morning After (1969)*	*What About Today? (1969)*
Hello Dolly (UK) (1969) US release with other titles issued, same as LP cover	*The Best Thing You've Ever Done (1970)*	*On A Clear Day You Can See Forever (1970)*

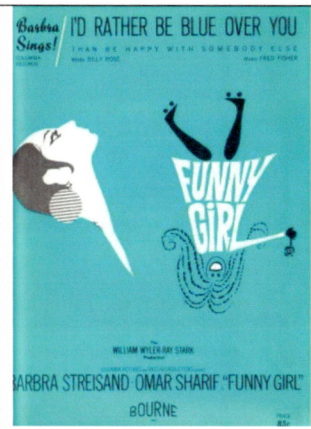

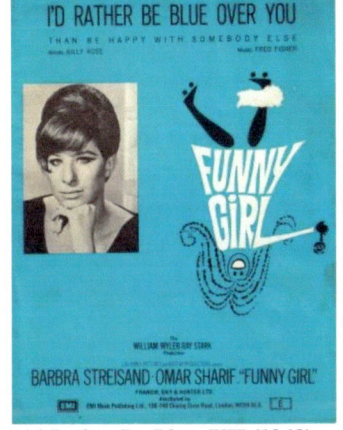

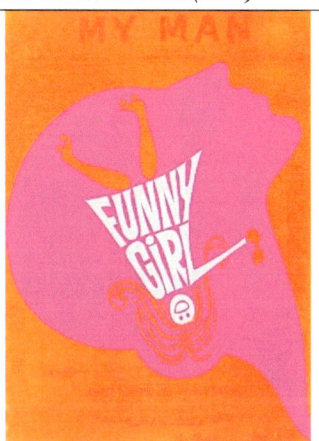

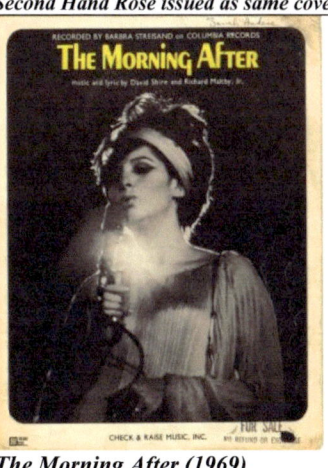

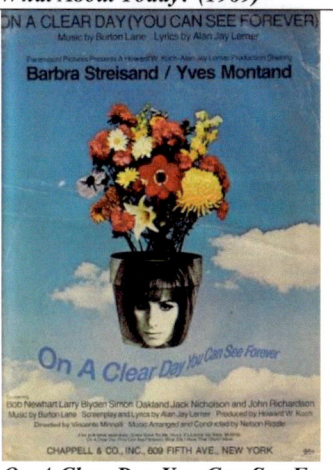

195

Hurry! It's Lovely Up Here! (UK) (1970) *(Also issued as other titles, same cover)*	*Stoney End (1970)*	*Time And Love (1971)*
Flim Flam Man (1971)	*Space Captain (1971)*	*Where You Lead (1971)*
You're The Top (UK) (1972)	*Sing (1972)*	*Make Your Own Kind Of Music (1972)*
Sweet Inspiration (1972)	*Sweet Inspiration/Where You Lead (1972)*	*Sweet Inspiration/Where You Lead (1972)*

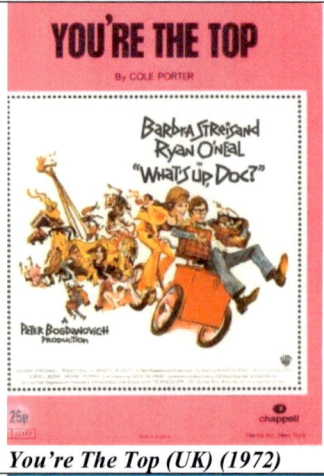

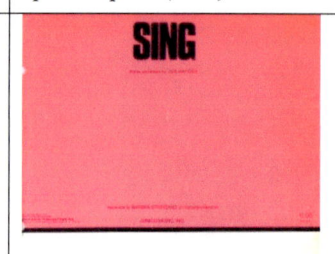

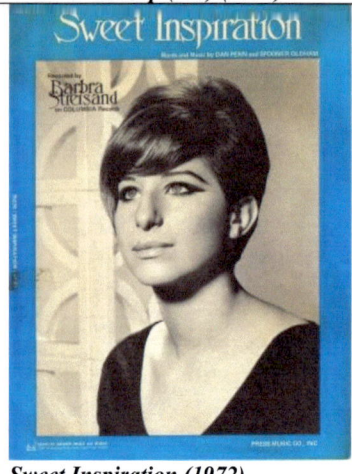

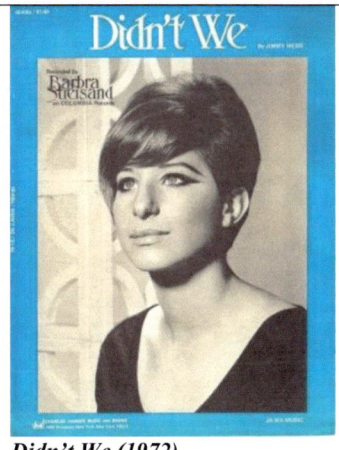

Didn't We (1972)	*The Way We Were (1973)* *(Reissued with blue & red boarders)*	*The Way We Were (1973)*
The Way We Were (UK) (1973)	*All In Love Is Fair (1974)*	*I've Never Been A Woman Before (1974)*
Guava Jelly (1974)	*How Lucky Can You Get (1975)*	*Great Day (1975)* *Also issued More Than You Know, similar cover*
More Than You Know (1975)	*My Father's Song (1975)*	*You And I (1975)*

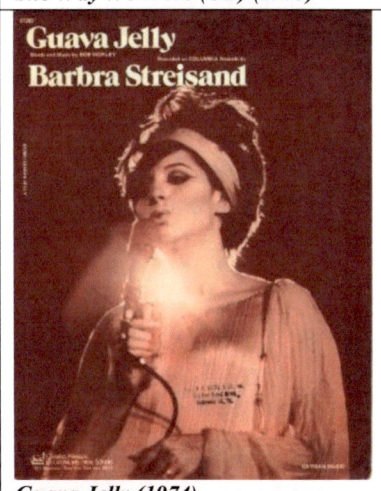

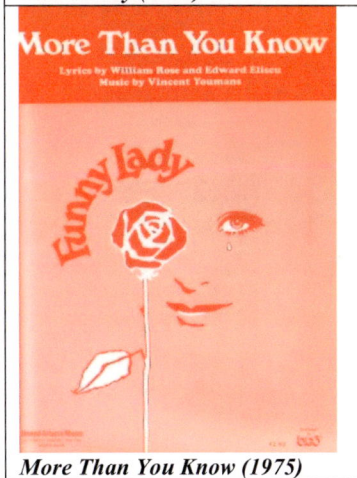

I Loved You (1976) Pavane issued as same cover	**Evergreen (1977)**	**Evergreen (France) (1977)**
Watch Closely Now (1977)	**My Heart Belongs To Me (1977)**	**My Heart Belongs To Me (1977)**
Superman (1977)	**Songbird (1978)**	**Prisoner (1978)**
You Don't Bring Me Flowers (UK) (1978)	**The Main Event/Fight (1979)**	**No More Tears (Enough Is Enough)(1979)**

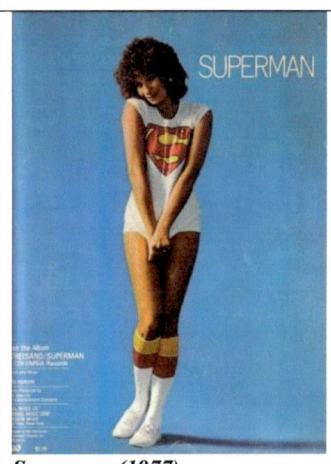

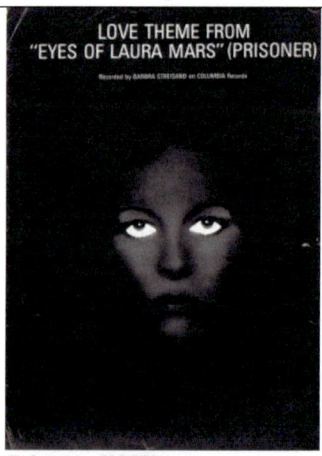

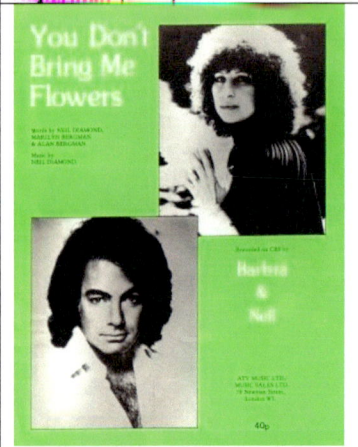

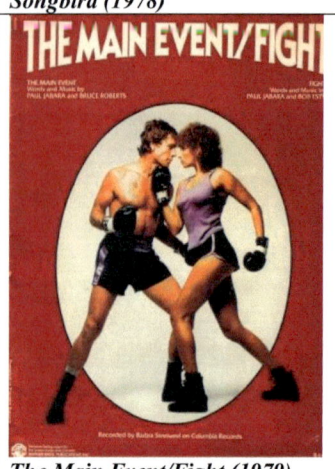

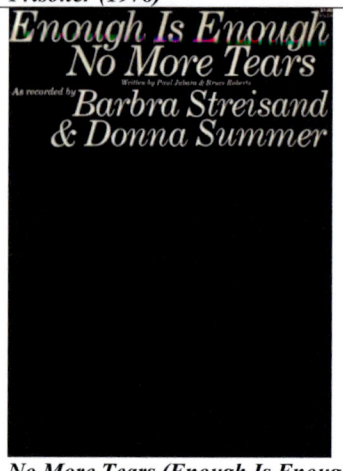

Kiss Me In The Rain (1979)	*Woman In Love (1980)* (Guilty, What Kind Of Fool, & Promises issued as same cover)	*Comin' In And Out Of Your Life (1981)*
Memory (1982)	*The Way He Makes Me Feel (1983)*	*Papa, Can You Hear Me? (1983)*
Till I Loved You (UK) (1988)	*Places That Belong To You (1991)*	*I Finally Found Someone (1996)* (All Of My Life also issued as same cover)
My Man (1997 reissue)	*Tell Him (UK) (1997)*	*Stranger In A Strange Land (2005)*

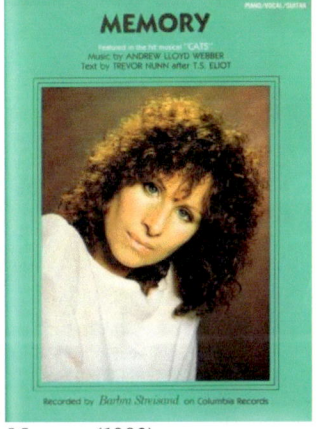

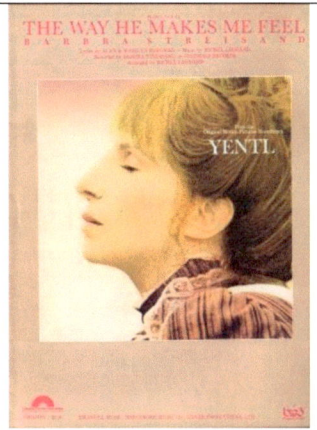

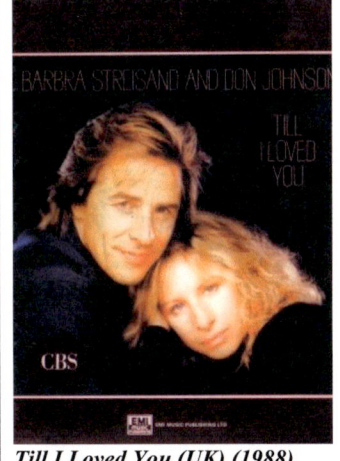

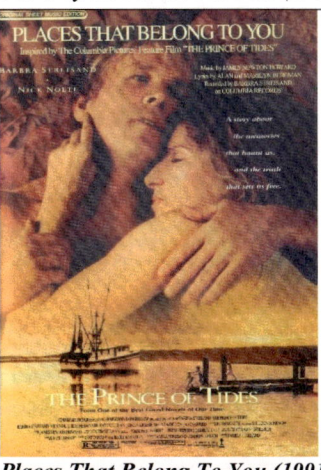

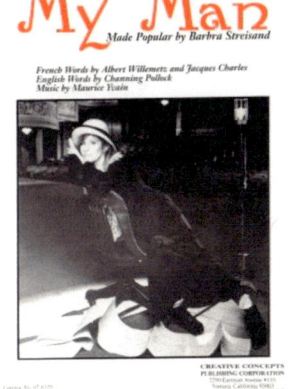

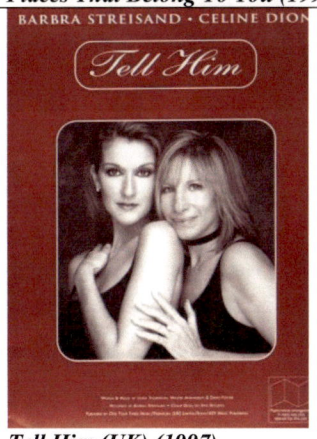

An American Institution

Barbra Streisand is one of the most successful artists of our time. She has sold over 72 million albums in the US and over 140 million worldwide. She is the only recording artist to have number one albums in six consecutive decades, the 60's, 70's, 80's, 90's, 2000's and 2010's. She has 52 Gold albums, 30 Platinum, 18 Multi-Platinum, 9 Gold singles, 5 Platinum singles, and countless awards including 2 Oscars and 10 Grammy's.

Some online searches show Madonna and Mariah Carey as the top selling female recording artist in the US. But according to the RIAA, the Recording Industry Association of America, Streisand is the highest selling female recording artist in the US.

RIAA's List of Top 20 Best-Selling Music Artists in the US (Certification in millions):

1. The Beatles — 178
2. Elvis Presley — 134.5
3. Garth Brooks — 134
4. Led Zeppelin — 111.5
5. Eagles — 101
6. Billy Joel — 81.5
7. Michael Jackson — 76
8. Pink Floyd — 74.5
9. Elton John — 73
10. Barbra Streisand — 72
11. AC/DC — 71.5
12. George Strait — 69
13. Aerosmith — 66.5
14. Rolling Stones — 66.5
15. Madonna — 64.5
16. Bruce Springsteen — 64.5
17. Mariah Carey — 63.5
18. Metallica — 62
19. Whitney Houston — 57
20. Van Halen — 56.5

RIAA has updated their list with Streisand remaining the only female in the Top 10. Now celebrating six decades with another number one gold album; she's remained an icon and an American Institution. Columbia Records has extended Streisand's recording contract, and to commemorate six decades, Sony is planning on releasing a multi-disc DVD set. And with a remake of the Musical Gypsy in the works, the legacy continues…

The End

Made in United States
Troutdale, OR
12/11/2023